EVERY KILLER
LEAVES A TRACE

*The Fatal Mistakes That
Finally Exposed America's
Most Elusive Killers*

DENNIS CARSON

WILDBLUE
PRESS

WildBluePress.com

EVERY KILLER LEAVES A TRACE published by:
WILDBLUE PRESS
P.O. Box 102440
Denver, Colorado 80250

Publisher Disclaimer: Any opinions, statements of fact or fiction, descriptions, dialogue, and citations found in this book were provided by the author, and are solely those of the author. The publisher makes no claim as to their veracity or accuracy, and assumes no liability for the content.

WILDBLUE PRESS is registered at the U.S. Patent and Trademark Offices.

ISBN 978-1-964730-81-3 Hardcover
ISBN 978-1-964730-82-0 Trade Paperback
ISBN 978-1-964730-80-6 eBook
Cover design © 2025 WildBlue Press. All rights reserved.

Interior Formatting and Book Cover Design by Elijah Toten
www.totencreative.com

EVERY KILLER
LEAVES A TRACE

CONTENTS

PREFACE

Every Killer Leaves A Trace offers a compelling exploration of the darkest recesses of human behavior. Chronicling 26 chilling true crime cases from modern history, this book goes beyond recounting acts of violence—it is a tribute to the pursuit of justice, the resilience of survivors, and the relentless efforts of those who seek truth in the aftermath of horror.

Each chapter dissects the final, fatal act that ultimately exposed a murderer and unraveled their ability to hide in plain sight. These are not merely accounts of crimes but human stories with emotional wreckage, investigative triumphs, and enduring grief.

They reveal how some of the most cunning, manipulative, and unrepentant offenders operated under the radar for years, sometimes decades, often using charm, deception, and constant mobility to evade capture. Many exploited jurisdictional boundaries, disappearing across state lines and reappearing with new identities and victims.

What distinguishes *Every Killer Leaves A Trace* is its depth of sourcing and investigative rigor. The cases are reconstructed using various authoritative materials: federal and state court documents, including indictments, trial transcripts, and appellate rulings; police and FBI case files obtained through public records requests; and detailed coroner and autopsy reports outlining causes of death and toxicology findings.

The book draws on peer-reviewed journals in criminal profiling, behavioral science, and forensic methodologies to ground each narrative in forensic and psychological accuracy. Significant media coverage—including ABC News, CBS, NBC, and *The Los Angeles Times* reporting—provides contextual framing. At the same time, documentary footage and televised courtroom proceedings lend further detail.

Most critically, firsthand interviews with law enforcement professionals, forensic experts, and surviving family members, along with private correspondence and case notes from retired detectives and professional collaborators, lend unique insight and authenticity to each case.

These carefully vetted sources form the book's foundation, ensuring that each chapter is factually precise, professionally grounded, and respectful of victims, investigators, and the broader justice process.

While each chapter is a self-contained account, together they form a larger narrative that examines how patterns emerge, how interagency cooperation has evolved, and how forensic breakthroughs now play a pivotal role in unmasking those who once believed themselves untouchable.

The book examines the rise of itinerant killers—murderers who used mobility as a weapon—and how law enforcement's growing ability to detect and connect across jurisdictions has finally turned the tide.

These are not overexposed stories. While some cases in *Every Killer Leaves A Trace* have received prior media attention, most have not been entirely told, indeed not with this level of investigative depth, forensic insight, and narrative cohesion.

This book doesn't simply rehash headlines or sensationalize crimes; it reconstructs the final act that brought each killer to justice, revealing investigative breakthroughs, overlooked mistakes, and the human toll in a manner that has never before been compiled.

Every Killer Leaves A Trace is not just a catalog of crimes but a testament to the tireless pursuit of justice. Through scientific innovation, unshakable intuition, or sheer perseverance, investigators refused to let these cases fade into silence. Each story captures that crucial moment when truth overcame deception and when justice, however delayed, prevailed.

These are not simply murder stories. They are narratives of reckoning, revelation, and an unwavering resolve to ensure those who kill are ultimately brought into the light.

CHAPTER ONE

Dating Game Killer –
Rodney James Alcala

Rodrigo Jacques Alcala-Buquor, referred to as Rodney James Alcala, was born in San Antonio, Texas, on August 23, 1943. After his father left, their mother raised Alcala and his sisters in a suburban neighborhood of Los Angeles.

In 1960, Alcala joined the United States Army as a clerk. Following a reported "nervous breakdown" in 1964, he was diagnosed with antisocial personality disorder by a military psychiatrist, leading to his medical discharge.

Despite a complicated past, Alcala, claiming to possess a "genius-level" IQ, graduated from UCLA's School of Fine Arts. He later registered at New York University under "John Berger," where he studied film with Roman Polanski.

Rodney Alcala, a convicted serial killer and rapist, was sentenced to death in California in 2010 after being found guilty of a minimum of 50 murders. However, authorities believe the number might be as high as 130, mostly committed between 1977 and 1979.

In September 1978, Rodney Alcala was featured as Bachelor No. 1 on *The Dating Game*, a popular TV show where contestants interviewed potential dates without seeing them. At the time, neither the audience nor the producers were aware that Alcala was already a convicted child molester. This gap in background checks led to significant changes, including the creation of a national crime database and improved vetting procedures.

He was characterized as "a successful photographer whose journey started at 13 when his father found him in the darkroom."

While on stage, bachelorette Cheryl Bradshaw prompted him to characterize the kind of meal he represented. Alcala replied, "I'm known as 'The Banana,' and I look amazing... Just peel me."

Alcala's crimes were marked by extreme cruelty. Prosecutors revealed that he "toyed" with his victims, strangling them to the brink of death, only to let them regain consciousness, repeating the torture multiple times before finally ending their lives.

Investigators discovered hundreds of photos taken by Alcala depicting women and teenage boys. This finding heightens concerns regarding his possible connections to numerous other murders throughout California.

He is viewed as a suspect in at least two unsolved homicides in New York. Authorities have drawn parallels between Alcala and Ted Bundy, cautioning that as fresh evidence emerges, he could eventually be acknowledged as one of the most notorious serial killers in American history.

Between 1971 and 1979, Rodney Alcala murdered at least eight women across New York, California, and Wyoming. His vicious crimes also included the sexual assault of two girls, one in 1968 and another in 1979.

On September 25, 1968, 8-year-old Tali Shapiro walked to school on Sunset Boulevard in Los Angeles. Her family temporarily resided at the famous Chateau Marmont Hotel, known for its ties to the entertainment industry.

As Shapiro was walking down the street, Rodney Alcala approached her and offered her a ride. At first, she said no, but when Alcala mentioned that he knew her parents, she reconsidered.

Considering her father's connections in the music industry, which frequently hosted legends like Mama Cass, Jim Morrison, and Lenny Bruce, his assertion seemed credible. "He might have known my parents," she reflected later. "Our home was constantly bustling with visitors. It felt like Grand Central Station."

After that, Shapiro entered the car. Alcala claimed he was a professional photographer and wanted to show her a poster at his place. But as soon as they arrived at his apartment, everything went dark.

"He brought me to his home, and I entered with him, but that's all I remember," she stated. "I can't recall anything further. He hit me on the head immediately afterward, and that was the conclusion of it."

Inside, Alcala brutally raped the young girl before bludgeoning her with a metal bar. By sheer luck, a witness had seen Alcala luring Shapiro into his car and reported the suspicious interaction to police.

Donald Haines, a bystander, followed Alcala to his apartment but was too afraid to confront him, worried he might be armed. Instead, he located a nearby payphone and dialed 9-1-1.

"I fixated on the little girl, which troubled me," he later told the police. "I saw rage in his eyes."

The police arrived promptly to offer Shapiro crucial medical aid.

Officer Camacho successfully pried open the door and found Shapiro unresponsive on the floor, lying in a pool of blood with a metal bar tightly secured around her neck. Initially, they presumed she was dead.

As Camacho lifted the bar, a faint breath escaped her lips— she was still alive. They urgently called for an ambulance and quickly took her to the hospital.

While officers focused on helping Shapiro, Alcala seized the opportunity to escape by slipping out the back of his apartment. During the chaos, Camacho discovered Alcala's ID at the scene—this was a crucial piece of evidence for investigators to find him. "They had to choose between saving me or pursuing him," Shapiro later said.

Shapiro spent 32 days in a coma and several months hospitalized.

"After the attack, I needed more than 27 stitches in the back of my head," she later testified. "He struck me at the back of the head."

While she survived, that day profoundly changed Shapiro. Her testimony was vital in ensuring that Rodney Alcala— one of America's most brutal serial predators—could not hurt another victim.

Authorities spent over two years tracking down and arresting Rodney Alcala for the brutal rape and attempted murder of Tali Shapiro. When the trial began, Shapiro's parents chose not to have her testify, concerned about the emotional toll it would take on their young daughter—an option she later expressed gratitude for.

"At that moment, I didn't know any of this, and it didn't concern me," Shapiro recalled. "Discovering these truths years later helped me cope, since they weren't intertwined with my identity. That didn't burden me. But, if I had known back then, it would have utterly destroyed my childhood."

Because Shapiro couldn't testify, however, prosecutors didn't have a key witness in the case, and Alcala ended up pleading guilty to child molestation and serving just 34 months in prison. He went on to commit at least eight other rapes and murders in California, New York, and Wyoming.

In 1971, two campers spotted Rodney Alcala on an FBI wanted poster at a post office and alerted the camp directors, which resulted in his arrest and extradition to California. Unfortunately, Tali Shapiro's family had moved to Mexico during the trial and chose not to permit her to testify. Lacking this key witness, prosecutors could not obtain a conviction for rape. They pursued charges of attempted murder, ultimately leading to Alcala pleading guilty to a lesser offense.

Alcala served just 34 months in prison under the preferred "indeterminate sentencing" program, which enabled parole boards to release offenders depending on their evaluated rehabilitation before being paroled in 1974.

Less than two months later, Rodney Alcala was arrested once more, this time for breaching his parole and providing marijuana to a 13-year-old girl who alleged she had been kidnapped. In spite of his prior offenses, he received an indeterminate sentence. He was released on parole after two years in custody.

Alcala's skill in manipulating individuals, despite being convicted as a sex offender, remains one of the most disturbing facets of his crimes. His involvement with *The Los Angeles Times* during the Hillside Strangler investigation highlights how effortlessly he assimilated into settings that allowed him to monitor law enforcement actions and possibly hone his methods.

His position as a professional photographer was profoundly misleading. The haunting portraits of young women he captured acted as trophies and a silent testament to unresolved crimes. To this day, the FBI has shared hundreds of his photographs to help identify potential victims. Nevertheless, some women depicted in these images have neither come forward nor been found.

Morgan Rowan met Rodney Alcala in 1965 when she was 13 years old. She spotted him while spending time with her friends in the parking lot of a popular teen nightclub.

"He was tall, charming, and captivating," she remembered. "He laughed easily and told stories. Young girls looked up to him. I never thought it was problematic, but it actually was."

Alcala flashed a smile in their direction, his presence effortlessly commanding attention. Rowan gently scratched his arm with her fingernails, wanting to draw his focus. When he asked her to stop, she didn't—so he grasped her arm and pulled her into the dark alley behind the club.

"I think he slammed my head into the wall when I was passed out," she stated.

After that night, Rowan avoided Alcala for three years.

In August 1968, she met him again.

Rowan and her family were preparing for their move to New York. Just four days before the move, she and her friends decided to host a farewell party on the Sunset Strip. While they enjoyed the lively atmosphere, Rowan recognized a familiar face—Rodney Alcala. An inexplicable chill swept over her, creating a wave of anxiety. Although he vanished into the crowd, surrounded by others, something about him left her profoundly disturbed. Later, she reflected on this feeling as being "creeped out," though she struggled to explain why.

That evening, Rowan and her friends crammed into a car heading to a local restaurant. She was wedged in the back seat, enveloped by her friends' joyful chatter and laughter. But when Alcala settled into the driver's seat, fear washed over her. Every instinct screamed for her to flee—yet she stayed put.

At the restaurant, Rowan went to the restroom. Just as she returned to her table, she turned a corner and almost collided with Alcala, who was standing there. "We're ready to head back to the Strip," he said calmly.

The group quickly jumped into the car, eager to return to the lively streets. However, Alcala unexpectedly detoured, stopping in front of a house. Without saying anything, he exited the vehicle and gestured for them to follow. Once inside, he distributed a bag of marijuana. The living room was blaring with music as Rowan's friends smoked, laughed, and created a hazy, dreamlike ambiance for the night.

In a flash, Alcala seized Rowan's arm. Before she could respond, he yanked her into a bedroom and shut the door, locking it firmly behind them.

Rowan felt her heart pounding in her ears as she cautiously stepped back, her breath shallow. The room seemed to close in around her, making her feel trapped. She kept moving until she hit the wall, her back pressed against its chilly surface.

Alcala inched nearer.

"He took off his belt and wrapped it around his fist," she recalled. "I tried to be brave and declared, 'No, you can't keep me here.' Then he hit me—right between the eyes, with all his force."

Rowan's head struck the wall, causing her to collapse to her knees as her vision exploded into a blur of stars. Though dazed, she remained aware. Alcala loomed over her, his eyes glazed, his face red and twisted with fury. He gripped a knife tightly in his hand.

He pressed the blade to the tie of her blouse and sliced it away from her neck. The metal grazed her skin, leaving a shallow cut.

"I felt the blood start to trickle down my chest," she recalled. "And I remember thinking, 'He's cut my neck. I'm going to die.'"

She felt paralyzed, her limbs refusing to respond. "His face was swollen and red. His eyes appeared wild. He had lost all semblance of humanity—he had turned into a beast," she recalled. "I wasn't praying to survive; I was praying for release from life."

Upon awakening, Rowan felt a weight on her chest. Alcala had pushed a large industrial dumpster onto her. She called out for help.

The club owner and his wife heard her screams and quickly rushed outside. They rescued her from behind the dumpster and placed ice on the swelling on her head.

Troubled by the assault, Rowan struggled to sleep in her new home and chose to lie on the floor next to her parents' bed. However, she never disclosed to them what had occurred.

After relocating to New York City, she received a letter from a friend that included a newspaper clipping about Alcala's violent rape. He also attempted to murder another woman, Tali Shapiro. Overwhelmed by guilt, Rowan held herself accountable for Shapiro's suffering, convinced that if she had reported Alcala's assault, it might have been prevented.

"I ought to have intervened. I should have talked to my parents," she confessed. "I regret not returning there to confront him myself. I felt entirely responsible, thinking I should have acted."

Several years later, in 2010, Shapiro testified against Alcala during his sentencing.

"All I felt was a commitment to justice, I told the Court. I purposefully refrained from looking at him. I steered clear of any attention—no glances, no recognition, and I never referred to his name. I deprived him of any satisfaction."

Then, Robin Samsoe followed.

Her abduction and later murder represented a pivotal moment in the case against Alcala. The finding of her earrings in a Seattle locker created a strong link to the crime. Alcala's numerous convictions, appeals, and eventual death sentence underscore the difficulties encountered by the justice system in ensuring complete accountability.

Alcala's skill in effortlessly moving across different jurisdictions, adopting various aliases, and blending into artistic circles illustrates the concept of itinerant killers—those who leverage geographical mobility to evade capture.

In 1980, Rodney Alcala was tried, found guilty, and sentenced to death for the murder of Robin Samsoe. However, the California Supreme Court later reversed his conviction, ruling that the Orange County Superior Court judge had wrongly permitted the jury to hear prejudicial details about his criminal history, which comprised the violent assault on Tali Shapiro, as well as several convictions for rape and kidnapping.

In 1986, Alcala underwent a retrial, resulting in another conviction and a death sentence. However, because of due process issues, the Ninth Circuit Court of Appeals overturned this conviction. The appellate panel concluded that the trial court wrongfully barred a critical defense witness from testifying. This witness could have bolstered Alcala's assertion that the park ranger who found Robin's remains had been "hypnotized" by police, which could have called the credibility of his testimony into question.

While preparing their third prosecution in 2003, investigators in Orange County discovered that Rodney Alcala's DNA— collected under a new state law despite his objections— matched the semen found at the rape-murder scenes of two women in Los Angeles.

Additional evidence was revealed when a set of earrings discovered in Alcala's storage locker tested positive for DNA from one of the victims.

The subsequent year, a DNA match from a cold case connected Alcala to more crimes, leading to his indictment for the murders of four additional women. Jill Barcomb, just 18 years old, was killed in 1977 and was initially thought to be a victim of the Hillside Strangler.

Georgia Wixted, 27, was bludgeoned to death in her Malibu apartment the same year. In 1978, Charlotte Lamb, 31, was raped and strangled in El Segundo, and in 1979, Jill Parenteau, 21, was murdered in her Burbank apartment.

The collected forensic evidence revealed a disturbing account of Alcala's series of murders, exposing a prolonged history of violence.

Ultimately, it was evident that Alcala was accountable for the murders of two young women in New York City: 23-year-old Cornelia Crilley and Ellen Hover.

In June 1971, Crilley was raped and strangled with her stockings inside her Manhattan apartment. Six years later, on July 15, 1977, Hover vanished after writing in her calendar that she was meeting someone named "John Berger"—an alias Alcala was known to use.

Authorities found her remains in Westchester County in 1978.

In 2016, Alcala was charged with the murder of 28-year-old Christine Ruth Thornton, which occurred in Wyoming in 1977. Nonetheless, prosecutors opted not to extradite him for trial.

Investigators suspect that Alcala murdered Pamela Lambson in the San Francisco Bay Area during the same period. However, the absence of trustworthy DNA evidence from the crime scene hindered the filing of formal charges.

Some of Alcala's victims survived. In 1968, he brutally assaulted 8-year-old Tali Shapiro in Los Angeles, leaving her near death. In 1979, he raped and attempted to kill 15-year-old Monique Hoyt, who managed to escape.

Both women later testified against him as adults, and their courage was vital in securing the convictions. In 2010, authorities published a series of Alcala's photographs to aid in identifying unknown individuals he photographed—some of whom might also have been victims. Many individuals stepped forward.

In 2003, prosecutors sought to merge the murder charges against Robin Samsoe with those of four newly identified victims. The California Supreme Court supported the prosecution in 2006 despite Alcala's objections. This resulted in Alcala's retrial in 2009. Defending himself, he presented a disjointed and lackluster case, asserting he was at Knott's Berry Farm during Samsoe's abduction. Notably, he did not address the murders of the other four victims.

In his closing argument, he played a portion of Arlo Guthrie's song "Alice's Restaurant," where the main character expresses to a psychiatrist his desire to "kill." He was found guilty on all five charges. A shocking witness in the penalty phase of the trial was Tali Shapiro, Alcala's first recognized victim. In March 2010, Alcala received a death sentence for the third time.

As Alcala awaited execution, California's death penalty system encountered multiple legal challenges, suggested reforms, and significant public attention.

In March 2019, Governor Gavin Newsom introduced a temporary moratorium on executions. While Alcala's sentence stayed the same, this order ensured he would not be executed.

Alcala died in prison on July 24, 2021, from unspecified natural causes while undergoing hospital treatment.

CHAPTER TWO
Railroad Killer – Ángel Maturino Reséndiz

On August 29, 1997, a calm evening turned unsettling for 20-year-old Holly Dunn, a junior at the University of Kentucky. She and her boyfriend, Chris Maier, had left a dull party near campus to unwind by the railroad tracks, enjoying beers and the tranquility of the night.

They stayed there, enjoying the tranquility of the warm night. The distant sound of cars blended with their soft laughter as they talked, fingers intertwined. Eventually, they stood up and strolled hand in hand along the tracks, reluctant to let the moment go yet prepared to return to the party.

They unwittingly entered the domain of a predator—an individual notorious for his violent criminal past, which has resulted in a blood-soaked legacy nationwide.

Ángel Maturino Reséndiz, known as "The Railroad Killer," was a fugitive on the FBI's Ten Most Wanted list. He traveled across the U.S. by freight train, attacking randomly and potentially leaving behind an astonishing number of victims, possibly up to thirty.

For over ten years, his reign of terror resulted in a shocking number of victims, spanning from Texas in 1986 to Illinois in 1999. His murders were marked by both brutality and randomness—horrific violence unleashed on innocent strangers who unwittingly crossed his path.

On the night Reséndiz met Holly and Chris, he glided through the system like a ghost, attacking abruptly and claiming lives without facing any repercussions.

A sudden rustle shattered the silence as Holly and Chris approached an electrical box near the tracks. A man stepped out of the shadows, and the atmosphere grew tense, amplifying the feeling of imminent danger.

"Give me your money!" Reséndiz yelled, brandishing an ice pick.

Holly's voice shook. "We don't have any money. We're just broke college students... but we do possess ATM cards... and you can take our car."

Reséndiz directed the ice pick at Chris. "Hand over your backpack and kneel down."

Chris complied. The man rummaged through the backpack, overlooking its contents. What he truly craved—what fulfilled him—was control.

Reséndiz secured Chris's hands behind his back with cold precision using the backpack straps. He forced both of them to lie on the grass and stuffed rags into their mouths. Thinking quickly, Holly stuck out her tongue as he pushed the rag in, letting it fall uselessly to the ground. That small act of defiance infuriated him. He ripped off her belt and used it to bind her wrists, then briefly left to climb back toward the tracks.

Holly worked furiously at the belt. Her fingers bled and ached, but at last, it gave way. Her feet were still tied, but she was able to reach Chris and pull the gag from his mouth.

"Are you able to escape?" she asked softly. "Should I dash for it?"

There was no time to answer. Reséndiz returned, this time carrying a large rock. Before either could react, he raised it and brought it down with devastating force onto Chris's head. The sound was sickening—bone-shattering under the stone. Chris died instantly.

Holly barely had time to scream before Reséndiz turned his attention to her. With ruthless efficiency, he pulled down her skirt and panties and forced her onto the ground. She froze as he climbed on top of her, unzipping his fly. His breath was hot and foul. Terror paralyzed her as he violated her, his movements cold and mechanical, devoid of humanity.

Then, he took out a knife. He pressed it against her throat and whispered, "Look how easily I could kill you."

Without hesitation, he drove the blade into her neck.`

Pain coursed through her body, yet Holly's focus sharpened. She scrutinized him, noting every scar, every feature, and every detail in her memory.

She grasped the ground, her nails digging into the soil, striving to leave a mark of her existence in case she didn't survive. Blood marked her skin, and her vision blurred, yet she urged herself to speak.

"I can't bear this pain any longer," she whispered. "I swear I won't tell anyone."

Reséndiz grabbed a wooden board and struck her face with it once, twice, again, and again. She raised her arms in defense, but he flipped her over and continued beating her, each blow a savage attempt to silence her forever.

He hovered above her, feeling fulfilled. She lay still, appearing lifeless to him.

Amid the despair, Holly clung to life. Despite her jaw being immobilized and her thoughts scattered, her resolve to survive grew stronger.

His breath was hot and foul as he climbed on top of her, unzipping his fly. Terror paralyzed her as he violated her; his movements were cold and mechanical, devoid of humanity.

She felt trapped under him, her thoughts racing. She knew the danger was real. He had already taken Chris's life; there was no chance he would allow her to survive.

Pain enveloped her, yet her mind became sharper. She focused on him, committing to memory every scar, every tattoo, every detail. *Remember it all*, she implored herself, *for I will seek you out one day.*

Her breaths became slower. Reséndiz lingered over her, watching intently. After confirming her death, he left, abandoning her, shattered, injured, and alone.

Ultimately, Holly was alive.

Despite facing unimaginable horrors—rape, beatings, stabbings—she decided to persevere.

Unsure of how long she had been out, she woke to find he had left. A dull pain pulsed in her head, and her jaw felt askew. Her mind was clouded. Still, one clear thought emerged through the discomfort: She needed to persevere.

She must make sure this monster was held accountable for its actions.

Once liberated from her bindings, Holly walked around 200 yards along the rough trail beside the tracks.

At approximately 3:00 a.m., university senior Chad Goetz was relaxing on his patio, preparing for an upcoming exam. The soothing sounds of the night and the light from his study lamp were his only companions. He preferred studying at night, a habit that allowed him to absorb numerous pages of notes.

From the corner of his eye, he noticed a movement.

At first, he wrote it off as an illusion created by the shadows. However, when he shifted his gaze, he was taken aback. A young woman staggered through the front yard, her body wobbling with exhaustion. Despite the low light, he noticed her features—her face was battered and swollen, with blood staining her skin.

Heart racing, he rushed to her side, gently helping her onto the sofa. She sank into the cushions, her breathing quick and uneven. Shaking, Chad grabbed his phone, dialed 9-1-1, and urgently requested both an ambulance and the police.

"I honestly thought she might not survive," Goetz reflected later. "There was no question about it. She would start to speak, but I kept losing her as she faded away. I continued my conversation, hoping she wouldn't lose consciousness before the paramedics arrived."

"My friend is still out there," she whispered, her eyes fluttering. "Please, you must find him. He is still out there."

Paramedics arrived within minutes, followed shortly thereafter by Detective Craig Sorrell and his partner from the Lexington Police Department.

As paramedics attended to Holly, she struggled against her pain, urgently attempting to explain the situation to Detective

Sorrell. Despite her trembling voice, her memories were sharp and clear.

"He looked Hispanic, around five feet eight inches tall, with wavy black hair and glasses," she remembered. "Though not particularly muscular, he had a slender build. I recall his Mexican accent."

Her mind abruptly turned to Chris. She continually mentioned him as if holding onto his memory. "He was incredibly grounded, adored nature, and seemed carefree." Her voice faltered, tears pooling in her eyes. "I can still picture the moment the rock struck him... and—" She swallowed with difficulty. "It took his life. Chris didn't make it through the attack."

Detective Sorrell knelt next to her, his face unreadable. "We can discuss this later," he murmured, then waved to the paramedics. "Take her to the University of Kentucky Hospital."

Heather Dunn Niemeier, Holly's sister, reached the hospital in under an hour. It was devastating to witness Holly; her face was swollen and dazed, her eye socket fractured, and her jaw broken.

Her mouth was bound with wires, and bruises, severe cuts, and staples marred her face and head. As the doctors couldn't cut her hair, they resorted to stapling through it in a desperate attempt to stop the bleeding.

Heather remembered feeling intense gratitude and love for her sister's survival, but she struggled with significant guilt for not being there.

However, Holly's journey was just beginning. She faced significant challenges in coping with the physical pain from her injuries as well as the emotional distress brought on by the attack. After spending five days in the hospital, she unfortunately could not attend Chris's funeral.

She constantly felt fear, believing he still recalled her.

"I sensed he was aware I was still alive and that he would return for me," she shared with her family.

Holly was overwhelmed by fear. Believing that distance was her only protection, she made a daring decision: she relocated to England. There, she started school, hoping to escape from the man who haunted her dreams.

At that time, no one understood the full extent of the horror. Before the brutal murder of Chris and the savage assault on Holly, Ángel Maturino Reséndiz had already been on a killing spree—one that left a trail of victims across the country.

After the horrifying attack on Chris and Holly, Reséndiz continued his murderous spree. Unaware that Holly had survived and was now working closely with law enforcement, Reséndiz roamed freely, raping and killing with cold precision.

Even with Holly's firm resolve and the hard work of investigators, Reséndiz remained elusive, causing more victims in his path.

July 19, 1991 – San Antonio, Texas

Michael White was brutally murdered with a brick, and his body was discovered in the front yard of an abandoned house in downtown San Antonio.

The scene provided minimal clues, devoid of witnesses, a weapon, or a clear motive, which caused the investigation to stagnate quickly. The case remained unresolved for years, posing a perplexing mystery within police records.

In a chilling confession, Ángel Maturino Reséndiz—infamously known as the "Railroad Killer"—acknowledged the murder. He asserted that he killed White due to his belief that White was homosexual, exposing not only the senseless cruelty of the act but also the perverse bias that motivated his crimes.

The confession revealed yet another tragic victim on Reséndiz's extensive list, emphasizing the irrational and unsettling mentality that fueled his deadly spree.

March 23, 1997 – Ocala, Florida

Jesse Howell, age 19, was brutally bludgeoned to death with a railcar air brake hose coupling—a tool turned into a weapon of savage force. His lifeless body was discarded beside the railroad tracks that carved through the heart of Florida, left exposed to the elements as a grim and silent witness to the violence that had stolen his future.

March 23, 1997 – Ocala, Florida

Wendy Von Huben, age 16, was raped, strangled, suffocated with duct tape, and buried in a shallow grave in Sumter County, Florida. Von Huben and her fiancé, Jesse Howell, age 19, had met Reséndiz near Jacksonville.

July 5, 1997 – Colton, California

Roberto Castro, a 54-year-old drifter, faced a tragic demise in the lonely expanse of a railway yard—a site that reflected his nomadic way of life. For years, he had wandered from one location to another, existing on the fringes of society.

However, his journeys came to a violent and definitive conclusion on that desolate stretch of tracks.

He met a horrific fate due to a piece of plywood. This primitive weapon evoked a chilling picture, starkly illustrating the brutality he experienced. For someone accustomed to a nomadic lifestyle, the rail yard—previously a passage to his next journey—turned into his ultimate destination.

October 4, 1998 – Hughes Springs, Texas

Reséndiz broke into the home of 87-year-old Leafie Mason by slipping through an open window. Once inside, he launched a brutal and unprovoked attack, bludgeoning Mason repeatedly in the head with an antique fire iron.

The brutal assault was fatal, taking yet another innocent life and continuing Reséndiz's unyielding rampage of terror and violence.

December 10, 1998 – Carl, Georgia

Fannie Whitney Byers, age 81, was ruthlessly murdered in her home, mere steps from the CSX Transportation railroad tracks. She suffered a fatal beating with a heavy tire rim—an act of shocking violence that left her community in stunned grief.

The brutal nature of the attack raised troubling questions: What prompted such extreme violence? Did the attacker know her, or was he an unknown individual who slipped through the crowded transit area? Fannie Byers' murder not only broke the community's sense of safety but also heightened concerns about the security of residents near transit routes like the railroad.

June 4, 1999 – Houston, Texas

Reséndiz broke into the home of 26-year-old schoolteacher Noemi Dominguez, where he viciously raped her before striking her down with a pickax. Departing from his typical pattern of traveling by train, he stole Dominguez's white Honda Civic. He drove to the small town of Schulenburg, Texas.

Later that same day, wielding the same pickaxe, Reséndiz savagely murdered 73-year-old Josephine Konvicka in her farmhouse. The weapon, still stained with Dominguez's blood, was left embedded in Konvicka's skull—a gruesome signature that investigators believed was an intentional and taunting message.

1999 – Gorham, Illinois

Just before dawn, Reséndiz broke into the home of 80-year-old George Morber in Gorham, Illinois. That day, George's 51-year-old daughter, Carolyn Frederick, was there to help clean her father's house, a routine act of kindness that sadly took a tragic turn.

Morber, a retired correctional officer and Army veteran, had earned a life of quiet dignity in his later years. But that morning, peace gave way to terror. Reséndiz bound George to a chair and executed him with a single shotgun blast to the back of the head.

Carolyn's ordeal was even more horrific. Reséndiz sexually assaulted her, then struck her with the butt of the shotgun—delivering such a violent blow that the weapon shattered. Neither George nor Carolyn survived the attack.

Before the sun finally rose, Reséndiz slipped into the predawn darkness, leaving behind a house drenched in blood and a sight almost too terrible to comprehend.

After two years, Detective Brian Sorrell received a call. An agent from the FBI's Violent Criminal Apprehension Program (ViCAP), representing the unit that identifies and tracks serial violent offenders, reached out.

"A homicide was reported near the railroad tracks in Texas," the agent said.

Sorrell hesitated briefly. This clue was subtle—another body had appeared near the tracks. After two years of chasing elusive leads, even the slightest indication warranted investigation.

What initially started as a mere suspicion developed into a more sinister truth. By examining timelines, locations, and victim profiles across multiple states, investigators revealed a concerning pattern. The killer extended beyond a 150-mile radius around Houston. He was, in fact, mobile, using trains to traverse jurisdictional boundaries and leaving a path of destruction behind him.

This was not just a murderer; it was a serial killer with a unique method and strategy—someone skilled at taking advantage of communication gaps in law enforcement. A true master of the art of vanishing.

He kept killing with ease, showcasing a frightening precision and steadfast resolve.

In just one day, he took the lives of two women approximately 90 miles apart. Four days later, he entered a new state. Fear gripped the community as residents locked their doors, drew their curtains, and feared the coming of night.

The race had begun. They needed to catch him fast, or more victims would emerge.

What started as a string of gruesome murders swiftly evolved into a nationwide pursuit. A serial killer roamed free—his assaults were violent, and his actions erratic.

Texas Ranger Drew Carter remarked, "Many of his assaults caught victims off guard. They were often asleep in their beds during these attacks. He resembles the boogeyman sneaking into your home, emphasizing the unsettling truth that genuine evil exists in our world."

The newest clue directed investigators to Texas. Detectives Brian Sorrell and Drew Carter pursued the lead, uncovering a troubling finding.

This wasn't just a killer; this was a ghost.

Ángel Maturino Reséndiz was an undocumented wanderer who quietly crossed borders, rode freight trains, and vanished into the night after each murder. He left no traces and showed no apparent patterns—just turmoil.

Although violence had characterized the past, law enforcement remained ill-equipped for the terror he would unleash.

Born on August 1, 1959, in Izúcar de Matamoros, Puebla, Mexico, as Ángel Leoncio Reyes Recendis, Reséndiz earned the nickname "The Railroad Killer" for good reason: nearly all of his documented murders occurred near train tracks. Trains served as his escape route—his lifeline. He traveled from Mexico to Canada and through various cities across the United States with ease, leaving a trail of blood in his wake.

Although he had family in Mexico, Reséndiz never felt a sense of belonging there. His childhood was marked by instability and emotional wounds. At the age of six, he went to live with relatives, which sparked feelings of abandonment and isolation. When he was 13 or 14, he faced a traumatic sexual assault by older boys after swimming in a nearby river. This event would profoundly impact his life. By 1973, he had left Mexico and entered the U.S., beginning a turbulent journey that would soon lead him into a world of crime and violence.

Government records show he was deported to Mexico a minimum of four times after entering the United States in 1973. Nevertheless, he managed to return each time, slipping across the border like a ghost and disappearing into America's vast railway network.

At that point, the manhunt had expanded from Ohio to the Texas-Mexico border. Authorities hurried to apprehend a murderer who was perpetually on the run, attacking unexpectedly and leaving one certainty in his wake: he was bound to kill again.

Helicopters hovered above the train tracks, their searchlights cutting through the darkness as locomotives came to a standstill. Authorities combed the rail lines in a frantic search for Ángel Maturino Reséndiz, who always eluded capture, remaining just out of reach. The widening dragnet intensified Holly Dunn's anxiety.

Simultaneously, an FBI profiler observed the escalating urgency of the manhunt: Reséndiz faces increasingly limited options. Lacking allies and with a significant bounty on his head, he was being chased by not one but two nations.

The source of the disturbance was surprising: a mysterious phone call from an unfamiliar relative. The caller urged the investigators to head to New Mexico and suggested they contact Reséndiz's sister, Manuela.

Caught between fear and obligation, Manuela emerged as the vital connection between her fleeing brother and U.S.

law enforcement. She feared he could kill again or be chased, possibly by Mexican bounty hunters. After enduring days of distress, she reached a firm decision.

She notified the authorities, "My brother will arrive in the United States on July 12. He intends to cross at the International Bridge."

On the morning of July 12, 1999, an unsettling tension permeated the U.S.–Mexico border in El Paso. Devon Anderson, newly appointed Harris County District Attorney, stood on the American side of the International Bridge. Meanwhile, Texas Ranger Drew Carter quietly observed from across the bridge, his gaze locked on the horizon.

Questions arose regarding Reséndiz's arrival. Would he approach peacefully, or would he come prepared for a confrontation?

Time seemed to elongate. Suddenly, a pickup truck crept across the bridge. Carter felt a wave of tension; his senses heightened. Inside the truck were three people, and he concentrated closely on the man in the center.

His presence was undeniable.

"Incredible, this is going to happen," Carter whispered to Anderson, his voice soft yet filled with enthusiasm.

As the truck drew nearer, Ángel Maturino Reséndiz sensed the imposing presence of law enforcement—Texas Rangers, U.S. Marshals, and Border Agents, all ready and well-equipped.

He experienced a jarring epiphany as if struck by a freight train. There was no way out.

Reséndiz complied without resistance. The events unfolded seamlessly. He accepted his fate, feeling an overwhelming sense of inevitability. The Texas Rangers arrived, placed him in handcuffs, and took him into custody. They then transported him back to Houston, where justice that had long been overdue awaited.

Drew Carter stated, "Reséndiz is linked to six murders in Texas, two in Illinois, and one in Kentucky."

Assistant District Attorney Devon Anderson was excited about Reséndiz's first court appearance. The impact was immediate and remarkable.

"I remember it as an extraordinary moment," Holly recalled. "Yet, he radiated intimidation. Although he was small and slender, he possessed considerable strength, with muscular arms."

She hesitated, her voice laden with recollections.

He carefully scanned the courtroom, noting each person present. His gaze met everyone's before settling on me. At that moment, his eyes showed nothing—cold and emotionless. It was as if a dark veil had obscured his sight, unrelenting and lifeless, merely conveying a sense of emptiness.

Anderson took a deep breath, pushing past his discomfort. "I collected my thoughts and reminded myself that this conversation must center on the victims, their families, and the lives he has devastated. Furthermore, we need to persuade a jury that he deserves the death penalty. And he does. He has undeniably earned it."

The primary witness was Holly Dunn, a survivor of exceptional strength. Displaying immense bravery, she recounted the harrowing experience that forever altered her life. Her account transcended a mere retelling of the assault she faced; it evolved into a moving depiction of the violent incident that took Chris Maier's life.

It is challenging to understand the bravery required to face the man who tried to silence her permanently. In this pivotal moment, Holly found her inner strength again. Her resolute voice broke the stillness. She wasn't just recounting her experience; she was insisting on justice.

Anderson looked forward to witnessing Reséndiz's response when he learned that someone had survived—someone who could confront him and expose the truth he wanted to keep concealed.

Holly stood as the only living witness, her voice the sole challenge to him, not through hearsay or courtroom evidence but through the unfiltered truth of her survival. At that moment, she shifted from a passive observer to a formidable reckoning force.

In May 2000, the trial began in a Houston courtroom filled with eager anticipation. Amid heavy security, Ángel Maturino Reséndiz arrived.

Overwhelmed with emotion, Holly inched closer to prosecutor Devon Anderson and murmured, "He appears so different. I suppose jail has altered him—he's gained weight, has that jailhouse pallor, and his hair looks greasy. But there's still not a shred of humanity in him. He doesn't deserve to live among us. Today, I'm going to put him down."

The trial commenced following the vicious murder of Dr. Claudia Benton, a 39-year-old physician and researcher at Baylor College of Medicine in Houston, Texas.

Just eight days before Christmas in 1998, Benton was found in her West University Place residence with sexual assault, multiple stab wounds, and blunt force trauma from a bronze statue. Like many of Reséndiz's crime scenes, her home was near railroad tracks.

Days later, investigators discovered her stolen Jeep Cherokee abandoned in San Antonio. Reséndiz's fingerprints on the steering column established a haunting and irrefutable connection, positioning him as the driver and the focal point of the Railway Killings.

Although law enforcement linked Reséndiz to many murders in various states, prosecutors concentrated solely on Benton's case. This approach was deliberate. With ample physical evidence and the seriousness of the offense, achieving one conviction was sufficient to seek the death penalty.

Reséndiz claimed insanity as his defense since it was the only viable option against the substantial evidence presented.

Following hours of heated debate, the jury delivered their verdict: guilty of capital murder.

Holly's case was the last one presented.

By then, the jury had already endured the grisly testimonies and forensic evidence tied to Reséndiz's trail of destruction. They had seen the photographs and heard the accounts. They had witnessed the carnage he had left behind. It had been a horror show—bodies beaten beyond recognition, knives driven deep into flesh, murders so vicious they seemed almost inhuman.

They were ready to hear another one.

Holly stood as the last victim; this was her opportunity to speak out.

The prosecutor gently guided her to the location. "What did you do over the weekend?"

Holly inhaled deeply, her voice calm even as the pain in her chest grew.

"I completed my college education."

She felt joy as she conversed with the man who had tried to take everything from her. He had the power to ruin her future and leave her profoundly hurt, but she persevered. Still, he remained unresponsive, and she sensed he always would.

Holly detailed everything she remembered about that night, her tears flowing freely—each terrifying instance, each brutal act. The courtroom was silent, broken only by her cries. Looking at the jury, she saw their eyes glistening with tears.

Detective Craig Sorrell approached his voice a mix of sorrow and respect.

"During these instances, we tend to face solely the terror— the violence—without a means to articulate it. Yet, Holly, you gave that voice. You allowed Chris and the others an opportunity they had long been missing: to convey their pain to the world."

She continued to share her story, and finally, the world would pay attention.

The critical moment in the trial came. The prosecutor kept a firm but steady tone while asking the question that would decide the defendant's fate.

"Is the person who attacked you in the courtroom today?"

Until now, Holly had steered clear of eye contact with him. There was no reason for it; his presence had eclipsed every breath and heartbeat since she assumed her place on the stand. However, at this moment, she finally raised her eyes.

With tears still flowing down her face, she responded softly, "Yes."

The prosecutor leaned in slightly, tilting his head. "What is he wearing?"

She faced him, their eyes meeting for the first time since that night.

Angel Maturino Reséndiz sat there, seemingly content and untroubled, like a spectator of another's misfortune. His eerie composure was unsettling. The atmosphere felt dreamlike, akin to a disturbing nightmare.

"He has on a white button-up shirt."

To Reséndiz, it must have seemed as if she had been given a second chance—her testimony marked the pivotal moment that shaped his destiny.

The jury deliberated for nearly ten hours, showing no signs of sympathy. When they returned, they issued a swift and clear verdict: guilty of first-degree premeditated murder.

In the sentencing phase, the jury determined that Ángel Maturino Reséndiz continued to be a threat to society and was deemed mentally fit for execution.

Given this conclusion, the judge was left with no alternative but to issue him a death sentence.

Reséndiz faced the court with a defiant smirk.

"I deny the idea of death. Although the body may fade, my spirit lives on. I will exist eternally," he proclaimed, his voice ringing with eerie certainty. "I embody both human and angelic qualities. You cannot bring about my end because I refuse to embrace my mortality."

He was discreetly led out of the Houston courtroom.

After the trial, Reséndiz was transferred to death row at the Texas State Penitentiary in Huntsville, which houses the busiest execution chamber in the country.

For Holly Dunn, the verdict was a great relief. He could no longer inflict harm. She had endured and battled, and now she was prepared to take on a new chance at life that she planned to fully embrace.

Later, while working at an outdoor supply store, Holly met Jacob Pendleton. He became the first man she dated following the attack, and they ultimately tied the knot. When their first son arrived, they named him William Christopher to pay tribute to Chris Maier.

Two years after the attack, Holly started sharing her story as Reséndiz's last recognized victim.

"Expressing my emotions, sharing thoughts, and shedding tears played a crucial role in my recovery, particularly after a long period of distance," she stated. "Being Reséndiz's sole survivor is one part of my journey, but helping fellow survivors in a professional role brings an entirely new array of challenges."

Taking a deep breath, she shared, "To conquer my survivor's guilt, I needed to realize that I'm not just living for myself or Chris—I'm also living for all the victims of Reséndiz. They never had this chance, but I do. Hence, I strive to live for them. I want their stories recognized. I hope they would find pride in my journey."

The Harris County District Attorney, Devon Anderson, commended Holly's resilience: "Holly is a hero for refusing to let her past define her. Instead, she has transformed her experience into a source of motivation to succeed and to help others."

Investigator Craig Sorrell considered the case's enduring impact.

"This was among the most difficult cases I've encountered, one I have thought about repeatedly. On my desk lies a small memento—a rock from the crime scene and a railroad spike from Texas. It represents the most crucial case I've handled and underscores the value of perseverance. With commitment and continuous effort, success is attainable in any situation. Therefore, cling to your determination. Never give up."

Despite Reséndiz committing murders in multiple states, he was only prosecuted for the crime that resulted in his conviction. He had already received the death penalty, and after his last appeal was rejected, a date for his execution was established.

Ángel Maturino Reséndiz was executed by lethal injection at the Huntsville Unit in Texas on June 27, 2006.

His final words were "I hope you can find it in your heart to forgive me. If not, I understand. I've allowed the Devil to steer my life. I seek your forgiveness and implore the Lord for His mercy after being deceived by the Devil. I am thankful to God for His unwavering patience. I know I don't deserve to hurt you; you don't deserve this. I accept the repercussions of my actions."

The Railroad Killer was pronounced dead at 8:05 p.m. CDT. He was 46 years old, marking this execution as the 13th conducted in Texas that year.

George Benton, whose wife, Dr. Claudia Benton, had fallen victim to Reséndiz, served as a witness.

Benton remarked, "Reséndiz represented true evil. He was a heartless entity, lacking any conscience, showing no regret, and exhibiting complete disregard for the sanctity of human life."

Holly decided against attending. For her, the execution symbolized the darkness she had worked hard to flee. Instead, she opted to spend time with her loved ones, placing peace above reliving the trauma.

Devon Anderson, instrumental in Reséndiz's capture, shared his thoughts on the arrest and later death: "I'm grateful I was at the International Bridge on July 12, 1999, when he was apprehended. That day remains one of the most rewarding in my career."

After a brief pause, he continued, "I came across a report on the execution which mentioned that just before they injected him, his feet trembled beneath the sheet. I wished that he felt at least some of the fear that Holly did. Knowing he felt scared gave me a fleeting sense of satisfaction."

During his years-long spree, Reséndiz murdered over a dozen people across six states, using rocks, pickaxes, and other blunt objects to brutally bludgeon his victims. He often lingered at the scenes, raiding refrigerators or taking sentimental keepsakes before disappearing into the night, always by rail.

While investigators found that some of his female victims were sexually assaulted, they believed that his crimes were not primarily driven by sexual motives.

He preyed on the vulnerable—smaller, weaker, or less likely to fight back. In several instances, the bodies were found covered as if he were trying to conceal the horror he had inflicted.

Despite enduring severe trauma, Holly found a way to take charge of her life. She established Holly's House, a center focused on assisting children and adults by offering a safe environment for victims of intimate crimes to report their experiences and begin their healing journeys.

She transformed her pain into purpose by offering survivors the support and resources they had previously lacked. Holly Dunn confronted a ruthless and sadistic killer—an international fugitive on the FBI's Ten Most Wanted list.

CHAPTER THREE

Killer Clown – John Wayne Gacy

John Wayne Gacy, one of America's most notorious serial killers and rapists, was born on March 17, 1942, in Chicago, Illinois, to John Stanley Gacy and Marion Elaine Robison. Gacy went on to murder at least 33 teenage boys and young men in Cook County, Illinois, between 1972 and 1978.

Gacy, the second of three children, was raised in a troubled family. His father, a World War I veteran and auto repair machinist, battled alcoholism and frequently exhibited violent behavior.

He often punished Gacy and his sisters with a razor strap for what he viewed as misbehavior. Moreover, Gacy's father consistently verbally abused him, labeling him as weak, stupid, and inferior to his sisters.

Gacy stated, "My father was very controlling. He drank a lot, and during those times, he was abusive to both my mother and me. However, I never fought back because I respected what he represented."

Despite Gacy's relentless attempts to gain his father's approval, he faced only ridicule and physical abuse, which profoundly affected his troubled mind and later manifested in horrific ways.

During his childhood, Gacy faced several health issues, particularly a congenital heart condition that resulted in multiple hospitalizations.

He also struggled with obesity and social challenges that made it difficult for him to connect with peers at home and school. His congenital heart condition limited his ability to engage in sports and social gatherings, which worsened his sense of isolation. Furthermore, Gacy's father, a domineering alcoholic, viewed his son's health problems as weaknesses. He displayed minimal empathy or understanding and continued to suppress him.

In his teenage years, Gacy dealt with persistent health problems that often led to hospitalization. Instead of showing concern, his father dismissed these issues as simple cries for attention, which deepened the rift in their emotional connection.

Gacy earned the nickname "The Killer Clown" due to his use of a clown costume and makeup at community events. His childhood was fraught with abuse and isolation, contributing to his difficulties with sexuality and worsening his already fragile self-esteem. This internal conflict and a strong desire for acceptance led him down a perilous and dark path.

In his childhood, Gacy suffered abuse from a family friend who was a contractor. From ages 10 to 12, he was accused of inappropriately touching a young girl.

Gacy's psychosexual development began between the ages of six and ten when a family friend's teenage daughter reportedly undressed and engaged with him.

He led a dual existence, captivating his neighbors while hiding gruesome offenses.

Despite leaving high school early, John Wayne Gacy enrolled at Northwestern Business College, where he refined his persuasive techniques and acquired essential management and sales skills. His charisma and drive hinted at a bright future, leading him to marry Marlynn Myers. He relocated to Iowa to oversee his father-in-law's KFC franchises. Gacy skillfully built an image as a respected businessman and community figure, gaining the trust of those around him. Yet, beneath this polished exterior lay a predator whose sinister urges would soon reveal themselves through horrifying acts against young men.

After leaving Chicago, Gacy moved to Las Vegas, where he worked part-time as a janitor at Palm Mortuary. A few months later, unhappy with his circumstances, he returned to Chicago.

Despite encountering academic and social challenges, Gacy demonstrated exceptional abilities in business and sales. His determination and charm swiftly propelled him to professional achievement, eventually securing a managerial position in the fast-food industry at a young age.

By marrying into a wealthy family, he gained the financial stability he had always sought, allowing him to move to Iowa. There, he shaped a persona as a thriving entrepreneur and committed community member. His charm and generosity helped him blend into social circles, winning the trust and admiration of those around him. However, behind his polished façade of success and respectability, a troubling darkness lingered that he struggled to conceal. Ultimately, it was only a matter of time before the carefully constructed illusion of his virtuous life fell apart, exposing the unsettling truth within.

Well-regarded in his community, John Wayne Gacy was instrumental in civic and political endeavors. He organized cultural events and actively participated in the local Jaycees chapter. His dedication to public service and skill in connecting with prominent individuals earned him admiration, which he later referred to as the happiest period of his life. Even his strongest critic—his father—gradually softened, offering him rare praise and acknowledging his previous misjudgment.

As his reputation grew and his confidence surged, Gacy considered a political career. "I thought about running for alderman, then aimed to become mayor, and if that went well, my ultimate goal was the state Senate. I saw no boundaries."

He might have been your neighbor, a coworker, a regular at the local bar, or even your father, who had two children from different marriages. Standing at 5'8" and weighing over 200 pounds, he had a solid build. His skin was oily, and his greasy, dishwater-blond hair, now mixed with gray, always appeared unkempt. Nevertheless, despite his scruffy appearance, he emanated a warm and welcoming vibe, charismatic in a way that made people feel at ease.

His charm made him ideal for playing the role of a clown, bringing joy to children's parties and hospital wards. His lively persona earned him accolades, recognition, and the Jaycee Man of the Year title in 1965. This allure helped him break into Chicago politics, famously illustrated in a photo of him smiling and shaking hands with First Lady Rosalynn Carter.

Gacy was a member of a local clown organization known as the "Jolly Jokers." He frequently wore clown makeup and costumes to entertain at children's parties, charitable events, and community fundraisers. By taking on roles such as "Pogo the Clown" and "Patches the Clown," he cultivated an image of joy and friendliness. However, hidden beneath this jovial facade was a menacing predator.

Years later, in observation, Gacy disclosed his clown-related actions to detectives, ominously stating, "Clowns can escape justice."

His first known killing occurred in 1972, when he lured 16-year-old Timothy McCoy into his home, stabbed him to death, and buried his body in the crawl space. When his crawl space could no longer accommodate more bodies, he began disposing of them in nearby rivers.

Gacy's downward spiral began in December 1978 at a pharmacy, where he lured 15-year-old Robert Piest after the boy's mother had left him to search for a job.

Following the teenager's disappearance, police quickly discovered that Gacy had been at the store shortly before, leading them to focus on him, especially after finding out about his previous conviction for sexually assaulting a teenage boy.

During a visit to Gacy's residence, a detective asked to use the bathroom and was overwhelmed by a strong smell of decay as the furnace fan kicked on. This odor and increasing suspicions led to a search warrant, revealing a shocking reality.

Beneath the house, in the cramped crawl space, investigators uncovered the first of many decomposing bodies. National news channels broadcast somber images of police teams meticulously recovering the remains, one after another.

Before murdering his victims, Gacy would handcuff them, detail his intended torture, and make them plead for their lives.

The remains of 29 victims were ultimately found on his property.

Richard Rappaport, representing John Wayne Gacy, said, "He staged a distorted reenactment of his childhood trauma. He needed them to embody his younger self—weak and scared—while he took on the father's role."

He admonished them for their frailties while expressing and contemplating the insecurities he struggled to accept in himself.

William Kunkle, an attorney in private practice and the lead prosecutor in John Wayne Gacy's trial, recalled Gacy describing how he met his first victim outside the Greyhound Bus Station on January 3, 1972. "He stated that his first victim was not strangled like the others," Kunkle noted, "but was instead stabbed twice in the chest."

Gacy stated, "After I picked up McCoy, we drove around before returning home. At my place, McCoy consumed some food and alcohol. Following that, we had consensual sex.

"Later that night, around 4:00 a.m., I awoke to find McCoy looming over me with a butcher knife. A fierce struggle ensued, and during this confrontation, McCoy accidentally fell onto the knife, resulting in his death."

An autopsy showed that McCoy had sustained several stab wounds.

Nevertheless, McCoy's family disputes the idea that he would have willingly associated with Gacy, claiming that the killer's account of events at his home is inaccurate.

Katherine Ramsland, a professor of forensic psychology at DeSales University, expresses her skepticism. She remarked, "I don't believe Gacy's account of how he killed McCoy or that there was any consensual sexual encounter between them. Gacy was a psychopathic narcissist, manipulator, and self-assured. This persona helped him attract victims and gain credibility with authorities. However, he was a self-serving liar who consistently blamed his victims. One undeniable truth about sexual predators is this: they will begin eliminating their witnesses. They will devise methods to evade capture."

Another significant detail noted by Ramsland is Gacy's confession to investigators that he experienced an orgasm after killing McCoy. This starkly contradicts Gacy's claim that the murder was impulsive and defensive—an act committed in a panicked haze after being abruptly awakened.

Ramsland explained that if Tim were Gacy's first murder victim and experienced an orgasm, it would arise from a pattern of developed fantasies.

She noted that this behavior is associated with a condition called erotophonophilia, in which sexual arousal or gratification results from the act of killing.

"When murder fails to fulfill the killer's fantasy, the desire may wane. However, when fantasy and reality align—when the act brings the anticipated thrill—it creates a foundation for repetition. That's when it paves the way for further killings."

The murder sparked a disturbing sequence of offenses. From 1975 to 1978, Gacy targeted young men, often luring them with job offers at his construction business, PDM Contractors.

Once inside his home, he bound, raped, and strangled his victims. Many were buried beneath his house, while others were discarded in the Des Plaines River, their lives erased by a man who hid his depravity behind a painted mask.

Gacy sometimes performed a macabre "rope trick," using a tourniquet to slowly asphyxiate his victims. In total, 33 victims were confirmed, though some remain unidentified.

His decline started in December 1978 after 15-year-old Robert Piest vanished. Piest had last been spotted talking to Gacy about a job opportunity. A search of Gacy's residence revealed unsettling evidence, such as driver's licenses, handcuffs, and items belonging to missing young men. Investigators also noticed a repugnant smell emanating from the crawl space. This troubling clue would soon expose the full scale of his offenses.

The excavation of John Wayne Gacy's residence uncovered far more than investigators expected—a chilling labyrinth of hidden horrors below. Beneath the crawlspace, an intricate system of tunnels emerged, a nightmarish underground network Gacy began constructing around 1972, shortly after completing his first prison sentence. Utilizing his building skills, Gacy ingeniously crafted concealed spaces and structures, transforming the foundation of his home into a covert burial site.

Gacy's construction company served as a sinister facade. He portrayed himself as a respected contractor, often providing job opportunities to young men and teenage boys. This seemingly innocent chance frequently signified their last moments. Once inside, they found themselves trapped in a horrifying atmosphere concealed beneath a veneer of suburban normality.

The chilling discoveries beneath the floorboards included:

Skeletal remains, numerous layers stacked in differing stages of decay.

The victims' personal belongings were carelessly tossed aside, though they held profound, lingering significance.

Evidence of torture exposes the unimaginable pain experienced by individuals who were tortured and never existed.

Gacy's terrifying double life serves as a stark reminder that many of the most dangerous predators disguise themselves as ordinary people. He actively participated in community events, performed at children's parties, and was viewed as a reputable businessman—all while concealing unimaginable wickedness. His prolonged ability to evade detection highlights the disturbing reality that the most atrocious acts can hide in plain sight.

The troubling history of the residence on Summerdale Avenue marks one of the most chilling chapters in American criminal history. The grim discoveries in Gacy's crawlspace stunned the world, forcing society to confront the truth that real evil is not always grotesque; it can sometimes reside just next door.

After relentless interrogation, John Wayne Gacy finally broke his silence by confessing to the brutal murders of more than 30 young men and boys. He even provided authorities with a detailed sketch of his crawl space, mapping out the locations where he buried many of his victims.

As investigators excavated beneath his suburban Chicago residence, they uncovered a horrific sight: multiple layers of human remains. This chilling discovery reverberated throughout the country, solidifying Gacy's position among history's most infamous serial killers.

Gacy's confirmed victims:

Timothy McCoy, 18 (January 3, 1972)
John Butkovitch, 17 (July 21, 1975)
Darrell Samson, 18 (April 6, 1976)

Randall Reffett, 15 (May 14, 1976)
Sam Stapleton, 14 (May 14, 1976)
Michael Bonnin, 17 (June 3, 1976)
William Carroll, Jr., 16 (June 13, 1976)
Rick Johnston, 17 (August 6, 1976)
Kenneth Parker, 16 (October 25, 1976)
Michael Marino, 14 (October 25, 1976)
Gregory Godzik, 17 (December 12, 1976)
John Szyc, 19 (January 20, 1977)
Jon Prestidge, 20 (March 15, 1977)
Matthew Bowman, 19 (July 5, 1977)
Robert Gilroy, 18 (September 15, 1977)
John Mowery, 19 (September 25, 1977)
Russell Nelson, 21 (October 17, 1977)
Robert Winch, 16 (November 10, 1977)
Tommy Boling, 20 (November 18, 1977)
David Talsma, 19 (December 9, 1977)
William Kindred, 19 (February 16, 1978)
Timothy O'Rourke, 20 (June 1978)
Frank Landingin, 19 (November 4, 1978)
James Mazzara, 21 (November 24, 1978)

One victim who miraculously survived John Wayne Gacy's sadistic torture was Robert Donnelly, a 19-year-old college student abducted from a Chicago bus stop. Gacy took him to his home, where he subjected him to a night of unimaginable horror—raping and torturing him relentlessly.

He repeatedly dunked Donnelly's head in a bathtub, holding him under until he lost consciousness, only to revive him and continue the torment. At one point, Gacy staged mock executions, pressing a gun to Donnelly's head and pulling the trigger. However, the weapon was loaded only with blanks.

The psychological and physical torment was so severe that Donnelly implored Gacy to alleviate his suffering, urgently begging for death.

But instead of killing him, Gacy let Donnelly go, warning him not to tell anyone. Shattered but alive, Donnelly defied his captor's threat and immediately reported the attack to the police. Inexplicably, when questioned, Gacy dismissed the incident as a consensual act of "sex slavery," and shockingly, authorities believed him. No charges were filed, allowing Gacy to continue his killing spree unchecked and undeterred.

In 1979, soon after John Wayne Gacy was arrested, authorities swiftly searched his home at 8213 West Summerdale Avenue in Norwood Park, Illinois, for evidence. After an extensive investigation, the house was partially taken apart.

By the following year, the entire property and all its buildings had been demolished, erasing all physical traces of the horrors hidden within. Ultimately, a new residence was constructed on the site. A worker who participated in the demolition hauntingly remarked, "If the devil exists, he lived here."

The trial of John Wayne Gacy began on February 6, 1980, at the Cook County Criminal Courts in Chicago. It lasted five weeks, and over 100 witnesses testified for the prosecution and defense. The evidence against Gacy was strong, leaving little room to question his guilt.

Consequently, the defense sought to establish that Gacy was legally insane at the time of the murders to escape the death penalty. Various psychiatrists testified on his behalf, depicting him as a man tormented by uncontrollable impulses and dissociative episodes. In opposition, the prosecution presented its mental health specialists, contending that Gacy was fully aware of his actions and had meticulously planned his crimes. The insanity defense failed to persuade the jury; after merely two hours of deliberation, they delivered a guilty verdict on 33 counts of murder—one for each of Gacy's recognized victims.

On March 13, 1980, Gacy received a death sentence and was subsequently moved to Menard Correctional Center in Chester, Illinois.

The Menard Correctional Center, a century-old brick building, is located by the Mississippi River. It operates as a maximum-security prison, accommodating several hundred more inmates, and serves as one of two death row facilities in Illinois.

The absence of windows creates a deep feeling of loss, significantly impacting your experience as you face numerous challenges and become aware of your limitations. For some unknown reason, the warden strictly prohibited chewing gum.

While at the Menard Correctional Center, Gacy took part in comprehensive psychological evaluations, dedicating hundreds of hours to consultations with doctors and participating in numerous tests.

He aimed to build his defense around claims of multiple personality disorder, asserting that his mind was divided into various identities, including a contractor, a clown, a politician, and a police officer named "Bad Jack." Gacy mentioned that Bad Jack held a strong disdain for homosexuality. He viewed male prostitutes—many of whom were his victims—as worthless, weak, foolish, and degraded.

Before his death, Gacy asserted that the families of his victims would find no comfort in his passing and accused the state of executing him. His alleged last words were, "Kiss my ass."

On the morning of May 9, 1994, Gacy was transferred to Stateville Correctional Center to be executed. That afternoon, he was allowed a private picnic on the prison grounds with his family. Gacy ordered a bucket of KFC, French fries, a dozen fried shrimp, fresh strawberries, and a Diet Coke for his last meal.

That evening, a Catholic priest performed the last rites before his transfer to the Stateville execution chamber.

In the hours leading up to Gacy's execution, over 1,000 people gathered outside the correctional center. While a vocal majority supported the execution, a small group of anti-death penalty protesters was also present. Among those advocating for the execution, some wore T-shirts referencing Gacy's past as a clown, featuring satirical slogans like "No tears for the clown."

At 12:40 a.m. on May 10, the procedure to administer the lethal injection began. However, the chemicals used in the execution solidified unexpectedly, clogging the IV tube. The execution team replaced the clogged tube, and the execution resumed.

The entire procedure lasted 18 minutes. Anesthesiologists attributed the issue to the prison officials' inexperience with executions. This mistake prompted Illinois to adopt an alternative method of lethal injection. One prosecutor at Gacy's trial, William Kunkle, stated, "He received a much easier death than any of his victims." Nevertheless, the impact of his crimes reached well beyond his immediate surroundings.

Amid significant local police criticism for their sluggish efforts to connect the missing victims to Gacy, federal and local law enforcement agencies started working together. They exchanged information about runaways and sex offenders, launched a national hotline, and set up a computer database to track missing persons.

Throughout the nation, police departments and schools worked together on comprehensive public service campaigns to inform parents and children about the risks associated with strangers.

Even after his execution, Gacy's legacy continues to serve as a chilling reminder of the evil that can lurk behind a charming exterior.

CHAPTER FOUR

San Diego Rapist and Killer – John Albert Gardner III

John Albert Gardner III is an American convicted double murderer and registered sex offender. He gained national attention after confessing to the rape and murder of 14-year-old Amber Dubois in Escondido, California, and the February 2010 rape and murder of 17-year-old Chelsea King in Poway, California.

John Albert Gardner III was born in Culver City, California, on April 9, 1979. His childhood was troubled and marked by instability and trauma. After his parents' divorce, he frequently moved throughout Southern California, living in places such as Lawndale, Palmdale, and Running Springs. In his teenage years, he settled in Running Springs. In this mountainous area, he reflected on his childhood, characterized by abuse and emotional distress.

In 1997, he graduated from Rim of the World High School with a 3.2 GPA and an IQ of 113, 13 points above the national average.

During high school, Gardner held various odd jobs, including working as a lifeguard at a rundown amusement park in Lake

Arrowhead. Although he appeared typical on the surface, deeper issues were developing. As a teenager, he received a trespassing conviction on his high school campus, marking the start of his escalating behavioral challenges.

After graduating high school, Gardner relocated to San Diego and briefly worked at a Big 5 Sporting Goods store. Diagnosed with attention deficit hyperactivity disorder (ADHD) and classified as "seriously emotionally disturbed," he began taking psychiatric medication at the age of six. At ten, he was hospitalized for 60 days in a psychiatric facility, where his mother, Cathy Osborn—a psychiatric nurse—managed much of his early mental health treatment. Gardner later stated that his father was an abusive alcoholic who frequently physically harmed him. By 16, he had completely stopped taking his medication.

In 2000, John Albert Gardner III was found guilty of molesting a 13-year-old girl from the neighborhood. He spent five years in prison and completed his parole in 2008. However, records indicate that Gardner violated his parole conditions at least seven times. A notable breach took place in 2007 when he was discovered living near a school, which was a direct violation of the restrictions placed on sex offenders.

Gardner was investigated by his parole officer for marijuana possession, but the charges were dismissed. While under supervision, he had to wear a GPS-monitoring ankle bracelet. Data from this device showed concerning behavior; he often came near schools, hung around a daycare center, and visited prison grounds to see a friend. Notably, the GPS monitoring stopped just four months before the kidnapping and murder of Amber Dubois, raising serious concerns about the oversight and enforcement of Gardner's parole conditions.

February 13, 2009

The day Amber had been looking forward to for a year had finally come. This event held great importance for her, as she had always dreamed of buying a lamb from a vendor at Escondido High School.

Amber had a profound love for animals. As a dedicated participant in her school's Future Farmers of America program, she eagerly anticipated raising a lamb, nurturing it, and forming a strong bond while diligently caring for it. She even selected a name—Nenette, a term of endearment in French. For weeks, her excitement was overwhelming, spilling into every conversation.

After months of pleading and heartfelt promises, Amber finally received her mother's approval for the purchase. That morning—an ordinary, drizzly Friday—she left the house beaming, her backpack fully zipped and a check securely tucked away. Her dream was now within reach.

Amber, however, did not arrive at school.

She disappeared under mysterious circumstances at the age of 14.

Carrie's mother spoke to the police with a trembling voice, saying, " I can't understand how this could happen to my cherished daughter." After gathering herself, she continued, "Just two weeks before her disappearance, she sent me a letter asking for a lamb. In it, she detailed how she would care for it and noted that it would enhance her resume. Amber has loved animals since childhood."

When detectives inquired about Amber to gain insights into her character, Carrie called her a "free spirit." Amber wasn't interested in trends or shopping but prioritized school, art, and her close-knit friends. "She promised herself not to skip any school days," Carrie remembered. "She wasn't fond of Facebook or spending time at the mall. Instead, she cherished peaceful moments spent reading and pursuing her dreams."

Her voice trembled. "My daughter adored books and aspired to be an animal behavior scientist. And now... she never got to go to school."

Amber's disappearance ignited a widespread search effort. Authorities, friends, and strangers combed the area, desperately looking for clues. However, a heavy sense of dread began to linger as time passed without any sign of her.

That afternoon, as Amber still hadn't returned home, her mother, Carrie, and stepfather, Dave Cave, felt their initial panic escalate into deep fear. They jumped into the car and sped to Escondido High, hoping it was a misunderstanding and that she had lost track of time.

As Carrie approached one of Amber's teachers, her heart raced. The teacher's chilling words were, "Amber didn't attend her classes today."

"In that moment, I felt a strong realization: Amber was gone."

With trembling hands, Carrie called the police. The nightmare had begun.

"Amber would never skip school," she said, incredulity clear in her tone. "She had that check for the lamb in her pocket—there's no way she'd miss it. Someone must have misled her. It had to be someone she knew, someone she trusted."

She struggled to hold back tears and said, "She's not the type of child to run away. She's responsible and thoughtful. Deep down, I believe she wouldn't just vanish. This is a parent's worst nightmare, realizing your child is out there, feeling helpless to assist her. It's just unbearable."

Dave clung to a glimmer of hope. "At first, I thought she might have found her lamb but lost track of time," he said.

Carrie and Dave sensed that an underlying issue was involved.

Subsequently, a witness came forward, claiming to have seen Amber near Escondido High at approximately 7:00 a.m. She conversed with a tall boy who appeared gentle and had a dark complexion. Despite being one of the few leads for investigators, it ultimately remained insufficient.

In the following days, Amber's father, Moe Dubois, resigned as an electrical engineer in Los Angeles. Along with his partner, Rebecca Smith, he moved to a hotel in Escondido to remain close to the investigation and actively participate in the search effort.

Moe said, "Amber, my daughter, is my sweetheart. She always wears a cheeky smirk, teasing me and joking about my receding hairline. That's just my girl."

Carrie expressed her fears and his comfort. "Amber wouldn't just disappear without telling us. This makes me believe she might have been kidnapped," she informed the police. As she pondered about her daughter, her voice softened. "She loves reading, has friends at school, and enjoys related activities. Makeup isn't her interest... she's truly a bookworm. When she acted out, I had to take away her books," she recalled with a warm smile. "She would snuggle under the covers with a flashlight just to continue reading."

Amber's disappearance ignited one of the most significant search operations in the area's history. More than 400 volunteers combed through over 200 square miles of challenging terrain around Escondido, desperately seeking any clues about the missing girl.

Her family went door-to-door, distributed flyers in the neighborhood, and actively sought tips. However, their fear turned into frustration as days became weeks, resulting in rising suspicion.

Doubts began to center on Dave Cave.

The lead search coordinator prohibited Dave from joining the missions without prior notice or explanation. When Dave asked for clarification, the coordinator's reply was unsettling: "If you locate Amber, the police will hold you responsible for the crime."

Was that the reason, or was there a deeper underlying issue?

After Amber's disappearance, detectives questioned Dave multiple times, and his account remained consistent each time.

"Amber repeatedly asked for the funds to purchase a lamb for her school's Future Farmers program," he recalled. "I gave it to her. That was the last time I saw her before she went to school."

Detectives were skeptical when they noticed several red flags. Dave did not show up for work that day. He claimed he had gone to the gym and spent the rest of the day working on his taxes.

His response to inquiries about a missed call was even more alarming. That day, Amber's school had left a message stating that she hadn't shown up.

Dave claimed he hadn't checked his voicemail, but investigators doubted him. Was he unaware of the message, or did he already know that Amber wasn't coming home?

As time passed, Carrie began to have doubts, too. One particular memory lingered in her mind.

"Dave arrived at my office with chocolate-covered strawberries and roses," she remarked. "He said it was to celebrate Valentine's Day, but it was February 13, not the 14th. Besides, Dave doesn't even celebrate Valentine's Day."

He stayed for about 45 minutes, with Carrie having to prompt him to leave.

She finally asked, " Dave, what are you doing here? Just go."

The unusual visit took place merely a day before Amber's disappearance.

A sudden realization emerged: the argument between Dave and Amber had escalated into a bitter feud.

Dave admitted, "Amber and I didn't always see eye to eye. Rules are crucial in a household. As a teenager, she sometimes pushed back against them. Certain disagreements were inevitable."

Carrie offered a different viewpoint. "They hadn't communicated for a month leading up to her disappearance," she remembered. "Each day felt like a struggle, as if I was walking on eggshells."

Despite the tension, Dave insisted that they had made amends in the days leading up to Amber's disappearance. "We went shopping the evening before she went missing," he recalled. "We visited a bookstore and genuinely enjoyed ourselves."

To clear his name, Dave voluntarily took eight polygraph tests, claiming that he passed each one. Investigators documented his physical condition with photographs, highlighting the absence of visible injuries or scratches. Nevertheless, skepticism persisted.

Six weeks after Amber's disappearance, Carrie took an unexpected step that astonished her closest friends and family. She packed her belongings, took Dave's biological daughter, Allison, and left.

"I couldn't share a bed with someone I suspected could harm my daughter," she told her friends.

As the investigation progressed, Escondido Police Captain Bob Benton delivered troubling news to Carrie and Dave: Amber's cell phone briefly activated the day after she vanished—for a mere twenty seconds. During this brief period, someone tried to access her voicemail. The signal connected with a nearby cell tower servicing her home and school.

During that period, the FBI became involved in the case.

"We are helping the Escondido Police Department with their investigation," said Special Agent Darrell Foxworth from the San Diego field office. "Our duties involve interviewing people and pursuing leads as they arise."

Investigators conducted a thorough search of the area, interviewed registered sex offenders, contacted Amber's friends and family, and pursued every possible lead. However, as time passed, frustration grew. Benton and his team sifted through over 1,200 tips and conducted over 500 interviews. Still, the case remained frustratingly challenging to resolve.

Benton later commented, "The more we investigated, the more dead ends we encountered. A classmate reported seeing Amber the Sunday before last, approximately half a mile from her home, accompanied by an unidentified individual.

We remain uncertain about the details of that encounter or that person's identity. However, it is extremely concerning that she is only 14 years old, has never gone missing before, and has not been seen for a long time."

As weeks passed into months, the community's tension grew, intensifying scrutiny on Dave. He became a central figure of public interest, with each of his actions being closely analyzed. The gravity of Amber's disappearance weighed heavily upon him.

Amber's photo was everywhere in North County—attached to lamp posts, displayed in shop windows, and handed out at gas stations. She was the community's missing girl, drawing everyone's attention.

In August 2009, Amber's grandmother hired a private scent detection and recovery dog team to find answers. This team traced Amber's movements from when she went missing on February 13. Sadly, their expert noses failed to pick up any significant scent trail. The opportunity to uncover new information had slipped away; the scent was no longer detectable.

Amber's situation became a puzzling mystery for both the Escondido Police Department and the FBI.

"With each passing day without a new lead," Police Chief Craig Carter later observed, "it became more challenging to maintain hope."

At that time, Carter served as a lieutenant overseeing media inquiries and became the public face of the task force. Reflecting on those early days, he remarked, "The investigation took two paths—one hypothesis suggested she had fled, while the other indicated she may have encountered foul play. Yet, every lead and motive we explored faced obstacles. Such a situation is uncommon. When a missing person case is this atypical, we quickly transition into task force mode."

Nevertheless, the community would not allow Amber's story to fade into obscurity.

Two weeks after her disappearance, Escondido High School hosted a candlelight vigil. Nearly 200 people gathered, creating a sea of flickering flames illuminating solemn faces, where grief mingled with hope.

Hailey Kosinski, a dear friend of Amber, recalls a sixth-grade moment showcasing her kindness. "I could always count on her to cheer me up when I was feeling low," she said softly. Amber would smile and reassure me, always making me believe everything would work out okay."

Amber's disappearance shattered the sense of security. "It was a jarring wake-up call," Hailey admitted. "You start to consider all the things that could go wrong... just from walking down the street or being alone for a moment."

Over the next few weeks, Hailey and her classmates distributed more flyers throughout the town, ensuring Amber's face remained visible and prominent.

Amber's mother, fighting back tears, spoke to the audience at yet another vigil. "Every night, I go to bed wishing she would come into my room and say, 'Mom, I'm home.'" She took a moment, her breath trembling. "But now... all that's left is emptiness."

Lisa Marquez-Vidaurri, a close family friend, expressed sentiments shared by many. "The community continues to honor and remember her."

Edna Hallbrook nodded somberly. "I can't miss Amber's memorial," she said. "However, I feel anxious about attending. She was extraordinary; her absence leaves a significant void in the world."

Amber's story dominated local headlines for months—every article and broadcast became a passionate plea for the truth. However, as time went on, media coverage dwindled. Leads vanished, taking hope with them.

Uncovering the truth was profoundly painful. Amber hadn't returned home.

A little over a year after 14-year-old Amber Dubois disappeared, her family received shocking news—another teenage girl had gone missing.

Amber's sister, Carrie, vividly remembered the moment with a sense of pain.

"My roommate rushed into my room, exclaiming, 'Carrie, Carrie, wake up! A 17-year-old girl has gone missing... Her name is Chelsea.'"

Chelsea King's shocking disappearance would ultimately lead investigators to a breakthrough in the Amber Dubois case.

The two notable cases had a profound impact on San Diego County, erasing any lingering sense of security. Parents became increasingly cautious, accompanying their children to school, monitoring bus stops, and meticulously organizing every pickup. Sleepovers became rare, permitted only after parents communicated extensively. Even typical school activities—such as sports events, concerts, and theater performances—were conducted with heightened security, as administrators hired external teams to ensure student safety. A constant, unsettling awareness overshadowed the daily freedoms once considered standard.

The Disappearance of Chelsea King

On the afternoon of February 25, 2010, 17-year-old Chelsea King wore her running shoes as she headed for a jog along the familiar trails near Lake Hodges. This area was just ten miles from where 14-year-old Dubois had gone missing the previous year.

Chelsea, born on July 1, 1992, to Brent and Kelly King, distinguished herself as an exceptional student at Poway High School. She excelled academically, showcased her piano skills with the San Diego Youth Symphony, and was just months away from graduating. Chelsea earned a reputation for her intelligence, ambition, and the affection she received from her peers.

When Chelsea didn't return home that evening, her parents immediately grew concerned. They quickly contacted the San Diego Sheriff's Department, initiating a search operation within hours. Sergeant Dave Brown stated, "Given the distance, we feared foul play. We can't determine if she is deceased or merely being held somewhere."

Authorities initiated an extensive search effort, with FBI agents examining over 300 homes in the vicinity of Lake Hodges. They pursued over 600 tips and interviewed registered sex offenders nearby. Chelsea's photograph was circulated on thousands of flyers. The community united, with neighbors, friends, and even strangers getting involved. Among the volunteers was the Dubois family, who were still grieving Amber's disappearance as they supported another family going through the same tragic experience.

The search concluded in sorrow after five distressing days. On March 2, 2010, a dive team located a shallow grave close to the lake, just half a mile from where Chelsea's black BMW was discovered. She had been sexually assaulted and strangled. On the same day, a searcher discovered one of her running shoes a mile from where her other clothing was found.

"That day was the worst of our lives," Kelly King told reporters, fighting back tears. "We'll never experience a pain this profound again."

After the incident, the King family faced challenges in moving forward. Eventually, Kelly relocated with her daughter and new husband to a tranquil home in northern Escondido—the same place she had been when Amber first went missing.

Amber's father, Moe Dubois, began his healing journey far from home. Struggling with grief, he left his engineering job and relocated with his partner, Rebecca Smith, to a charming fishing village along the central Oregon coast. In this new setting, he opened a small tackle shop with stunning sea views.

"I gave up my engineering career to sell dead fish," Moe said, a bittersweet smile on his face. "I may smell a bit worse, but I'm much happier."

The community quickly became aware of his past. Moe's store, situated near a school bus stop, was a refuge for children. He often watched them as they waited, a silent guardian shaped by deep sorrow.

"My daughter always makes me smile," he remarked. "Even though she's no longer here, that smile lingers. She brought it to my face when she was with me."

Ultimately, the major breakthrough that the researchers had anticipated occurred.

The forensic analysis of the panties and socks found near the trail confirmed the presence of Chelsea's DNA. It also revealed a second, unidentified male profile. This DNA matched John Albert Gardner III, a convicted sex offender whose information was already in the Combined DNA Index System (CODIS).

The FBI operates CODIS as a vital national resource for solving crimes. Organized into three tiers, it connects local, state, and national DNA profiles, enabling law enforcement agencies nationwide to compare forensic evidence swiftly. Its purpose is to bridge gaps between jurisdictions, and it has successfully achieved this.

The system indicated that it was focusing on Gardner.

John Albert Gardner III later admitted and pleaded guilty to attempting to rape 23-year-old Candice Moncayo in December 2009. She had been running along a trail when he tackled her. Despite the sudden and violent nature of the attack, Candice fought back and managed to escape with her life.

When police questioned her, Candice described her assailant as a linebacker-sized man who had appeared out of nowhere. "I was running when I was suddenly attacked and thrown off the trail," she recalled. "I was caught off guard. I thought he was going to rape me. As I lay on my back, I screamed in terror."

Her attacker growled, "Hand over your money and keep quiet."

Determined not to be victimized, Candice shot back, "You'll need to kill me first." He laughed darkly, replying, "That can be arranged."

As he held her face, she kicked and struggled until she freed herself. She ran toward nearby houses to call 9-1-1.

A police helicopter circled swiftly overhead as patrol units rushed to the scene. Officers searched the trail and nearby areas for hours, yet the assailant was nowhere to be found. Strikingly, despite the seriousness of the assault, authorities failed to collect DNA evidence from Candice—a significant oversight. This omission remained unexplained, resulting in the loss of crucial forensic evidence.

Candice, a graduate student from Colorado Springs, recognized Gardner's photo while examining a set of mugshots. She confidently declared, "That's him. Definitely."

At the time of the attack, Gardner was a convicted sex offender who had served a five-year prison sentence for molesting a 13-year-old female neighbor. Despite having violated his parole seven times, he was released in 2008. One of these violations led to an investigation for marijuana possession, but the charges were eventually dropped.

For a period of up to four months before the disappearance of Amber Dubois, Gardner wore a GPS ankle monitor. Data revealed 168 violations of parole. He loitered near schools, hovered outside a daycare center, and visited prison grounds. He was also tracked to a remote location—later identified as the site where Amber's remains would be discovered.

A forensic psychiatrist had previously noted that Gardner exhibited "significant predatory behaviors" and continued to pose a threat to young girls. The psychiatrist recommended a maximum sentence of ten years. However, Gardner was given only a six-year sentence and was released after serving just five years.

After the tragic murder of 17-year-old Chelsea King in February 2010, law enforcement intensified its efforts. Investigators were propelled by DNA evidence recovered from Chelsea's clothing and by Candice Moncayo's description of a man who had nearly killed her just months earlier.

On February 28, 2010, investigators followed leads to a Del Dios bar near Lake Hodges. There, they found 30-year-old John Gardner, covered in mud, wet, intoxicated, and disoriented.

When asked about Chelsea King's disappearance, he said he hadn't seen her. At one point during the interview, he erupted into strange, uncontrollable laughter—an act that one detective later described as "psychotic."

Although DNA evidence linked Gardner to Chelsea's murder, investigators also suspected his involvement in the earlier disappearance of Amber DuBois. Their concerns intensified when Gardner unexpectedly mentioned her name during questioning without any prompts.

In March 2010, Gardner's attorney presented a noteworthy proposal to San Diego County District Attorney Bonnie Dumanis: "If you ensure that my client's assistance won't be used against him, he will lead you to Amber's body."

Despite the controversy, the agreement received approval.

San Diego law enforcement officers walked along a narrow dirt path, weaving through thick brush and gnarled trees until they reached an old, rusted water tank near the Pala Indian Reservation. This remote location, nestled in the San Luis Rey River Valley and just east of the tranquil community of Fallbrook, exuded an eerie silence.

Investigators uncovered a heartbreaking truth in a shallow grave beneath the hard-packed soil: the skeletal remains of 14-year-old Amber Leeanne Dubois, who had been missing for over a year.

The scene was grim. Forensic evidence indicated that Amber had been raped and fatally stabbed. The brutality of the crime painted a chilling picture of her final moments, ones marked by terror, pain, and the abrupt shattering of an innocent life.

Amber's parents received the call they had both dreaded and anticipated that evening.

"I can't say I'm ready for this," said Moe Dubois, her father, his voice heavy with sorrow. "But after months of searching, we're prepared for anything you can tell us." He paused before continuing, "Just give us an answer. Make this terrible nightmare stop."

Even with the recovery, law enforcement faced a new challenge: proving that Gardner was the murderer. "No evidence connected John Gardner to Amber," stated investigator Bob Benton.

Amber's family was divided in their opinions. Some thought he had murdered her, whereas others remained skeptical because of a lack of evidence.

In late March, Moe Dubois passionately voiced his conviction that John Albert Gardner III was behind the killings of both Amber Dubois and Chelsea King. "Come on," he insisted. "The parallels between these two cases are clear. It's time to face the truth."

Despite the certainty, perspectives differed among those involved in the case. Amber's grandmother, Sheila Welch, and the private investigator who was initially hired to find the missing teen suspected that someone else might be responsible for her death.

"Gardner's behavior is erratic," stated Michelle Bart, spokesperson for Welch. "He generally preys on girls in isolated locations for surprise attacks. Yet, Amber was on her way to school in broad daylight, surrounded by her peers. That morning, she was thrilled—she had Valentine's cards and a check for purchasing a lamb. This situation does not fit his usual methods."

There was a time when Amber's family seemed destined never to find the justice they sought—until Chelsea King's family made a significant, transformative decision.

Faced with compelling evidence, Gardner agreed to plead guilty to both murders and disclose the circumstances of each girl's case, provided the death penalty was removed as a possibility in Chelsea's situation.

Bonnie Dumanis, the San Diego County District Attorney, empowered Chelsea's family to choose. Although they were confident in their strong case for capital punishment, they opted for a broader approach to justice that could provide answers for themselves and the Dubois family. This decision ensured that Gardner's confession concerning Amber's case would be revealed, ultimately offering closure.

Before Gardner was sentenced, the families of Amber and Chelsea, along with survivor Candice Moncayo, delivered moving victim impact statements, each highlighting the profound sorrow and devastation caused by Gardner's actions.

"Over the past 14 months, the Dubois family has encountered difficult to comprehend challenges," said Brent King, Chelsea's father, during a press conference. "The unexpected revelation concerning Amber's murder has left us in a state of ongoing uncertainty."

Amber and Chelsea had never crossed paths. Yet, their tales became eternally linked in death—two spirited young lives abruptly ended by the same ruthless attacker, John Albert Gardner III.

During a subsequent prison interview, John Albert Gardner III confessed to being overwhelmed by intense rage during the attacks on Amber Dubois and Chelsea King. He explained that he couldn't control his actions and attributed them to years of disappointment and emotional abuse.

"I deeply loathe myself. There's no way to undo my actions. If I could, I definitely would. However, I lost control and could not restrain myself; I was completely out of control."

Those words provided no comfort to the families of the victims.

Chelsea's father described Gardner as "a monster and an animal," hoping the killer would "sink to the deepest level of hell" after his death. Similarly, Amber's father, Moe Dubois, echoed this sentiment, labeling Gardner as a predator.

Carrie McGonigle, Amber's mother, was overwhelmed by grief. Following the murder of Chelsea King, which ultimately led investigators to Amber, Carrie found it challenging to get out of bed for two weeks, just as a psychologist had predicted would occur once the shock wore off.

"For 15 months, I was perpetually in a hurry," Carrie said. "Then, suddenly, it dawned on me... this is what life is truly about."

Carrie chose not to return to work at a San Marcos printing company. Instead, she found a new calling. Now receiving disability benefits, she devotes her life to a private search-and-rescue team focused on locating missing girls like Amber and Chelsea.

Moe Dubois has faced obstacles in his journey forward. Now living in Orange County with his partner, Rebecca Smith, he has limited contact with Carrie. The emotional and financial toll remains substantial as they work to rebuild their lives.

"The last two years have thrust us into financial difficulties," Moe expressed. "I have found it especially hard to return to work."

Motivated to honor Amber's legacy, Moe and Rebecca founded the More Kids Organization, an advocacy group to reform how law enforcement handles missing child cases. Following Amber's abduction, they discovered concerning issues, notably the absence of standardized procedures during the crucial initial hours when a child is reported missing.

Resources were available to aid the search efforts, but a notable lack of knowledge and coordination persisted. Moe and Rebecca advocated for legislation to address these gaps, improve agency communication, and establish precise, urgent protocols. Their mission was clear and urgent: to prevent any other family from enduring what they had suffered through.

Their efforts led to the passage of three significant California laws:

1. Mandatory reporting: Authorities must now report abductions to a national tracking system within two hours, instead of four.

2. Law enforcement coordination: Enhanced agency communication, faster response times, and standardized procedures.

3. Oversight position: Create a Director of Missing Children's Operations to manage and enhance abduction response programs.

"I truly want to advocate for more legislation," Moe stated. "The issue is that there's no financial compensation for it— not a dime. It can be quite expensive."

Since 2011, Brent and Kelly King have honored their daughter, Chelsea, by hosting Finish Chelsea's Run. This annual 3.1-mile race provides funding for college scholarships through the Chelsea's Light Foundation.

Before Gardner was transferred to prison, Carrie and Moe visited him. In her quest for closure, Carrie sought answers about Amber's final moments, the details of her abduction, and the ordeal she faced. To her astonishment, Gardner's explanations were ones she found credible.

He had difficulty making eye contact with her during their conversation.

"I thought I was seeing a ghost when I first saw you in the courtroom the day I pleaded guilty," he told Carrie. "You bear such a striking resemblance to Amber. Everywhere I go, I see her face. It torments me daily. But I didn't want to go back to prison, so I stayed quiet. And then I killed again."

As Carrie exited the jail, she spotted Gardner curled up in a tight ball, crying and drenched in sweat.

"He was a wreck, and I found it exhilarating," she remarked.

Afterward, Carrie channeled her grief into proactive efforts by founding Team Amber Rescue, an organization committed to assisting in the search for missing children and adults. Moreover, she has emerged as a vital source of support for other grieving parents, providing comfort, empathy, and the assurance that they are not alone.

On April 16, 2010, the San Diego County Superior Court was filled with victims' families, investigators, and media as John Albert Gardner III awaited sentencing. The King family, represented by attorney Michael Fell, had fought to prevent disturbing crime scene and autopsy photos from being included in the proceedings. Gardner sat shackled, occasionally sobbing, while family members delivered poignant victim impact statements.

In an attempt to avoid the death penalty, Gardner admitted to the kidnapping, rape, and murder of Amber and Chelsea. He also confessed to a previous assault on a female jogger, Candice Moncayo, who bravely addressed the hearing: "Today, I'm here to remove this man from our lives... Nightmares still plague me. I've suffered countless hours of nausea and dread, just like a frightened rabbit."

On May 14, 2010, Judge David Danielsen of the Superior Court sentenced Gardner to life in prison without the possibility of parole. He received two consecutive life sentences for murder, in addition to 25 years to life for attempted rape and 24 years for prior offenses.

During their statements, the families of Amber and Chelsea expressed their profound sorrow and the unimaginable horror caused by Gardner, who had taken the lives of two innocent individuals and discarded their bodies as if they were worthless.

Moe Dubois informed the court, "His risk of death in the general population exceeds that of using a needle. He's no longer on the streets and cannot face this again. What else could you ask for? Yes, I would love to spend a week alone with him, but that's unlikely."

Amber's family created a touching video tribute showcasing her love for reading and boundless kindness. Chelsea's family honored their daughter as an outstanding student with infinite potential, valuing her laughter, empathy, and the deep conversations they shared.

Brent King, Chelsea's father, expressed the profound grief of a parent whose child has been a victim of violence.

"Chelsea epitomized virtue, standing in stark contrast to him, who personified evil. I am overwhelmed by an anger I never knew existed."

Gardner remains incarcerated at Mule Creek State Prison in Ione, California. This high-security facility accommodates inmates in "Sensitive Needs Yards," which include sex offenders and individuals who require protective custody. It currently houses over 4,000 inmates despite being initially designed for just 3,284.

CHAPTER FIVE

Girl In The Box Killer – Cameron Hooker

Colleen Stan, born on December 31, 1956, is an American woman known for her survival story, regarded as one of the most harrowing kidnapping cases in modern history.

On May 19, 1977, 20-year-old Colleen departed from her home in Eugene, Oregon. She was hitchhiking to Westwood, California, to celebrate a friend's birthday. She was an experienced hitchhiker who exercised caution. She had already turned down two rides earlier that morning. However, when an ordinary young couple in a blue van offered her a lift, she felt comforted. The man introduced himself as Cameron Hooker, with his 19-year-old wife, Janice, seated beside him and holding their infant child.

This choice would alter her life forever.

What started as a typical journey transformed into a seven-year nightmare.

While held in captivity at the Hookers' residence in Red Bluff, California, Colleen Stan endured severe physical, mental, and sexual abuse.

For much of her captivity, she was confined in a coffin-like box beneath the couple's bed, cramped, dark, and lacking air, remaining inside for up to 23 hours a day.

Cameron Hooker used manipulation and sadism to dominate her, convincing her that a shadowy, omnipotent organization called "The Company" would kill her and her family if she attempted to escape.

The fear was paralyzing. The control was absolute.

From 1977 to 1984, Colleen endured harsh conditions, stripped of her freedom, identity, voice, and sense of reality.

Her rescue was not forced; it stemmed from a change of heart. Janice Hooker, Cameron's wife and complicit partner, ultimately felt overwhelmed by guilt. She disclosed to Stan that "The Company" was a fabrication and assisted her escape. In exchange for her cooperation and testimony, Janice was granted complete immunity.

Cameron Hooker was apprehended and later found guilty of several offenses, including kidnapping, torture, and sexual assault.

The FBI described the case as "unprecedented" in terms of psychological manipulation and the severe brutality of the conditions Colleen had endured. Her experience has inspired books, documentaries, and dramatized films, acknowledged by experts as one of the most disturbing and complex instances of coercive control and prolonged captivity ever documented.

Colleen never anticipated that her hitchhiking trip to a friend's house would result in her abduction by a sadistic captor, who would make her his sex slave, prisoner, and victim.

She felt a false sense of security from the family's presence. As she climbed into the van, she remained unaware that she was stepping into a nightmare that would last for seven years.

While stopping at a gas station, Colleen went to the restroom. When she returned, she noticed an unusual item in the backseat—a rough, handmade box that hadn't been there before. Though uneasy, she kept quiet and returned to the van. As they ventured deeper into rural Northern California, Colleen felt persistent discomfort. Despite a voice urging her to escape, she stayed where she was.

Suddenly, Hooker veered off the highway onto a secluded dirt road. He drew a knife, pressed it against her throat, and conveyed his intentions.

Before Colleen could grasp the danger, Hooker pressed a heavy custom wooden contraption—a 20-pound "head box"—onto her head. Designed to block light, sound, and airflow, it would serve as both her confinement and a tool for psychological torment.

That day signaled the start of one of the most distressing kidnapping cases in recent history.

When Colleen arrived at Hooker's home near Red Bluff, California, she was taken to the basement. There, Hooker and Janice removed her clothing, gagged her to prevent her from making noise, and suspended her from the ceiling beams.

Blindfolded and vulnerable, Colleen endured repeated whippings while Janice looked on. The couple then engaged in sadistic sex acts beneath her suspended body. When they were finished, Hooker forced Colleen to perform oral sex on his wife.

Colleen would later recall, "I was let out only once a day—but only to be mercilessly beaten, electrocuted, whipped, my pubic hair burned, my head held underwater—then raped and forced to do disturbing and demeaning sexual activities.

"By the end of the first month, I had lost 22 pounds. I relished my first bath in August, three months after my admission."

Before abducting Colleen, Hooker had struck a disturbing agreement with Janice. A former victim of his bondage and torture, Janice was growing weary of his abuse. They agreed that he could take a "slave"—a woman to replace Janice as his subject of control and sadism.

The couple's agreement included one condition: Hooker was prohibited from engaging in penetrative sex with the new victim. However, similar to his previous commitments, he ultimately chose to disregard this.

For months, Colleen was confined in that wooden box resembling a coffin for 23 hours each day, only being taken out to be mistreated.

In January 1978, Hooker coerced her into signing a handwritten "slave contract," which he believed legally bound her to a life of complete servitude.

The contract referred to Hooker as her "master," requiring her to seek permission to eat, breathe fresh air, or use the bathroom. Although Janice ultimately destroyed the original document, a surviving copy was later discovered, serving as evidence of the disturbing psychological coercion Colleen endured.

Hooker stripped her of her name and assigned her a new one, obliterating her identity and replacing it with an objectified form of existence.

He exerted total control over every aspect of her life. He formed a secret organization called "The Company"—an all-seeing, omnipotent group that would hunt down and eliminate her and her family if she ever tried to escape. This psychological tactic was arguably even more paralyzing than physical torture.

Colleen's prolonged captivity left her with lasting medical complications, including nerve damage, back problems, injuries, and significant trauma. While sleeping in a box beneath Hooker and Janice's bed, she made a troubling discovery: a photo of another young woman, 18-year-old Marie Elizabeth Spannhake.

On January 31, 1976, Marie vanished from Chico, California, following an argument with her boyfriend at a flea market. After he was cleared as a suspect, the investigation stalled. Authorities now believe she could have been Hooker's first confirmed victim.

Marie's photo, discovered in Colleen's box, hinted at a more profound, darker truth that investigators would soon begin to uncover.

Years later, plagued by insomnia and a heavy conscience, Janice Hooker could no longer endure her secrets. In November 1984, she entered a police station and disclosed details that startled investigators.

Janice admitted that she and her husband, Cameron Hooker, had abducted, assaulted, and tormented a young woman several years prior. The name on the victim's ID was Marie Elizabeth Spannhake. However, disturbingly, Marie was not their first captive; she would not be the last either.

According to Janice, it was January 1976 when Marie was lured into their home in Red Bluff, California. Once there, Cameron suspended her from the rafters in their basement, where he subjected her to unspeakable torture for his sadistic pleasure. "She was like his toy," Janice later told police.

But the horror didn't end with physical abuse. One night, Cameron led Marie into the bathroom. There, he sodomized her repeatedly with an array of objects—extra-large dildos, Coke bottles, wooden spoons, and even a pair of scissors. Then, in a gruesome escalation, he severed her vocal cords in an attempt to silence her forever.

"The violence was overwhelming," Janice recounted to investigators. "Marie began to bleed profusely." As Marie's health deteriorated, Cameron lifted her fragile, injured body back to the basement and restrained her once more.

Minutes later, he shot her in the stomach before finally strangling her to death. Janice admitted to helping dispose of the body. "We loaded her into the car and drove toward Lassen Volcanic National Park," she said. "Cameron dug a shallow grave, and I helped him bury her."

Marie's remains were never found. Due to the lack of a body or concrete evidence, prosecutors could not file murder charges against either Cameron or Janice.

It took years for authorities to grasp the full extent of Cameron Hooker's depravity. Eventually, another victim, Colleen Stan, surfaced with a story that tested the limits of human endurance.

Colleen recounted how Cameron had exerted psychological control over her, most alarmingly through an imaginary organization he called "The Company."

"He convinced me they were observing my every action," she stated. "If I attempted to flee, they would track me down, torture me, sodomize me, and hurt my family."

Cameron Hooker's seven-year reign of terror profoundly affected Colleen. At one point, Janice returned home in a knee brace after her surgery. Cameron informed Colleen that The Company had punished Janice for attempting to escape, deepening the illusion that defiance would lead to tragedy. The message was unsettling: disobedience would have dire repercussions.

Dr. Michele Galietta, a psychology professor at John Jay College of Criminal Justice, investigated the effects of this psychological warfare. "Her faith in The Company was logical given her circumstances," Galietta noted. "It might seem incredible, but keep in mind—she was locked away for years in a box beneath a bed. When every notion of safety and predictability is taken from you, what remains of your mind?"

Galietta analyzed Janice's involvement in the abuse. "She was a collaborator," she stated, "but I don't believe she matches the psychopath profile. These issues go beyond psychology—they involve morality. From the evidence, Janice seems to have been so mentally restricted and deeply enmeshed in the control dynamic that she lost her capacity for independent thought."

Dr. Mark Olver, a forensic psychologist specializing in psychopathy and sexual deviance, shared his thoughts on Hooker's twisted relationship with Colleen. He stated, "While it's challenging, it's not implausible that a psychopathic individual like Hooker could form an emotional connection with a victim. Despite the sadistic and unreciprocated nature of their relationship, it raises the question: Was this genuine attachment or merely the loss of a human object for sexual use?"

In April 1978, the Hookers moved to a mobile home in Red Bluff, bringing Colleen with them. Once again, she was confined inside a wooden box beneath the couple's waterbed. Her existence became one marked by darkness, suffering, and subservience.

Cameron married Janice on January 18, 1975, when she was still a teenager. From the beginning, Janice understood that Cameron derived sexual gratification from inflicting pain. One of his early rituals involved hanging her naked from tree branches and whipping her with a bullwhip as she dangled helplessly. Over time, Janice could no longer tolerate the abuse and began refusing to participate in his escalating fantasies.

Initially, Janice regarded Colleen as a threat, a rival. However, by 1984, that perspective began to change. When Cameron announced that he wanted to abduct another woman to serve as a second sex slave, Janice made him promise not to have intercourse with the new victim. For her, that was the line.

Colleen—now referred to only as "K"—was forced to call Cameron "Master" and forbidden to speak without permission. Hooker's obsession with dominance went so far that he tried to mold her into a real-life version of O, the submissive protagonist in Story of O, a 1954 French erotic novel. In the book, the woman is stripped, chained, blindfolded, beaten, branded, and forced into absolute sexual obedience. For Cameron, it was not fiction—it was the blueprint.

Even though Janice eventually admitted to her role and helped Colleen escape, the shadow of Marie Spannhake still loomed. True justice for Marie sadly remained out of reach due to the lack of a body or tangible evidence, along with only a long-forgotten confession.

Unlike Story of O, Cameron Hooker refrained from vaginal intercourse with Colleen. He claimed that doing so would violate his vow to Janice. Instead, he subjected Colleen to brutal sexual assaults using foreign objects—many of which he had previously used to torture Marie Elizabeth Spannhake.

Despite the great suffering she faced, Colleen later stated, "My faith in God and my hope for escape helped me to persevere. My greatest fear, which Hooker emphasized every day, was The Company."

To avoid Hooker's punishments, Colleen made significant efforts to meet his demands. Eventually, he granted her a few limited privileges: she was allowed to jog, do yard work, care for the Hookers' children, and assist in constructing expanded confinement areas, including an underground dungeon.

Despite occasionally having access to open doors, nearby neighbors, and a telephone, Colleen remained trapped by psychological manipulation. The fear instilled by the myth of The Company kept her submissive, maintaining her silence and confinement.

In 1980, Colleen confessed her affection for Cameron—a truth she later revealed was a fabrication for her protection. While she was under his influence, she had permission to contact her family. The following year, she was able to meet them in person, with Hooker posing as her boyfriend. Fearing the truth might be uncovered, she hid her struggles from them.

Colleen reflected on that visit, sharing, "My family believed I was involved in a cult due to my handmade clothing, financial struggles, and long periods of silence. They hesitated to press me for explanations, fearing I might vanish again."

Three months later, Janice Hooker reported the incident to the police. She confided in Lt. Jerry D. Brown of the Red

Bluff Police Department, saying, "From our first date, Cameron tortured me, brainwashed me, and called me a 'whore.' I coped through denial and compartmentalization. He kidnapped, tortured, and murdered Marie Elizabeth."

In August 1984, Janice sought advice from a pastor. After revealing her situation, she was urged to separate from her husband. Acting on this suggestion, she spoke to Colleen at the motel where she worked and disclosed the shocking news—The Company was a fabrication and she was free to walk away.

During the trial, Colleen shared her experiences of captivity. "I was thrilled to reunite with my family, and they took a picture of Cameron and me smiling. However, after our return, Hooker feared he had allowed me too much freedom, so he placed me back in the box under his waterbed. For the next three years, I was confined there for 23 hours each day.

"I never knew what was coming next. I had to use a bedpan with my feet. His children were told I'd gone home. But once they were asleep, Hooker would let me out—to feed me or to torture me. I had to stay silent, still, with barely enough air. In the summer, the heat in the box would climb past 100 degrees. I ate leftover scraps nobody else wanted."

In a later interview, Colleen described her escape: "In late August 1984, while Cameron was at work, Janice and I took the children and left. She dropped me off at the bus station, where I called Cameron to inform him of my decision to leave. He cried. After that, I boarded a bus and went home. I wanted to start anew."

Despite her escape, Colleen didn't report him immediately. She often reached out to him. During the trial, she explained that Janice had encouraged her to give Cameron a chance to change.

Over time, Colleen started to recover from her trauma, taking back control of her life. She recounted her survival story: "You learn to navigate your thoughts. You escape reality and journey to a comforting place where you are cherished. That's how I managed."

Ultimately, Janice worked with prosecutors to secure immunity despite initially helping Cameron destroy evidence. Her testimony and Colleen's played a crucial role in ensuring a conviction.

Cameron Hooker was sentenced to 104 years in prison for kidnapping, rape, oral copulation, sodomy, and using a knife during his abduction and assault. Initially, he was ineligible for parole until 2023; however, he received a hearing in 2015 under California's Elderly Parole Program. On April 16, 2015, his request for parole was denied, with his next eligibility date set for 2030.

During sentencing, Judge Clarence Knight remarked, "Hooker is the most dangerous psychopath I have ever encountered. His threat to women will persist throughout his life. Colleen Stan's ordeal is unparalleled in FBI history."

Cameron Hooker is currently incarcerated at the California Substance Abuse Treatment Facility and State Prison in Corcoran, which caters to inmates with substance use disorders.

In the years following the trial, Colleen Stan focused on rebuilding her life. She married four times, earned a degree in accounting, and cherished moments with her grandson. However, despite her efforts to restore a sense of normalcy, the profound trauma from her captivity continued to haunt her.

Colleen chose not to let her past define her; instead, she transformed her pain into purpose. She became actively involved with the Redding Women's Refuge Center, dedicating herself fully to assisting other survivors of abuse. Through her advocacy work, Colleen Stan continues her story so it will be remembered not only for her suffering but also as a powerful testament to resilience, bravery, and hope.

CHAPTER SIX
Highway Killer – Adam Leroy Lane

Adam Leroy Lane, born on August 7, 1964, in Jonesville, North Carolina, is a convicted murderer and an alleged serial killer infamously known as "The Highway Killer" due to a series of violent assaults and murders occurring near major highways along the Eastern Seaboard.

Lane, a long-haul truck driver, exploited his job to stalk, assault, and, in some cases, murder women in their homes, instilling fear across several states during the summer of 2007.

Lane seemed to lead an ordinary life, graduating from high school and working as a truck driver at a local chicken processing plant. He shared a trailer with his wife and three daughters, embodying the image of an everyday working-class family man. Yet, beneath this facade lay a deeply troubled individual harboring an unsettling obsession with violence.

This darker reality became evident after Lane's arrest when authorities searched his truck and discovered disturbing items: two large hunting knives, a length of choke wire, black gloves, and a leather mask with holes cut out for the eyes and mouth.

A DVD of *Hunting Humans*, a low-budget horror film about a serial killer, was also found. Prosecutors later referenced this discovery to illustrate Lane's violent fantasies and planning.

Murders and Attacks

July 13, 2007 – West Hanover Township, Pennsylvania

Lane's first known murder occurred when 42-year-old Darlene Ewalt was ambushed while talking on the phone in her backyard. Lane slit her throat and stabbed her multiple times with a long hunting knife, mere feet from her family, who remained unaware inside the house.

July 17, 2007 – Conewago Township, Pennsylvania

While Patricia Brooks slept on her couch, Lane entered her home and stabbed her multiple times; however, she was able to survive the attack.

July 28, 2007 – Bloomsbury, New Jersey

Monica Massaro, 38, was murdered inside her duplex. Lane broke in and attacked her as she slept, stabbing her in the head, neck, and chest and slashing her throat. It was a savage, unprovoked killing—and it would be his last known murder.

July 30, 2007 – Chelmsford, Massachusetts

Lane's most notable attack took place when he exited I-495 and invaded the McDonough family's residence.

Fifteen-year-old Shea McDonough, the daughter of Jeannie and Kevin, was a thoughtful and bright teenager who adhered to a strict noon curfew. On that warm Sunday evening in Chelmsford, Massachusetts, she returned home approximately fifteen minutes early—tired yet satisfied after a lovely night with friends just a few houses down.

She quietly approached the back door to check if it was unlocked, and it was. Anticipating her older brother Ryan's return later, Shea left it ajar to avoid being suddenly woken by a message asking her to let him in. This small gesture highlighted her thoughtful nature as a sister who cared for her brother.

She was unaware that Ryan would not be home that night because he had already informed their parents that he was staying at his friend Ricky's house.

What Shea didn't realize—what no one could foresee—was that the door she had left open for Ryan would invite a monster inside instead.

Before dawn, she would be the last victim of the man who had caused havoc across multiple states, earning the chilling title of The Highway Killer.

At 58, Adam Leroy Lane was a long-haul trucker covering New Jersey, Pennsylvania, and Massachusetts. His life on the road—characterized by countless hours of isolation, quick meals, and growing frustration—transformed him into a menacing 245-pound predator. Under the cover of the night, he prowled peaceful neighborhoods, searching for victims.

At 3:55 a.m., fueled by a sinister urge to attack once more, Lane quietly maneuvered through the peaceful streets of Chelmsford. He had already tried to enter three homes before quietly slipping through the McDonough unlocked back door.

He believed he was on the verge of executing another perfect crime.

He selected the wrong house and the unsuitable family instead.

Lane slipped into the house, grabbed two purses, and headed to the back deck. He rummaged through one, discovering Shea McDonough's school ID. After a quick glance, he tossed it aside and quietly returned indoors.

He moved silently like a shadow toward the bedroom where 17-year-old Shea lay asleep, the air conditioner's hum disguising his entry. Clad from head to toe in black and equipped with gloves, a mask, and a utility belt filled with knives, a choke wire, and a throwing star, Lane towered over her.

He then made his move.

Shea jolted awake as a gloved hand clamped over her nose and mouth, cutting off her breath. A 15-inch hunting knife pressed cold and unforgiving against her throat.

"Make a sound or move, and I'll kill you," warned a deep voice.

A wave of panic engulfed her. She flailed frantically, her body striking the headboard as she kicked and fought, desperately trying to be heard, hoping her parents would rescue her.

Fate stepped in from above.

That evening, the McDonough family's air conditioner broke down—an unexpected occurrence that might have saved their daughter's life. Just before Lane's arrival, Jeannie McDonough had stood up to get a glass of water, preventing her and Kevin from falling into a deep sleep.

Shea's gentle whimpers shattered the silence.

Kevin and Jeannie hurried into the room.

Kevin momentarily halted, struck with terror at the sight before him: a masked intruder looming over his daughter, a sharp blade threateningly poised against her throat. It felt as if a nightmare had come to life.

Instinct immediately took charge.

Kevin and Jeannie charged at Lane. Despite their smaller size—Kevin weighed 160 pounds and Jeannie 135—they successfully overpowered the 245-pound attacker.

A violent and chaotic confrontation arose as they fought to wrest the knife from his grip.

"Call 9-1-1! Get the gun!" Kevin shouted to Shea.

It was a deception. They had no weapon, yet the intimidation was effective. Lane hesitated for a moment.

Kevin seized the moment, wrapping his arms around Lane's neck as he had in his high school wrestling days. With a firm tug, he pulled Lane backward, and they both collapsed.

Jeannie reached for the knife, gripping the blade tightly as she yelled, "What do you want from us?"

Blood oozed from her hands.

Lane spoke with a thick Southern drawl, saying, "I was just looking for some cash. I'm a nobody. Just let me go."

Kevin's voice was raw with rage. "You're not going anywhere, you fat piece of shit."

Shea swiftly picked up the phone, her hands shaking as she dialed 9-1-1. Injecting a bit of humor, she commented to the dispatcher about handling the situation before rushing back into the room.

Blood was splattered all around.

"I couldn't tell its origin," Shea remembered. "When I glanced down, I noticed my mom was tightly holding the knife. She refused to release it."

That evening, they achieved what many had failed to do: they stopped The Highway Killer.

Minutes later, Chelmsford police arrived to find Kevin still holding Lane in a headlock. He did not release him until the officers had handcuffed and secured the attacker.

Lane was swiftly apprehended and charged with attempted murder.

The McDonoughs hurried to the hospital because Jeannie needed urgent medical care. Meanwhile, the doctors had to assess Shea, who, despite being physically unharmed, had faced a challenge no teenager should encounter.

Only after it ended could the McDonough family finally breathe, relieved of the weight of survival.

Chelmsford Police Chief James Murphy remarked, "The night's events were remarkable. Some individuals might hesitate, while others step up. Without that courage, the outcome could have been significantly worse."

They were celebrated as heroes—an everyday family that triumphed over a brutal predator. However, beneath the relief lay a storm of emotions: vulnerability, disbelief, anger, and deep guilt. If they truly were heroes, why did they feel so disturbed?

Jeannie McDonough remarked, "We behaved as any parent would: we safeguarded our child and shifted into survival mode. We are simply survivors. That's all there is to it."

When detectives examined Adam Lane's truck, the sobering reality of their situation became evident. The McDonoughs had not merely faced an intruder; they had prevailed against a callous member of society.

Unwittingly, they had confronted pure evil. Driven by instinct and determination, they brought it to an end.

Adam Leroy Lane, who had left high school before graduating, moved between jobs as a truck driver and a worker at a chicken processing plant. He lived in a trailer with his wife and three daughters, exemplifying a modest working-class life.

But behind that façade lurked something monstrous. In his truck, investigators found two large hunting knives, a choke wire, and a leather mask with the eyes and mouth crudely cut out—tools of terror that hinted at the dark satisfaction Lane derived from stalking and killing.

Just three weeks later, the McDonoughs discovered a startling truth: Lane had embarked on a brutal killing spree. This horrifying series of events began on July 13, 2007, with the murder of 42-year-old Darlene Ewalt.

Darlene lived in a peaceful suburban house in West Hanover Township, near Harrisburg, Pennsylvania. At around 2:00 a.m., she enjoyed the warm night air on her patio, conversing with her friend Chet Gerhart about the cruise she and her husband had planned.

Unknown to her, a predator was watching her closely.

From the shadows, Lane emerged and launched a frenzied attack. He slashed Darlene's throat and stabbed her repeatedly, leaving her lifeless on the wooden deck. Her husband, Todd, had been asleep inside.

Haunted by that memory, Gerhart recalled the last words he heard before the call was disconnected "She cried, 'Oh my God, oh my God.'"

Upon arrival, investigators discovered the scene to be both horrific and confusing. What could drive someone to commit such violence in a peaceful neighborhood? The FBI was called due to the home's proximity to Interstate 81. Federal agents speculated that the assailant might be a truck driver—someone who could use the highway to stalk, kill, and vanish without a trace.

They believed the murderer simply returned to his truck at a nearby stop and disappeared into the darkness.

The Ewalt family encountered profound tragedy.

Nicole Pogasic, Todd and Darlene's daughter, vividly recalls the time when her life fell apart. "I received a call from my brother around 6:45 a.m. He said, 'Nicole, Mom's dead.' In disbelief, I replied, 'What? You're joking. Please tell me that's not true.' He answered, 'No, she was murdered.' In that instant, my entire world crumbled."

Dauphin County District Attorney Ed Marsico Jr. subsequently stated, "Our experience indicates that homicides taking place in a residence are often perpetrated by someone known to the victim. This occurrence appeared intentional."

Investigators focused on Todd Ewalt, identifying him as the primary suspect—either as the murderer or the mastermind behind the crime.

Nicole remembered the day her father was arrested. "The officers took me to the Pennsylvania State Police barracks, where he was in custody."

Overwhelmed with shock and sorrow, Todd recalled the instant his daughter emerged. She turned the corner, dashed into his arms, and embraced him tightly. He felt helpless to alter the situation; he could only hold her close.

Despite their efforts, law enforcement remained skeptical. They rigorously questioned Todd about his marriage, alleged financial struggles, and accusations of infidelity. They even claimed that he had failed a polygraph test, which was false. The pressure on him was relentless.

Nicole remained resolute. "You're mistaken; this is clear. I never questioned my dad's innocence concerning my mom's death; I was utterly convinced. She had no adversaries; everyone loved her. Who could possibly wish her harm, let alone end her life?"

She paused before replying, "And who could that monster be? I can assure you, I never go out alone at night anymore."

Nick Ewalt, Darlene's 24-year-old son, encountered significant challenges after his mother's tragic murder. He expressed, "The painful memory of my mother's death haunts me. I often find it difficult to sleep or even go to bed. I lie awake, pondering everything that has occurred."

Four days later, on July 17, 2007, Adam Lane targeted 31-year-old Patricia Brooks, roughly 25 miles south of the Ewalt residence.

"I was dozing on the sofa at my home on Bowers Bridge Road in rural York County, Pennsylvania," Patricia later recounted to the police. "At 2:05 a.m., I was abruptly awakened by a man in black who was stabbing a knife into my shoulder."

Lane had slashed her neck and fled as Patricia screamed and sat up. Blood poured from her wound as she clutched her throat and staggered to another sofa, dazed, watching the intruder slip out through the unlocked back door.

The scene felt familiar: a partially open door, a solitary female victim, and a stealthy attacker armed with a knife.

After Patricia called 9-1-1, she was swiftly transported to York Hospital. Although she survived, she sustained minor injuries and ongoing nerve damage. She recalled that her assailant was a White male with a noticeable pot belly, dressed in dark pants resembling a correctional officer's uniform. He wore a hat but did not have a mask.

Patricia later identified Lane in a photographic lineup.

A different witness described noticing a suspicious person in black gloves hanging around Locust Point Road that morning. A tractor-trailer was stationed at the junction of Locust Point Road and Susquehanna Trail close to Interstate 83.

A Pennsylvania State Police detective believed there was a connection between the Brooks attack and Darlene Ewalt's murder. However, Dauphin County District Attorney Edward M. Marsico Jr. dismissed this idea without explanation.

Fewer than two weeks later, Lane struck once more.

Monica Massaro, a 38-year-old loan officer and skilled amateur photographer, enjoyed a relaxing moment in her cozy Victorian home in Bloomsbury, New Jersey. A devoted and free-spirited individual, she had chosen this picturesque town for its peacefulness, charm, and security.

She was oblivious to the predator lurking in the neighborhood while she changed into her pajamas, brushed her teeth, and prepared for bed.

At around 8:30 p.m., Lane parked his truck at the nearby Bloomsbury T&A Truck Stop and went inside for a quick meal. While seated at the counter, he began tapping his right index finger and foot—nervous habits that signaled his urge was returning.

The urge to end a life.

With a knife, Lane slipped out of the truck stop and quietly navigated through the sleeping neighborhood. He steered clear of houses with barking dogs or bright windows until he reached Monica's—dark, serene, and welcoming.

He slipped in through the back, noticed her keys on the kitchen table, and went outside to unlock her car. After rifling through her purse, he went back inside. Quietly positioned in a dark doorway, he watched Monica as she stepped into the bedroom. For a fleeting moment, he believed she hadn't seen him. But once she did, she screamed.

Lane lunged at her, tackling her onto the bed and covering her mouth to stifle her cries. Monica resisted with all her strength, even biting his hand in defiance.

Enraged, Lane drew his sharpest knife and sliced her throat, then mutilated her body in a frenzy, slashing her abdomen, thighs, and breasts.

Before fleeing, he yanked a necklace from her neck and returned to his truck at the rest stop.

No DNA, fingerprints, or witnesses were found. Monica died alone, without assistance.

Detective Sergeant Geoffrey Noble of the New Jersey State Police later stated, "The initial major injury occurred to her throat. It was lethal—she lost a lot of blood in mere minutes. Even after she died, he continued stabbing her heartlessly. Monica died alone in the hands of that inhuman, violent monster. She didn't have time to run. She had nowhere to go."

After the murder, Lane parked his truck nearby and tried to sleep. The next day, he drove north to Chelmsford, Massachusetts, ready to kill again.

Around 11:00 p.m. on July 29, a resident of an apartment complex noticed a man hiding in the bushes and promptly called the police. However, by the time the officers arrived, he had disappeared. A few hours later, another 9-1-1 call came from a nearby trailer park, reporting a masked man dressed in black who was attempting to break into a woman's home.

Kathy Crowley shared, "My daughter thought she saw someone watching our house. I stepped outside to check, and that's when I spotted a man in a mask—he resembled a ninja. When he faced me, I felt a surge of anxiety. He barged into my home, and I was terrified as he banged on the door. How could this be happening?"

The police acted swiftly once more. Lane had vanished again.

In New Jersey, the murder of Monica puzzled investigators. The closest home was near the Bloomsbury Truck Stop at Exit 7. Seeking help, local law enforcement reached out to the FBI, which had recently initiated the Highway Serial Killers Initiative, a national database created in 2005 designed to link unsolved murders and assaults along highways. This database has grown to encompass over 500 victims, facilitating connections between crimes across various jurisdictions.

The critical moment happened when Monica's case was linked to the attack on Shea McDonough, which had occurred close to a truck stop—specifically, an old I-495 in Chelmsford, Massachusetts.

That morning, surveillance cameras recorded a big rig arriving at the lot just before 5:00 a.m. Subsequently, investigators verified that the license plates belonged to Adam Leroy Lane.

As a result, a judge issued a search warrant for Lane's truck. Inside, police discovered critical evidence, including receipts from the Bloomsbury truck stop and a blood-stained knife.

Forensic analysis confirmed that the blood was Darlene Ewalt's.

This was the opportunity authorities had been looking for.

Investigators began to piece together Lane's troubling pattern. He utilized America's highways as both a hunting ground and an escape route—slipping off exits, selecting victims in quiet neighborhoods, and vanishing into the night.

Lane was arrested without any incident.

During the interrogation, he confessed to murdering Darlene Ewalt and Monica Massaro and to attempting to kill Patricia Brooks. However, detectives suspected he had not disclosed the full extent of his criminal activities.

A thorough inspection of Adam Lane's truck revealed a hidden compartment filled with startling evidence.

Among the items were large hunting knives, bloodied gloves, wire rope, Monica Massaro's stolen necklace, and a copy of *Hunting Humans*. The findings provided investigators with a chilling insight into Lane's disturbed psyche.

Authorities retained Lane's truck for three weeks, meticulously documenting the evidence. A surprising mistake occurred when the trucking company's owner discarded Lane's personal belongings in a dumpster at the Massachusetts impound yard. As a trash hauler was about to empty it, detectives arrived—just in time.

For hours, investigators meticulously sorted through the packed refuse, uncovering Lane's clothing, shoes, and socks—each item a potential source of DNA evidence. Their diligent efforts would soon prove essential in connecting Lane to multiple violent crime scenes.

In New Jersey, Detective George Tyros was determined to interview Lane about his brutal multistate crime spree that occurred from July 13 to July 30, 2007. Despite colleagues warning him that Lane had refused to cooperate with investigators from Massachusetts, Tyros believed the potential benefits outweighed the risks.

Detective Kevin Noble initiated the interrogation, and suddenly, Lane, who had once been uncooperative, appeared eager to talk.

Noble stated, "We aren't here because of anything that happened in New Jersey. We're here because we're certain you did something."

Lane remained motionless, acutely aware of the gravity of his situation. After a prolonged silence, he abruptly stated, "I'm done."

Noble confidently switched off the recorder and exited the room. Moments later, Lane signaled his readiness through the small door window.

What ensued was a haunting revelation.

Lane confessed to illegally entering Monica Massaro's home with plans to rob her. However, their confrontation turned fatal, resulting in a violent murder. Lane's family later disclosed to investigators that he harbored profound misogynistic beliefs and a longstanding animosity toward women, indicating that his actions were driven not only by opportunism but also by deep-seated, violent rage.

Lane's confession provided authorities with the solid evidence they needed.

His former wife, Miriam M. Benge, who divorced him in 1993 after five years of marriage, later told police, "He thought women were beneath him. He hit me once. He abused his mother, too. He'd cuss her out, call her names, and, believe it or not, he hit on her."

Later, experts described Lane's behavior towards his mother as a significant instance of child-to-parent violence, which is often overlooked as a form of domestic abuse.

Lane's confession was graphic, almost gleeful in detail. "I had the knife," he said, mimicking stabbing motions. "It was on the bed. It was about that long. She rolled against it and cut right here." He motioned to his neck.

In the video, Lane appeared exhausted and unkempt, portraying himself as a defeated individual: a truck driver burdened by a back injury, struggling with financial difficulties, and reliant on medication for diabetes and hallucinations. He emphasized his respectful demeanor, commitment to the law, and politeness.

"I possess good manners," he asserted. "I treat others as I would like to be treated."

Detective Noble identified the deception.

"No doubt about it," he later told his colleagues, "Adam Lane is the most dangerous man I've ever seen. Because there is no explanation. There is no why. And I believe he killed Monica Massaro just for the damn sport of it."

Weeks later, forensic analysis uncovered a startling find: the DNA of Monica Massaro and another victim, Darlene Ewalt, was detected on Lane's knives.

District Attorney Ed Marsico Jr. of Dauphin County found the results conclusive.

"After discovering Darlene's blood on the knife," he remarked, "I talked to Todd Ewalt to let him know we had identified the killer and to apologize for any confusion he experienced during the investigation. I promised him we would do all we could to ensure that Adam Lane is held accountable."

On October 4, 2008, Detective Noble at a Massachusetts jail asked the pivotal question that resolved the case.

"Adam, could you describe what happened during your visit to the Route 78 rest area in New Jersey?"

Lane recounted the events of the night of July 29, 2007. After leaving the rest stop, he entered Bloomsbury and checked several doors before finding one unlocked. Inside, he found 38-year-old Monica Massaro asleep in her bed. He stabbed her to death.

In his videotaped confession, Lane claimed, "As we wrestled on her bed, she turned into the knife, slicing her throat. I panicked and mutilated her body to throw the police off— make it look like a sex crime."

His words were unsettling. His intention was clear.

With the awareness of his crimes laid bare, justice became unavoidable.

On May 21, 2009, Adam Leroy Lane admitted guilt to charges in New Jersey and Massachusetts, resulting in a 75-year prison term. He was subsequently extradited to Dauphin County to address homicide charges stemming from the violent murder of Darlene Ewalt, which had been initiated almost a year earlier on August 6, 2008.

The arraignment took place almost two years after Ewalt's death. Dauphin County District Attorney Edward M. Marsico Jr. declared his plan to pursue the death penalty.

On June 28, 2010, Lane pleaded guilty to avoid the death penalty. He received a sentence of 25 to 50 years for the Chelmsford attack, 50 years for the murder of Monica Massaro, 10 to 20 years for the attempted murder of Patricia Brooks, and a life sentence for the killing of Darlene Ewalt.

Authorities suspect that Lane may have committed additional murders nationwide, using his long-haul trucking routes as an ideal cover. However, no new evidence has surfaced so far. Lane has chosen not to communicate with investigators or the public.

Today, Adam Leroy Lane is serving his sentence at the State Correctional Institution in Fayette, Pennsylvania. This maximum-security facility houses over 2,000 inmates. However, for the families he terrorized, this sentence offers little peace.

Jeannie McDonough later shared, "You always feel something surprising might occur. You start to think about every possible outcome. Nevertheless, I find calmness every night amid it all."

CHAPTER SEVEN
Night Stalker – Richard Ramirez

Richard Ramirez was born on February 29, 1960, in El Paso, Texas, to Mexican immigrants Mercedes Muñoz and Julián Tapia Ramirez, who faced significant difficulties while raising their large family. Julián, a railway worker, struggled with alcoholism and was notorious for his violent outbursts, which often escalated into physical confrontations. His anger was frequently directed at Mercedes and their children, resulting in a chaotic and traumatic home environment. Their youngest child, Richard, would later gain a more sinister reputation.

Angel grew up in a Catholic household, but by age ten, he started to separate himself from that upbringing. He began to experiment with marijuana and alcohol, signifying a difficult childhood that was rapidly transforming into more significant problems.

Psychiatrist Dr. Michael Stone characterized Richard Ramirez as a psychopath who was "made" rather than "born." He highlighted how Ramirez's schizoid personality disorder significantly contributed to his emotional detachment and lack of empathy.

Stone mentioned that Ramirez suffered several severe head injuries before turning six. In these events, he lost consciousness, putting his life in danger. Stone proposed that these early injuries could have led to the development of temporal lobe epilepsy, seizures, heightened aggression, and hypersexual behaviors.

At 14, Ramirez started using LSD frequently. He bonded with his cousin Mike over their mutual interests in drugs, Satanism, and the occult.

As his sexual development progressed, his fantasies grew darker, fusing sex with acts of violence, mutilation, domination, and murder.

While still in school, Ramirez worked at a Holiday Inn, using a master key to enter rooms and rob sleeping guests. On one occasion, he molested two children in an elevator, though the incident was never reported or prosecuted.

He lost his job after trying to sexually assault a woman in her hotel room. However, her husband stepped in, causing a confrontation. Because they were out of state, the couple decided against returning to testify, resulting in the dismissal of the criminal charges.

At just 15, Richard Ramirez experienced a traumatic event that would forever affect him. On May 4, 1975, he witnessed his older cousin, Miguel "Mike" Ramirez—a Vietnam War veteran—murder his 26-year-old wife, Jessie Valles, during a tumultuous domestic dispute.

At close range, Mike shot Valles, hitting her in the face and instantly killing her.

After the shooting, Mike Ramirez became more withdrawn, exhibiting signs of moodiness and isolating himself from family and friends. Although Mike was arrested, he was later acquitted of murder due to insanity, as the court linked his violent actions to post-traumatic stress disorder stemming from his military service.

At 22 in 1982, Richard Ramirez relocated from Texas to California. He started using cocaine, which quickly developed into a serious addiction. To support this habit, he engaged in theft and burglary, leading to a transient lifestyle along the California coast, moving between Los Angeles and San Francisco until his arrest.

Over 14 months, Ramirez committed a series of brutal home invasions, leaving a trail of death, sexual violence, and terror in his wake. He was ultimately convicted of 13 counts of murder, five attempted murders, 11 sexual assaults, and 14 burglaries.

Ramirez turned to violence due to his complex and chaotic upbringing.

In the following years, Ramirez's fascination with violence deepened. He became increasingly obsessed with Satanism and the occult, which later emerged as a troubling aspect of his criminal signature.

Ramirez moved quietly through neighborhoods, frequently entering homes through unlocked doors or windows.

His assaults were characterized by severe brutality, including shootings, stabbings, beatings, sexual assaults, and mutilations, often infused with ritualistic or Satanic elements.

He employed many weapons, including knives, guns, a machete, a tire iron, and a claw hammer. In some cases, he strangled his victims, used ligatures, or stomped them to death.

He inflicted torture on a woman using an electrical cord. He ridiculed others, compelling them to "swear to Satan" or praise the devil.

Survivors often recalled his unsettling gaze, foul odor, and decayed teeth, all of which shaped society's perception of Ramirez as a terrifying predator.

The media hype surrounding the Night Stalker case escalated as his crimes spanned multiple jurisdictions. In addition to his acts of violence and depravity, he exhibited various patterns that complicated efforts to track him down.

Public anxiety peaked in August 1985, when a mob from East Los Angeles identified and captured him after his photo was published in the newspapers. He did not resist, infamously declaring, "It's me. Hail Satan."

Victims

June 28, 1984 – Jennie Vinco, 79, Glassell Park
Jennie Vinco was found brutally murdered in her apartment. Her throat had been slashed, and the scene showed signs of forced entry.
Charges: Murder, burglary.

March 17, 1985 – Dayle Okazaki, 34, and Maria Hernandez, 20, Rosemead
Maria Hernandez survived an attack in her garage, but her roommate, Dayle Okazaki, was shot and killed inside the home.
Charges: Murder, attempted murder, robbery.

March 27, 1985 – Vincent Zazzara, 64, and Maxine Zazzara, 44, Whittier
The couple was attacked in their home. Vincent was shot; Maxine was stabbed multiple times and mutilated.

Charges: Two counts of murder and sexual assault-related charges.

May 14, 1985 – Bill Doi, 66, Monterey Park
Bill Doi was shot and killed in his home. His disabled wife Lillian was sexually assaulted.
Charges: Murder, robbery, sexual assault.

May 30, 1985 – Carol Kyle, 41, Burbank
Carol Kyle was raped, sodomized, and forced to submit to oral copulation.
Charges: Burglary, robbery, sexual assault-related charges.

June 1, 1985 – Mabel "Ma Bell" Bell, 83, and Florence "Nettie" Lang, 80, Monrovia
The sisters were bludgeoned in their home. Mabel died of her injuries. Satanic symbols were scrawled on the walls.
Charges: Burglary, robbery, sexual assault-related charges.

July 2, 1985 – Mary Louise Cannon, 75, Arcadia
Mary Cannon was beaten and had her throat slashed in her home.
Charges: Murder, burglary.

July 5, 1985 – Whitney Bennett, 16, Sierra Madre
Whitney was savagely beaten with a tire iron in her bedroom but survived the attack.
Charges: Attempted murder, burglary.

July 7, 1985 – Joyce Lucille Nelson, 61, Monterey Park
Joyce Nelson was found beaten to death in her home.
Charges: Murder, burglary.

July 7, 1985 – Sophie Dickman, 63, Monterey Park
Sophie was sexually assaulted and robbed in her home on the same night Joyce Nelson was murdered.
Charges: Burglary, robbery, sexual assault.

July 20, 1985 – Max Kneiding, 68, and Lela Kneiding, 66, Glendale
The Kneidings were both shot to death and mutilated in their home.
Charges: Murder, burglary.

July 20, 1985 – Chainarong Khovananth, 32, Sun Valley
Chainarong was shot to death. His wife and son were both sexually assaulted during the home invasion.
Charges: Murder, robbery, burglary, and sexual assault-related charges.

August 8, 1985 – Elyas Abowath, 35, Diamond Bar
Elyas was shot while sleeping in his bed. His wife was raped during the break-in.
Charges: Murder, robbery, burglary, rape.

The intensity and speed of the attacks quickly drew media attention, instilling fear throughout the Los Angeles area. Witnesses described a man with long, curly hair, bulging eyes, and widely spaced, decayed teeth.

Ramírez's mugshots were released to the public, and his image was featured in major newspapers and on television throughout California.

The reign of terror ended on August 31, 1985, when he was caught in East Los Angeles while trying to steal a car. Identified from news reports, a group of locals came together to chase him down.

They captured him, restrained him, and began to assault him, angry and unyielding against the man who had instilled fear in countless others. The police arrived just in time to rescue him from the infuriated mob, arresting him and putting an end to the terror of the Night Stalker once and for all.

Richard Ramirez is often seen as one of the most unsettling figures in American criminal history—a ruthless murderer whose actions, motivations, and impact continue to be both captivating and disturbing.

Trial and Conviction

The jury selection for Richard Ramírez's trial began on July 22, 1988, marking the start of one of the most infamous and widely publicized criminal trials in American history. Over several weeks, nearly 1,600 potential jurors participated in a rigorous voir dire process as attorneys from both sides sought individuals capable of managing the unsettling evidence and extensive media attention surrounding the case.

The courtroom was charged—an intense atmosphere filled with trauma as memories collided with fear. Over 100 witnesses testified; some struggled, their memories hazy from time or muddled by anxiety, while others were resolute, delivering compelling testimonies and unmistakably pinpointing Ramírez as the source of a terrifying wave across California.

The trial, which spanned more than a year, ended on September 20, 1989, as the jury issued a clear verdict: guilty on 43 felony charges, including 13 counts of murder, five counts of attempted murder, 11 sexual assaults, and 14 burglaries.

These figures illustrate a grim reality. The decision represents a profound awakening—unmistakable and accusatory in essence.

Just two weeks into the trial on August 3, 1988, *The Los Angeles Times* reported a chilling development. Jail officials had allegedly overheard Richard Ramírez plotting to smuggle a gun into the courtroom with the intent of assassinating the lead prosecutor.

The revelation rippled through the high-stakes proceedings. Authorities swiftly reacted by setting up metal detectors and stationing armed guards at each entrance, turning the courtroom into a fortress. The existing tense atmosphere deepened with discomfort. This threat highlighted the defendant's unpredictability and the life-and-death importance of the case taking place in that courtroom.

Suddenly, a shocking event shook the very foundation of the courtroom. On August 14, juror Phyllis Singletary failed to appear. Later that day, her lifeless body was discovered, shot in her Los Angeles apartment. The timing was ominously precise. Whispers surged through the jury box: Had Richard Ramírez orchestrated a hit from prison?

Tension filled the courtroom. The trial paused. Anxiety simmered just beneath the surface.

"I think many of us have tears in our eyes," said Superior Court Judge Michael Tynan to the panel in his emotion-filled voice. He stressed, however, that the murder of Ms. Singletary "is unrelated to this case." He encouraged the jurors to set aside their sadness and focus solely on the evidence presented during the trial.

Ultimately, investigators concluded that Singletary's boyfriend had committed a murder-suicide unrelated to the case. The psychological effects were significant; the alternate juror who replaced her was so shaken that she decided not to return home, fearing she might become the next victim.

By then, Ramírez had become more than merely a defendant; he had morphed into a dark cultural icon. He garnered a loyal fan base, receiving correspondence from fans and women who romanticized the monster behind the murders.

Among them was Doreen Lioy, a freelance magazine editor who sent nearly 75 letters to him. 1988 Ramírez proposed, and they married on October 3, 1996, in a small ceremony at San Quentin State Prison. Lioy later claimed she would take her own life if Ramírez were executed. Her loyalty, much like Ramírez's crimes, transcended logic.

On November 7, 1989, Richard Ramírez was sentenced to death by the jury, a sentence that was to be carried out in California's gas chamber. However, the pursuit of justice encountered numerous obstacles.

Ramírez spent over twenty years on death row. Although there was a lasting public fascination with the "Night Stalker," California's death penalty process faced extensive appeals, legal standstills, and shifts in political attitudes. Consequently, the execution that many families of his victims had eagerly anticipated never took place.

Ramírez died of natural causes at Marin General Hospital in Greenbrae, California, on June 7, 2013. His family did not come forward to claim his body. Like many of his victims, he died alone. Consequently, his remains were cremated.

CHAPTER EIGHT
Cross Country Killer – Israel Keyes

Israel Keyes was born in 1978 in the tranquil town of Richmond, Utah. He was raised in a strict Mormon family and was homeschooled alongside his siblings. In the early 1980s, his family relocated to a remote, rugged area near Colville, Washington, adopting an off-the-grid lifestyle that lacked electricity and running water.

Keyes is thought to have committed his first documented violent crime by abducting and sexually assaulting a teenage girl in Oregon between 1996 and 1998.

Even after enduring the traumatic event, the assault marked the beginning of a decade-long spree of violence, leaving a trail of victims across the United States.

Later, Keyes confessed to murdering at least four individuals in Washington State during the late 1990s and early 2000s. Although the details of these murders remain unclear due to ongoing investigations, his admissions suggest a broader and more serious pattern of violence than previously recognized. Despite these alarming confessions, Keyes had no felony convictions in Washington. His recorded offenses were minor, including a DUI and driving without a valid license.

Keyes largely remained under the radar while living in various parts of Washington State, including Colville, the Makah Reservation at Neah Bay, and near Olympia. Adapting to different communities enabled him to operate without drawing attention. Consequently, law enforcement officials are revisiting cold cases of unsolved homicides and missing persons in these areas, searching for potential links to Keyes.

In addition to his known activities in Washington, Keyes confessed to a murder in New York State, though the victim remains unidentified. In April 2009, he also carried out an armed bank robbery in Tupper Lake, New York. Furthermore, he admitted to trespassing into a Texas residence and setting a fire there. The FBI considers his admission regarding the New York murder credible, even as investigators continue their efforts to determine the victim's identity.

Modus Operandi

Israel Keyes defied the conventional patterns of serial killers. He showed no preference for victim profiles; age, gender, and race did not dictate his choices. Instead, he operated with chilling calculation and discipline, meticulously planning his crimes months or even years in advance. His murders stemmed from opportunity rather than compulsion, and he intentionally avoided establishing a recognizable pattern.

Keyes crisscrossed the United States, traveling thousands of miles from his home in Alaska in 2007 to carry out his attacks. To facilitate his crimes, he buried so-called "murder kits" in remote locations across the country—containers stocked with weapons, restraints, cash, and cleaning supplies. These caches, sometimes hidden years before being used, allowed him to kill quickly and efficiently, then vanish without a trace.

He fixated on avoiding detection. He exclusively used cash, disabled his cell phone during trips, and never visited the same location more than once, steering clear of areas near his home. This calculated secrecy rendered him nearly undetectable by law enforcement.

The Murder of His Most Notable Victim – Samantha Tessla Koenig

At the time of her abduction, 18-year-old Samantha Tessla Koenig was thoroughly enjoying life in Anchorage, Alaska, with her father, James Koenig, and her boyfriend, Duane Tortolani II.

Born on August 30, 1993, Samantha was an energetic young woman with a profound love for animals, music, photography, and poetry. She cherished fishing and camping adventures with her dad. She enjoyed playing *Call of Duty* with Duane, her partner and best friend. She dreamed of working with animals in equestrian settings or with wildlife she adored.

Samantha attended West High School and Avail High School and worked at Subway and the House of Harley. In the weeks before her disappearance, she was employed as a barista at Common Grounds, a coffee stand on Tudor Road in Anchorage.

She could have enjoyed a peaceful, fulfilling life with her supportive family and boyfriend. However, fate had different plans.

On February 1, 2012, Samantha Koenig became the unsuspecting last victim of serial killer Israel Keyes. Her abduction and subsequent murder exposed the sinister secrets Keyes had concealed for years—his nationwide spree of kidnappings, sexual assaults, strangulations, and killings.

Before that evening, Keyes did not know Samantha, and his identity remained a mystery. However, the tragedy surrounding her case led to his arrest, revealing the full extent of his crimes through her story.

As the temperature dropped to 19 degrees Fahrenheit, Keyes stayed hidden in the shadows near the dimly lit coffee stand, his eyes fixed on the young woman inside. Samantha Koenig expertly worked behind the counter at Common Grounds, unaware of the predator observing her every move.

Despite being Alaska's largest city, Anchorage remains over 90 percent unspoiled. This vast area offers profound darkness and tranquility, establishing a perfect hunting ground for someone like him.

Samantha was unaware that Keyes had been watching her for several days. He knew her closing times and that a young man—her boyfriend, Duane Tortolani—usually picked her up. They remained oblivious to Duane's initial involvement in Keyes's plot. Investigators could not determine why Keyes altered his plans. However, Anchorage homicide detective Monique Doll later stated, "Duane was part of Keyes's original plan."

As Samantha commenced her closing routine to conclude another shift, a dark figure emerged from the shadows outside the window—silent, focused, and poised to strike.

Keyes showed up at the coffee stand wearing a hooded sweatshirt, a ski mask, and a baseball cap pulled low, all in a casual style.

"How do you feel about an Americano?" he asked casually.

Samantha smiled politely, unaware of what was coming. She prepared the drink, slid it across the counter, and reached for the register.

In an instant, Keyes drew a handgun, his voice shifting into a menacing growl. "Hand over all the cash."

A wave of fear washed over her. Shaking, she leaned against the counter, grabbed the cash bag, and handed over a stack of bills.

Without hesitation, Keyes snatched the cash and hurried through the order window into the cramped stand. "Where is your vehicle?"

"I don't have a car tonight," she said softly.

He huffed in frustration. "Turn off the lights; I don't want to be seen on the cameras."

The switch was only inches from the panic button. Samantha hesitated to push it, caught in fear or struggling to think clearly amid the chaos. Keyes was unaware that the surveillance cameras had already captured everything: his arrival, Samantha's desperate signal from below the counter, and the cash being handed over.

Feeling satisfied, he grabbed a handful of zip ties to bind her hands behind her back. Napkins stuffed in her mouth muted any cries for help. "Get down on the ground," he commanded sharply.

She agreed, and the camera continued recording.

Moments later, he told her to get up and took her outside. However, as they approached his truck, Samantha broke free and desperately tried to flee.

Keyes lunged and tackled her before she could escape. He pressed a knife to her throat and hissed a chilling warning, "My gun is loaded with silenced ammo. Don't force my hand."

Without uttering another word, he bound Samantha's hands, forced her into his truck, and vanished into the frigid night.

The vehicle was meticulously modified for abduction. Keyes eliminated identifying elements, such as removing the ladder rack, unbolting the toolboxes from the truck bed, and detaching both license plates.

A surveillance camera above a Home Depot parking lot captured a faint, grainy image of a hooded man walking toward a white pickup truck with a young woman. Although the footage was pixelated and distant, investigators later identified the vehicle as a 2004 Chevrolet Silverado—Keyes's truck. Extracted stills from the video became critical in building a timeline and tightening the noose around him.

Additional surveillance footage from local shops and a gas station captured the truck roaming Anchorage, displaying random and deliberate movements. Meanwhile, Samantha remained confined inside.

"I'm taking you for ransom and nothing else," he stated simply.

Nevertheless, it was a lie, and both knew it.

"Listen," Samantha tried to explain, "my family isn't wealthy. You likely won't receive a large ransom."

Keyes released a soft, eerie laugh. "Your family will gather resources—public appeals, donations, whatever it takes. Just cooperate, and you'll return home safely."

Still behaving as if it were only about money, he insisted she hand over her phone to fulfill his demand. "Where's your phone? Is it in your jeans?"

"No, I think I left it on the counter."

"Damn," he murmured.

He made a sudden U-turn, his tires screeching, and raced back to Common Grounds. He quickly slipped inside, grabbed her phone and other personal belongings, and drove away to a different part of town.

He texted Samantha's boyfriend and boss, inventing a story about her challenging weekend departure. After sending the messages, he removed the battery. He tossed the phone out the truck window, letting it tumble into the darkness.

As they approached her home, he looked at her once more. "Give me your debit card?"

"I don't have it with me," she replied. "I share it with my boyfriend, Duane, and we keep it in the car."

"Where is that car?"

"It's parked in front of my father's house."

He looked at her, assessing her response. Then he said, "All right. Give me the PIN."

At 2:00 a.m., Samantha realized she was tied up in a shed behind Keyes's Anchorage house. The thin plastic cable ties had been replaced with a sturdier rope. Before offering her a bottle of water, he poured himself a glass of wine in the kitchen, trying to project an air of kindness.

It was merely an act. He was determined to prevent her from leaving.

He exited the shed and entered the house to check on his 11-year-old daughter, Sarah.

In the shed, Samantha whispered in puzzlement, "Why would he watch over his daughter while treating me poorly? A psychologist might find that fascinating."

When Keyes returned, the temperature inside had climbed to 90 degrees from the space heaters he'd set up. Unbothered by the stifling heat, he pulled on a pair of leather gloves and picked up a large knife. With cold precision, he stabbed Samantha once beneath her right shoulder blade.

While music streamed from a radio he had brought into the shed, he struck her twice.

Once he finished, he hovered above her, his expression blank. Samantha's voice trembled as she asked if he intended to take her life. In desperation, she pleaded with him to stop, begging for a chance to live.

Keyes carefully sipped wine before saying, "I'll string you up with this rope."

Next, he acted.

After confirming her death, he wrapped her in a tarp, stored her in a lower cabinet, turned off the heaters, and securely locked the shed door behind him.

He prepared himself, entered the house, and took a shower— as if committing murder were as commonplace as mowing the lawn or washing the dishes.

Later that evening, Keyes headed to Samantha's father's house. He parked nearby, trying to remain inconspicuous. However, despite his precautions, he was spotted by an unexpected person—Samantha's boyfriend, Duane.

Around 3:00 a.m., Duane spotted a masked person lingering by his car. Concerned, he approached and discovered the man trying to steal Samantha's debit card. Understanding the risk, Duane hurried back inside to inform Samantha's father, James. Unfortunately, when they returned outside, they found that the masked thief and the debit card had vanished.

At the same time, reports of Samantha's disappearance surfaced, sparking a desperate search. Meanwhile, her body remained hidden in plain sight within Israel's shed, unbeknownst to investigators. As days passed, the community united, holding onto hope. The reward for information leading to her return increased to more than three times its original amount.

Exploiting the cold's natural preservation, Keyes orchestrated a grotesque deception. He braided Samantha's hair and applied makeup to her face. He sewed her eyelids open with a fishing line to simulate alertness in a chilling display of manipulation. He posed her next to a copy of *The Anchorage Daily News* dated February 13 to create the illusion that she was still alive. He took a photo—a staged "proof-of-life" intended to mislead.

The news hit Samantha's family like a shockwave. Keyes provided them with a glimmer of hope that she was still alive and could be saved. This cruel, calculated trick was designed to exploit her family's feelings.

Days later, after his deception was in motion, Keyes dismembered Samantha's body. Disguised as an ice fisherman, he drove to Matanuska Glacier Lake near Palmer, Alaska.

Under the pretense of ice fishing, he used a chainsaw to cut a hole and covertly submerged her remains in the freezing waters. This macabre burial hid the evidence of his crime.

But even after disposing of her body, Keyes continued his sadistic performance. On February 24, he used Samantha's phone to text her boyfriend, Duane, sending a cryptic message that led him to a local dog park.

Duane discovered the photograph—a chilling image of Samantha, looking alive, with the February 13 newspaper in her hands. The back of the photo bore a ransom note written in cold script: Keyes demanded that $30,000 be transferred to Samantha's bank account.

Clinging to hope inspired by the image, Samantha's family gathered funds and met the demands. As Keyes intended, they believed their efforts could bring her back home.

Keyes was prepared. Hidden beneath a baseball cap, sunglasses, and multiple face coverings, he withdrew ransom money from ATMs in various locations. He proceeded with caution, expecting surveillance and implementing measures to evade detection. Yet, he underestimated the increasing repercussions of his overconfidence—the evidence he inadvertently left behind.

At the same time, the Anchorage Police Department faced increasing public criticism regarding their handling of the case, particularly concerning their decision not to release surveillance footage related to Samantha's abduction. Detractors demanded greater transparency, but Lieutenant Dave Parker defended the choice. "We will not release the video because it won't assist the investigation," he explained. "The footage contains crucial evidence for investigators but sharing it wouldn't help since the suspected kidnapper's face isn't visible."

Unbeknownst to the public, the case was evolving. The façade started to crumble, and Israel Keyes's carefully maintained anonymity was about to vanish.

Keyes's meticulously crafted plan began to unravel in Arizona due to a significant blunder: he parked his rental car directly in front of a surveillance camera while withdrawing cash from an ATM with Samantha Koenig's debit card. The grainy footage captured a masked individual extracting money and fleeing in a white Ford Focus. Although the disguise concealed his identity, the car became crucial evidence for investigators monitoring the transaction.

On March 13, 2012, a highway patrol officer in Shepherd, Texas, spotted a white Ford Focus that matched the reported description in a hotel parking lot. The officer followed the vehicle closely until the driver committed a minor traffic infraction—speeding—which provided the officer with legal grounds to pull the car over.

At the wheel was 34-year-old Israel Keyes.

The arrest occurred swiftly and without complications. Texas Highway Patrol Corporal Bryan Henry and Texas Ranger Steven Rayburn quickly apprehended Keyes. Anchorage police investigator Jeff Bell recalled, "Agents had spent the entire night tracking his ATM cash withdrawals and images. We were just ten minutes behind him."

The search of Keyes's vehicle revealed chilling evidence: stacks of cash wrapped in rubber bands, Samantha Koenig's stolen debit card and ID, her cell phone, a .40-caliber Sig Sauer pistol, and a crude homemade mask with roughly cut eye holes. Additionally, a highlighted map indicating travel routes through California, Arizona, and New Mexico suggested broader intentions. The disguise captured in the ATM footage was also found.

An officer remarked, "Why not visit a nearby costume store to get a rubber Groucho Marx mask featuring bushy eyebrows, a prominent nose, and thick glasses?" However, the humor didn't land, leaving only silence as the agents absorbed the unsettling sight.

When he was captured, the public maintained hope. Authorities regarded the case as a ransom situation, causing many to believe that Samantha might still be alive. Even after

Keyes was charged, the only accusation was kidnapping, which helped sustain that sense of optimism.

That hope was extinguished on April 2, 2012. Investigators located Samantha's dismembered remains submerged in Matanuska Lake, a remote, icy body of water just north of Anchorage. It confirmed the community's worst fears, and Keyes was charged with her murder.

Before this incident, Keyes had a relatively minor criminal record. He had never been linked to violent crime. Therefore, when he was, questions arose: Who was Israel Keyes? And why had he abducted Samantha?

The answers were much more terrifying than anyone could have envisioned.

During his chilling confession, Israel Keyes admitted, "There wasn't a real motive. I simply wanted to kill. You know, I killed several other victims before Samantha."

Monique Doll, a homicide detective in Anchorage, conducted many interviews with Keyes and later noted his unsettling demeanor: "Israel Keyes didn't engage in kidnapping and murder out of insanity. Divine commands or a troubled past didn't influence his actions. Rather, he acted because he derived significant pleasure from it, similar to how someone with a substance use disorder enjoys drugs. Throughout the months of interviews, Keyes remained completely unrepentant and showed no signs of remorse. While he had previously demonstrated self-control, he lacked that restraint regarding Samantha."

While in custody, Keyes continued speaking with investigators over several months. In one conversation, he stated, "I want to be executed within a year to avoid publicity—and the negative attention my daughter might face. So, as you know, I killed a lot of people in several different states. I purposely killed people in different locations to avoid linking my victims' cases."

At that point, investigators recognized they were confronting a remorseless, methodical serial killer. Although he had already faced charges for Samantha's kidnapping and murder, authorities remained hopeful he might offer insights to help resolve other unsolved cases.

Nevertheless, he did not.

Meticulous in his methods, Keyes took extraordinary steps to avoid leaving a trail. During his murder trips, he turned off his phone and used only cash. He buried so-called "kill kits"—buckets filled with weapons, restraints, and body disposal tools—in remote areas near potential crime scenes, allowing him to travel light and strike without warning. Investigators believe he buried at least 12 of these kits across the country.

Keyes later confessed that he preferred strangulation as his method of killing because, in his words, he "liked to watch the light go out." He showed no remorse and took pride in how little evidence he left behind. Only Koenig's remains were ever recovered; the rest of his victims vanished without a trace.

During interviews, Keyes belittled other serial killers for their mistakes. He derided Dennis Rader, the BTK killer, for feeling remorse after his arrest, calling him a "wimp." When questioned about his reasons for murder, Keyes merely shrugged and replied, "Why not?"

Investigators believe that Keyes may have committed his first murder as a teenager in Colville, Washington. On March 2, 1996, 12-year-old Julie Marie Harris disappeared from the area. A month later, her prosthetic feet were found near the Colville River. The following year, her remains were discovered in a nearby wooded area, but the cause of death was never determined.

The Boca Raton Mall Murders and the Shadow of Israel Keyes

On December 12, 2007, Nancy Bochicchio, 47, and her 7-year-old daughter, Joey Bochicchio-Hauser, visited Town Center Mall in Boca Raton, Florida, eager for a joyful afternoon of Christmas shopping. What began as a festive outing quickly escalated into an unimaginable tragedy.

Surveillance footage later captured the pair leaving the mall that evening, seemingly unaware they were being watched. Not long after, they were ambushed and forced at gunpoint into Nancy's black SUV by an unknown assailant.

The assailant instructed Nancy to go to a nearby ATM, forcing her to take out $500.

Both the mother and daughter were bound with zip ties and duct tape. Blackout goggles were secured over Nancy's eyes—a troubling detail that indicated a methodical and experienced predator.

Just before midnight, a mall security guard patrolling the parking lot noticed something strange. Inside the SUV, both Nancy and Joey were discovered, executed with gunshots to the head at point-blank range.

The scene was shocking. The intentional brutality echoed throughout the community, quickly garnering attention from law enforcement and media nationwide.

Nonetheless, the fear persisted after that moment.

Earlier that year, a young mother and her 2-year-old son had been abducted from the same mall parking lot. Their experience was hauntingly similar; they were compelled to drive to an ATM and withdraw $600.

Similar to Nancy and Joey, they were also bound with zip ties, secured with duct tape, and blindfolded using blackout goggles. Astonishingly, they were set free, left in the parking lot by the same careful predator.

Days later, a 19-year-old woman was robbed at gunpoint in Mizner Park. The attacker tried to force her to drive to an ATM, but she ultimately handed him $200 in cash instead.

She also survived, but it was evident that someone was meticulously stalking and targeting women in Boca Raton.

During a thorough investigation, a crucial clue emerged: the zip ties and duct tape used in the abduction of Nancy and Joey were purchased in Miami-Dade County. This discovery made authorities suspect that the perpetrator lived in or frequently worked in South Florida.

The systematic strategy—employing restraints, blindfolds, and mandatory ATM withdrawals—was anything but impulsive. It was intentional, calculated, and entirely emotionless. As a result, some investigators started to suspect they were dealing with a serial predator potentially active in other regions of the country.

One name repeatedly emerged: Israel Keyes.

Though no direct evidence has tied Keyes to the Boca Raton cases, the parallels are hard to ignore. Keyes was known to target victims in public places—often parking lots—where he would abduct them, force them to withdraw money, and use zip ties, duct tape, and blindfolds to maintain control. He operated across state lines and was obsessively organized, often stashing kill kits around the country.

Keyes is believed to be responsible for the 2009 disappearance of 48-year-old Debra Feldman, a sex worker from Hackensack, New Jersey. She vanished from her apartment on April 8, never to be seen again. Investigators later discovered that Keyes had researched her case online multiple times. When shown her photograph during an interrogation, he paused before cryptically stating, "I don't want to talk about her yet." Authorities suspect that he may have buried her near Tupper Lake, New York, although her body has never been recovered.

The number of potential victims continues to increase.

Madison "Maddy" Scott, a 20-year-old Canadian woman, disappeared after attending a party at Hogsback Lake near Vanderhoof, British Columbia, on May 28, 2011. Her remains were not found until 2023, twelve years later. Hogsback Lake is a 33-hour drive from Anchorage, Alaska, where Keyes resided, and the remote nature of the crime scene aligns with his operational patterns.

In Texas, 58-year-old electrician James "Jimmy" Lamar Tidwell Jr. vanished after finishing a night shift on February 15, 2012. The following day, Keyes committed a bank robbery in Azle, Texas, wearing a white hard hat that resembled Tidwell's. Furthermore, Tidwell's dark hair resembled the wig Keyes donned during the heist. When questioned about the wig, Keyes smirked and remarked, "You don't have to buy real hair to get real hair."

This single sentence has haunted investigators for years.

Despite speculation, the Boca Raton Mall murders remain unsolved. However, the calculated nature of the crimes, the signature use of restraints, the ATM withdrawals, and the control exerted over the victims all indicate a killer who clearly understood his actions.

Was it Israel Keyes, or could another equally organized and cold predator be operating in South Florida, still evading capture?

A question lingers, just as troubling now as it was during Keyes's arrest.

Why Did Israel Keyes Kill?

A widely accepted theory suggests that his motive was both straightforward and unsettling: pure enjoyment.

"While he provided some motivation, I find it difficult to categorize his reasons for this," U.S. Attorney Tristram Coffin said in December 2012. "He informed investigators that this was a deliberate choice on his part. He was capable of controlling it and took pleasure in doing so. The rationale behind this behavior remains unknown to everyone."

Nonetheless, the murder of Samantha Koenig stood out.

She was his last known victim—and the only one whose case gave investigators a complete view of his brutal methodology: abduction, sexual assault, strangulation, and disposal. Her murder, committed in Anchorage, Alaska, ultimately unraveled the hidden world of a calculating serial killer whose crimes spanned the country—from Alaska to New York, Vermont to Washington—over more than a decade.

On May 23, 2012, Keyes attempted to escape during a routine court hearing. He used wood shavings from a pencil to pick the locks on his handcuffs but was quickly subdued with a Taser and returned to custody. Keyes later explained that his attempt to escape was a spontaneous reaction driven by stress and a feeling of dishonesty from the prosecutors.

Two months later, on July 20, authorities publicly connected him to the 2011 disappearances of Bill Currier, age 49, and his wife, Lorraine, 55, in Essex, Vermont. Annoyed by the media scrutiny, Keyes remained silent for several weeks. When he eventually chose to engage again, he continued withholding crucial information, keeping his secrets tightly guarded.

Keyes obtained a genuine razor blade despite enhanced security measures and isolation at the Anchorage Correctional Complex. On December 2, 2012, he took his own life by slashing his wrists and hanging himself with a makeshift noose tied to his foot. Below him lay a blood-stained suicide note—an eerie, poetic homage to murder—yet it offered no further information regarding victims or motivations.

In 2020, the FBI released disturbing drawings discovered beneath his mattress: eleven skulls and a pentagram with the words "WE ARE ONE" scrawled underneath. Investigators believe the number of skulls could represent his total victim count.

Israel's passing denied justice to law enforcement and victims' families.

"While we take no joy in dismissing the charges against Mr. Keyes, it is our legal duty," stated Assistant U.S. Attorney Kevin Feldis, who led the prosecution.

Before his suicide, Keyes faced severe limitations—isolated from fellow inmates, fully restrained during transport, and prohibited from having razors or pencils. Despite these measures, they were ineffective.

"How could anyone mistakenly give a real razor blade to someone in segregation?" James Koenig, Samantha's father, asked in disbelief.

Despite the alarming seriousness of his crimes, the complete truth about Israel Keyes may still be hidden.

CHAPTER NINE

Panties Rapist and Killer – James Michael Biela

Brianna Denison, born on March 29, 1988, to Jeff and Bridgette Denison, was a sophomore majoring in child psychology at Santa Barbara City College. She had returned to Reno for winter break and was eager to reconnect with friends.

On January 19, 2008, she planned to participate in various activities at the Summer Winter Action Tours snowboarding festival—an annual event she had enjoyed in previous years. Before departing, she shared a list of events she intended to attend with her mother and told her she would stay at her friend K.T. Hunter's house that night.

Brianna and K.T. enjoyed the festival and capped off their night with an early mozzarella sticks and milkshakes breakfast at Mel's Diner in the Sands Regency Hotel and Casino. The evening felt typical, filled with laughter and the vibrancy of youth. Unbeknownst to anyone, it would be Brianna's final night.

Police reports indicate that the girls arrived at their friend's home at 1395 Mackay Court, near the University of Nevada campus, at approximately 4:00 a.m. Pacific Time on January 20, 2008. Four male friends drove off after letting the girls out, while the two young women entered the house.

Once Brianna was in her cozy pajamas, Hunter offered her two blankets, a cushion, and a teddy bear to support her pillow. At the same time, she settled in for the night on the leather sofa downstairs.

Brianna, who stood five feet tall and weighed 98 pounds, slept peacefully in view of the unlocked glass-paneled front door.

Meanwhile, Hunter went to her upstairs bedroom with her housemate, Jessica Deal. She brought her Chihuahua, locked the door, and fell asleep.

Hunter and her roommates woke up around 9:00 a.m., expecting to find Brianna curled up on the sofa. To their astonishment, she was nowhere to be found.

Initially, they assumed she had stepped out. But soon, they noticed it—the pile of her belongings. Brianna's phone, purse, clothes, and shoes were scattered across the floor alongside bloodied blankets. Usually a somewhat untidy yet reasonably maintained college hangout, the home now felt like the aftermath of something far more sinister.

Brianna had not merely taken a walk.

Then came the chilling discovery that would alter everything: a small, fresh bloodstain and a smear of mascara marked the corner of the pillow Brianna had used.

Hunter took a deep breath and glanced at Jessica before reaching for her phone. She called Brianna's mother, Bridgette Denison, trying to maintain her composure.

"When I woke up this morning, Brianna was gone," she said, clutching the phone tightly. "There's this bloodstain, roughly the size of a silver dollar, and some mascara on the pillow I gave her." She took a shaky breath. "I'm not sure... should I contact the police?"

Bridgette answered immediately, "Yes."

As Bridgette rushed to the house, Hunter's trembling fingers dialed 9-1-1.

Tears rolled down their cheeks as Hunter, Jessica, and Bridgette stood powerless, observing police detectives collect evidence. What started as a confusing morning swiftly became a nightmare, enveloping the community in fear, inspiring volunteers and rallies, and attracting national attention. Blue ribbons would adorn the streets in no time, a sincere plea to bring "Bri" back home.

Detective Dave Jenkins scanned the room before turning to the three women. His expression revealed nothing, but his words resonated ominously with them.

"Anyone glancing through the windows would notice Brianna sleeping on the sofa," he stated quietly. "Furthermore, I must point out that there were three separate bloodstains, all on one side of the pillow, positioned directly under the mascara smear."

An oppressive silence filled the room. The truth was clear: something dreadful had befallen Brianna.

She did not leave of her own accord.

Each bloodstain was irregular, varying in diameter from one to three inches. Forensic analysis later revealed that one stain contained a mixture of saliva and mucus or phlegm. Subsequent DNA testing confirmed that all the bloodstains belonged to Brianna Denison.

Eventually, authorities found male DNA on the sofa where Brianna slept, connected to at least two earlier sexually motivated assaults in the area—one on November 13 and another on December 16, 2007.

Detective Jenkins fixed his gaze on Bridgette, took a sharp breath, and remarked, "It's evident this isn't a voluntary disappearance. The blood on the pillow indicates that Brianna was forcibly taken. Additionally, there are no indications of a struggle within the house."

Investigators also observed apparent bite marks on the fabric, indicating that someone had forcefully pressed her face into the pillow. The evidence suggested an actively bleeding injury in or near her mouth, throat, or nose at the time of the attack.

Brianna's close friend, K.T. Hunter, informed detectives, "I didn't hear anything after I went to bed, and my dog didn't bark at all. When I realized she was missing, I called her mom first and then you."

Hunter and Jessica told detectives that one blanket Brianna had used was left on the sofa. At the same time, the other lay on the kitchen floor, approximately six feet from the couch and close to the path leading to the house's rear door. Oddly enough, Brianna's teddy bear was also missing.

That evening, Jessica described her return to the house. "I was tired and wanted to leave early. Instead of calling a cab, I flagged down a stranger in an SUV. I could have walked, but given the cold weather, I accepted a ride from someone departing the parking lot. I know—it was probably not the best decision."

Her comments sparked worries regarding an additional possible suspect. At the same time, the man who drove her home contacted the police, saying, "I heard about the missing girl and was worried I might be considered a suspect for giving someone a ride home."

He willingly provided his DNA and was cleared, leaving investigators with few concrete leads.

Fighting back tears, Hunter expressed, "Someone invaded my home, abducted my friend, and I can't imagine what was done to her. It feels surreal. She is genuinely the kindest person. She has a beautiful heart. It's devastating that this occurred."

During an interview, Brianna's younger brother, Brighton Denison, expressed, "We want her back. Whoever has her, please return her to us. We love her, and she belongs to us." He later participated in initiatives to raise awareness, contributing to the creation of blue ribbons for the "Bring Back Bri" campaign, which was visible throughout Northern Nevada.

Police reports show that Brianna likely left her ID, wallet, phone, and shoes, indicating she was probably barefoot when taken. Hunter told investigators she was last seen donning a white tank top featuring pink angel wings and rhinestones, with "Bindi" printed on the back. She may also have worn pink or light blue sweatpants and orange socks.

A crucial piece of evidence emerged when forensic investigators collected a substance from the back door's doorknob. Further analysis revealed an unidentified male DNA profile.

Did the suspect use the rear door for entry, exit, or possibly both?

Whether through diligent police efforts or mere chance, forensic experts obtained touch DNA from the doorknob, comprising shed skin cells and other biological remnants left during contact.

This type of forensic evidence transformed laboratory analysis and investigations. Recognizing its significance, a forensic investigator beamed at his team, raised his hand for a high-five, and shouted, "Wow, we just received our first major lead!"

He paused for dramatic impact before continuing, "What are we waiting for? Let's consider this as a kidnapping."

As the investigation deepened, authorities questioned nearly 100 registered sex offenders residing within a one-mile radius of the MacKay Court residence. The search for Brianna evolved into a significant operation, with approximately 1,700 volunteers combing a 100-square-mile area. Among the volunteers was then-First Lady of Nevada, Dawn Gibbons, the wife of Governor Jim Gibbons.

Gibbons stated, "As a mother of a child the same age as Brianna, I deeply empathize with the Denison family. I am continually impressed by the incredible support from the community and the commitment of many volunteers in the search efforts. This tragic case has touched many lives across the state."

For days, Reno police conducted a thorough search of Brianna, deploying search crews, K-9 units, and helicopters to examine the area, including the snowy foothills and other secluded spots. Undercover officers surveyed the neighborhood to locate a witness who may have seen or heard something suspicious.

Despite extensive efforts, the investigation yielded minimal results. The search was broadened to include the Truckee River, which flows through the town center next to the

Union Pacific railroad tracks. However, there was still no trace of Brianna.

Reno Police Commander Ron Holladay emphasized, "It's essential to solve a case like this within 24 to 36 hours. As time goes on, our likelihood of finding her alive diminishes."

Brianna's family portrayed her as dependable and compassionate, emphasizing that she would have contacted them if possible. Their concern for her safety intensified with each passing minute.

Investigators diligently pursued the truth behind Brianna's case. They examined previous non-fatal assaults on college women in the area, searching for connections—whether physical evidence, a suspect's pattern of behavior, or both— that might provide the crucial lead they so desperately sought.

At approximately 5:00 p.m. on November 13, 2007, a 21-year-old University of Nevada, Reno student was walking through the parking lot of an apartment complex in the 400 block of College Drive when an unknown male approached her from behind and forcefully applied a deadly chokehold.

The assailant forced the victim between parked vehicles, at one point throwing her to the ground and aggressively groping her. Despite this aggression, she resisted, kicking and screaming as loudly as she could while the attacker demanded that she "be quiet."

Fearing that the noise would attract attention, the attacker kicked the victim in the head and arm before fleeing the scene, leaving behind several unopened packages of condoms. DNA evidence from this assault was later linked to the December 16, 2007, attack and the disappearance of Brianna Denison.

Reno investigators, aware of the need to prevent public panic, were selective in sharing details about the suspect. They noted that he seemed to seek dominance and power over his victims, which intensified the severity of his attacks. Police reports indicated that all the female victims were petite and had long, straight hair.

In follow-up interviews, the victim from December 16, 2007, gave a detailed description of the attacker:

"He appeared to be a Caucasian male, likely aged between 20 and 30, standing around five feet nine inches to six feet three inches tall, with a robust or slightly heavy build and brown hair. His fingers were thick and meaty, and he spoke in clear, fluent English without a discernible regional accent."

She also remembered his vehicle:

"A contemporary pickup truck typically featured an extended cab, reclining bucket seats, and options for gray or black upholstery. It also included carpeting, a sleek raised center console with a hinged lid, and adjustable headrests. Furthermore, it was outfitted with an automatic transmission and interior cab lights above the rearview mirror. Getting into the vehicle necessitated a significant step up."

Impressed by her remarkable memory, Detective Jenkins shared the vehicle description with local auto collision repair shops and discovered several 2001 to 2006 Toyota Tacoma four-wheel-drive pickups that matched it.

By the third week of searching for Brianna Denison, the Reno police had pursued over 1,000 tips.

Ultimately, the search for Brianna reached a tragic conclusion in South Reno on Saturday, February 16, 2008.

While returning from his lunch break at a Subway restaurant, local resident Albert Jimenez spotted bright orange fabric in a ditch filled with discarded Christmas tree limbs. Upon further inspection, he recognized that the fabric was neon orange socks attached to a pair of feet. At first, he assumed it was a mannequin, only to realize soon it was the body of a deceased woman.

Jimenez, aware of Brianna Denison's kidnapping but uncertain whether the victim matched her photos, hurried back to his workplace at EE Technologies to contact the Reno police. When the officers arrived, they informed him that the victim was likely Brianna Denison.

An autopsy later confirmed that the body found in the South Reno lot was indeed Brianna Denison and that she had died from strangulation.

Investigators concluded that the body had likely been at the location for over a week, possibly longer, as the area had previously been covered in snow. The site was approximately eight miles from Hunter's house.

Beneath one of Brianna's legs, investigators discovered two pairs of thong-style women's underwear containing male and female DNA profiles that did not match Brianna's. However, one DNA profile matched that of the still-unidentified attacker. Police were uncertain whether the clothing items belonged to Brianna or if they had been left near her body as a taunt to investigators. Authorities urged anyone who might recognize the clothing to come forward, as it could hold crucial information about the perpetrator's identity.

Swabs taken from Brianna's body contained sperm. DNA tests confirmed that the profile matched the unknown male DNA found on the rear doorknob of the house from which Brianna had been abducted, as well as in two previous attacks.

The DNA profile obtained from the crime scene had no matches in law enforcement databases, suggesting that the offender was not a registered or known sex offender.

On November 1, 2008, a significant breakthrough occurred. An anonymous tip to the Secret Witness hotline led investigators to a new suspect—James Michael Biela, a 27-year-old from Sparks, Nevada. The caller, Biela's girlfriend, mentioned his suspicious actions after he returned from Washington State, where he had begun working in March 2008.

The Secret Witness Program enables community members to report criminal activities anonymously through a 24/7 hotline. In this instance, the caller's tip revealed a troubling detail: "I found someone else's sexy underwear in my boyfriend's truck."

Investigators quickly found that Biela had significant similarities to their suspect. He had recently owned a truck that resembled the vehicle described by a sexual assault victim, matched the physical traits outlined in a suspect sketch, and was employed as a pipefitter. Moreover, his hands were notably thick, a distinctive characteristic highlighted by a prior victim.

Before concluding the call, investigators asked the caller if she could provide a piece of Biela's clothing for DNA testing. She agreed without hesitation.

In the meantime, media reports circulated a police sketch and a description of a vehicle connected to a rape that had occurred a month before Brianna's abduction. Reno Police Department Chief Michael Poehlman later confirmed that these reports had generated new leads.

Detective Adam Wygnanski was tasked with investigating a lead from the Secret Witness Program. On November 7, he set up a meeting with Biela. In their discussion, Wygnanski revealed that Biela's name and several others had come up in the Brianna Denison case. He then asked Biela for a saliva swab to clear his name as a suspect, but Biela declined.

During the interview, Wygnanski noted that Biela exhibited clear signs of stress, including excessive sweating and avoiding eye contact. The detective felt confident that Biela matched the physical description provided by the victim of the December 2007 assault. When questioned about his work as a pipefitter on a construction project at the University of Nevada, Reno (UNR), Biela denied any involvement.

Biela similarly refuted any links to Brianna's murder, asserting that his girlfriend, who is the mother of his child, could provide him with an alibi. Lacking the physical evidence necessary for a conviction, Wygnanski was compelled to release him.

However, forensic analysis later confirmed that the DNA recovered from the clothing sample provided by Biela's girlfriend matched the DNA found at Brianna's crime scene and in a preceding assault. This breakthrough ultimately led to Biela's arrest and prosecution.

Police acted swiftly, armed with sufficient evidence to secure arrest warrants for James Michael Biela and collect his DNA. On November 25, 2008, he was arrested and charged with murder, first-degree kidnapping, and sexual assault. The arrest occurred while Biela was dropping off his son at the Reno Stepping Stones Children's Center, after which he was booked into the Washoe County Jail.

On November 12, 2008, Detectives Jenkins and Wygnanski interviewed Biela's girlfriend, who stated, "I have been with Biela for the past six years, and we have a 4-year-old child together." However, she could not verify his whereabouts in the early hours of December 16, 2007, or January 20, 2008.

During further questioning, she disclosed, "Our relationship was frequently rocky, and it was common for James to leave our home for several days at a time. He insisted he had been sleeping in his car during those absences. From March to September 2008, he traveled to Washington to work as a pipefitter. He also sold his Toyota Tacoma and acquired another vehicle. When he decided to return to Reno, I traveled to Washington to help him. While I was there, I discovered a woman's bloodstained thong panties in his vehicle. When I confronted him about it, he responded that he had taken them from a woman at a laundromat in Washington, which I found utterly illogical."

A significant breakthrough occurred on November 26, 2008.

Forensic testing conducted that day confirmed that Biela's DNA matched the DNA at the crime scene, clearly linking him to the murder of Brianna Denison and one of Reno's most chilling sexual assault cases.

On that same day, Carleen Harmon, a friend of Biela's girlfriend, submitted an anonymous tip via the Secret Witness Program that further blamed him.

After receiving the tip, detectives interviewed Biela again. He maintained his innocence, stating, "I had nothing to do with Brianna's murder."

At that moment, without direct physical evidence to secure a conviction, authorities had no choice but to release him.

When police re-interviewed Biela's girlfriend, she agreed to DNA collection from their 4-year-old son. The findings were incriminating—a genetic analysis confirmed that DNA found at the site of Brianna's abduction and a previous rape scene belonged to a close relative of the child.

This revelation completed the final piece of the puzzle that law enforcement needed. Biela's fate was sealed.

At a later press conference, Chief Poehlman stated, "The Washoe County Sheriff's Department crime lab tested Biela's DNA and found it to match the DNA from the Denison case and another rape."

During that press conference, Washoe County District Attorney Dick Gammick told reporters, "I will be prosecuting the case with one of my criminal deputies, Elliot Sattler, and my office will be seeking the 'maximum penalty' for Biela, including the death penalty.

"We learned that Biela was familiar with the university grounds because he had worked there on a construction job last year. His experience on campus made it easier for him to target women.

"Brianna was smothered with a pillow until she choked, then later raped and strangled with her best friend's thong underwear.

"Moreover, Biela sold his truck in Idaho, which resembled the vehicle linked to the earlier sexual assault. The car will be transported back to Reno for analysis and utilized as evidence in the case against him."

During Biela's trial on May 27, 2010, Brianna's boyfriend, Hooker Wilson Done, struggled to hold back tears as he shared with the jury, "Brianna and I disagreed on the day she was last seen. My last text to her at 4:23 a.m. was full of anger. She was my first girlfriend."

In court, Bridgette Denison testified, saying, "The last time I saw my daughter, she was packing an overnight bag to go to a friend's apartment before the concert. The next morning, I received a call from K.T. Hunter, informing me that Brianna had vanished. She noted seeing a bloodstain on the sofa where Brianna had slept."

The Brianna Denison murder case was combined at trial with the cases of two other women who alleged that Biela had sexually assaulted them. Both women testified during the first week of the trial.

One of the women recounted how she was attacked on campus, stating, "My assailant threatened me with a gun, raped me, and took my panties as a souvenir, although I never reported it to police."

When asked if her attacker was in the courtroom, she pointed to Biela.

The defense disputed the identification, noting that she had previously told a friend she was unable to describe her attacker to the police.

The second woman, a university student, testified, "I was abducted outside my apartment, driven to a dark area, and assaulted in the attacker's vehicle. The vehicle was an extended-cab pickup truck with a dome light and a toddler's shoe on the truck's floor. Before he let me go, he demanded my panties. Reluctantly, I gave them to him." DNA obtained from the victim's rape kit matched Biela's.

Biela's defense attorneys challenged the DNA testing method, arguing it was inaccurate. His public defender urged the jury to consider his lack of a previous criminal record and his difficult upbringing in an abusive, impoverished home in the Chicago area, where his father brutally beat his mother almost daily.

Despite his troubled upbringing, the jury determined that Biela was still responsible for Brianna's brutal rape and murder, as well as the various assaults he committed in 2007.

Biela showed little emotion, standing with his hands crossed at his waist as the verdict was read.

After deliberating for approximately nine hours, the jurors reached a unanimous verdict on five different counts:

GUILTY – Count 1: Sexual assault related to the October 2007 incident in the parking garage at the University of Nevada.

GUILTY – Count 2: Kidnapping of a woman abducted from outside her apartment in December 2007.

GUILTY – Count 3: Sexual assault against the abducted woman, which allegedly occurred in Biela's truck.

GUILTY – Count 4: The murder of Brianna Denison. This charge was categorized as open murder, indicating the jury would determine if it was first-degree, second-degree, or manslaughter.

GUILTY – Count 5: Sexual assault against Brianna Denison.

The same jury that convicted 28-year-old James Michael Biela deliberated for an additional nine hours before sentencing him to death by lethal injection.

Before exiting the courtroom, Biela was questioned about his feelings on Brianna's discovery. His unsettling reply was, "She probably had it coming." As he was escorted away, he expressed regret to his mother, stating, "Don't cry."

On July 30, 2010, Judge Robert Perry sentenced Biela to four additional life sentences for multiple counts of rape and kidnapping related to attacks on two other victims before Brianna's abduction and murder.

Biela requested the Nevada Supreme Court to review the Washoe County Second Judicial District Court's refusal of his 2012 habeas corpus writ. His appeal was ultimately dismissed on June 12, 2019. The Nevada Supreme Court declared, "After considering Biela's arguments, we conclude that they do not warrant relief. We ORDER the district court's judgment AFFIRMED."

Prosecuting Attorney Terry McCarthy, who oversaw the appeals for the District Attorney's office, avoided speculating on when Biela's execution might take place. "Inmates on death row typically wait around 15 years," he noted. "Naturally, this incurs costs to taxpayers, which is why many individuals grow frustrated with the death penalty process."

As of this writing in July 2025, James Michael Biela is still on **death row at Ely State Prison**, a maximum-security facility in White Pine County, Nevada.

CHAPTER TEN

Grim Sleeper – Lonnie David Franklin Jr.

Lonnie David Franklin Jr., a former LAPD garage attendant and city garbage collector, was born on August 30, 1952, and grew up in South Central Los Angeles. This community later became the backdrop for many of his crimes. He eventually married and had two children, creating what appeared to be a stable family life. However, beneath the surface, Franklin concealed a violent history.

His chilling nickname was earned due to a perplexing 14-year gap in his killing spree, which lasted from 1988 to 2002—a hiatus that mystified both investigators and the public.

In April 1974, Franklin and two fellow servicemen stationed in Stuttgart, West Germany, encountered a teenage girl who was walking and stopped to ask for directions. They offered her a ride home, and when she accepted, the situation turned violent.

Once inside the vehicle, they held a knife to her throat and drove her to a secluded field, where all three men repeatedly raped her. During the assault, they took photographs—an ominous foreshadowing of Franklin's later crimes, in which he would also document his sexual violence against women he raped and murdered.

The girl remained calm and feigned interest in Franklin by asking for his phone number. That courageous action allowed investigators to identify and apprehend him.

In 1989, Franklin was convicted of two counts of theft, one count of misdemeanor assault, and one count of battery. He served time only for one of the theft charges.

In July 2010, Franklin was ultimately arrested due to a groundbreaking yet controversial application of familial DNA. After several years of pre-trial motions and delays, his trial began in February 2016.

On May 5, 2016, a jury convicted him of murdering nine women and one teenage girl. A month later, on June 6, the same jury recommended the death penalty. On August 10, 2016, the Los Angeles Superior Court officially sentenced Franklin to death, one count for each of the ten victims mentioned in the verdict.

Confirmed and Suspected Victims

Sharon Alicia Dismuke, 21, was found in South Park, Los Angeles. Initially, her murder was not linked to the Grim Sleeper. However, after Franklin's arrest, investigators revisited her case and uncovered evidence that aligned with his methods. Consequently, her case was presented during Franklin's sentencing phase.

Debra Ronette Jackson, age 29, suffered three gunshot wounds to the chest. Her body was found on August 10, 1985, in an alley close to West Gage Avenue in the Vermont-Slauson area. Jackson is thought to be Franklin's first officially recognized murder victim.

Henrietta Wright, 35, was found dead on August 12, 1986, in an alley near the 2500 block of West Vernon Avenue in Hyde Park. She had been shot multiple times, and her body was partially concealed under a discarded mattress, suggesting she may have been killed elsewhere and dumped.

Thomas Sylvester Steele, 36, was found dead on August 14, 1986, at the intersection of 71st Street and Halldale Avenue in Harvard Park. Although Franklin was considered a suspect in Steele's murder, he was never charged due to insufficient evidence. Police believed that Steele may have known too much about Franklin's crimes or had a personal connection to another victim.

Barbara Bethune Ware, 23, was discovered in the 1300 block of East 56th Street in Central Alameda. She had been shot, and there were indications that her body had been discarded after her death.

Bernita Rochelle Sparks, 26, was discovered in a trash bin on April 15, 1987, in the 9400 block of South Western Avenue in Gramercy Park. She had been fatally shot and discarded like garbage—a signature move in many of Franklin's killings.

Mary Katherine Lowe, 26, was found dead on October 31, 1987, in an alley in the 8900 block of Western Avenue in Gramercy Park. Like others, she had been shot, and her body was discovered in a secluded area.

Lachrica Denise Jefferson, 22, was murdered and her body was dumped in the 2000 block of West 102nd Place in Westmont. She was found on January 30, 1988.

Inez Elizabeth Warren, 28, was shot on August 15, 1988, and found unconscious in an alley in Gramercy Park. She later died at a nearby hospital. Like Sharon Dismuke, Warren was not initially included among the Grim Sleeper's victims until the case was revisited after Franklin's arrest.

Alicia Monique Alexander, 18, was found dead on September 11, 1988, in an alley near 43rd Place and Western Avenue in Vermont Square. She had been shot, and her body showed signs of assault.

Enietra Margette Washington, 30, is the only known survivor. On November 20, 1988, she accepted a ride from Franklin in Gramercy Park. He shot her and pushed her out of the vehicle, leaving her for dead. She survived and later provided crucial testimony that helped identify Franklin decades later.

Georgia Mae Thomas, 43, was fatally shot on December 28, 2000, in South Park. Like Dismuke and Warren, her murder was not initially linked to the Grim Sleeper, but connections were established during the sentencing phase of Franklin's trial.

Princess Cheyanne Berthomieux, just 15 years old, was found strangled and beaten in an Inglewood alley on March 19, 2002. Her nude body was discovered in the shrubs by a passerby. Her family had last seen her alive on December 21, 2001.

Valerie Louise McCorvey, 35, was found on July 11, 2003, on Denker Avenue between 108th and 109th Streets in Westmont. She had been murdered and left in an abandoned area.

Ayellah Gbo Dzata Marshall, age 18, was last seen on February 1, 2005, at a medical facility in Hawthorne. Her body was never recovered. However, her school ID was found in Franklin's garage. Despite this evidence, prosecutors determined there was not enough to charge Franklin with her murder.

Rolenia Adele Morris, 31, disappeared on September 10, 2005, near the 9000 block of South Western Avenue in Gramercy Park. Her body was never found, but her Nevada driver's license and sexually explicit photographs were discovered in Franklin's possession. This evidence was presented during sentencing.

Janecia Lavette Peters, 25, was found on January 1, 2007, in the 9500 block of South Western Avenue. She had been shot, and her body was wrapped in a garbage bag.

Arrest

On July 7, 2010, *The Los Angeles Times* reported a significant development in the Grim Sleeper investigation: an arrest had been made. District Attorney Steve Cooley identified the suspect as 57-year-old Lonnie David Franklin Jr., who had worked as a mechanic for the City of Los Angeles's sanitation department from 1981 to 1989 and had had a brief tenure with the LAPD. This arrest was made possible by an innovative application of familial DNA analysis, an emerging forensic technique.

For many years, investigators faced challenges in accurately matching the DNA from the Grim Sleeper crime scenes with profiles in California's DNA database. In a novel strategy, they employed familial searching to identify partial matches that pointed to a biological relative of the unidentified suspect. This technique eventually guided detectives to a DNA profile that significantly matched the crime scene samples; it was traced back to Franklin's son, Christopher, known for a prior felony weapons conviction.

As suspicion grew, undercover officers devised a plan. One officer disguised himself as a waiter at a restaurant where Franklin dined. After Franklin finished his meal, the officer collected discarded pizza crusts, utensils, and glasses—

anything containing saliva. A lab confirmed it: the DNA on those items matched the genetic material found on several of the Grim Sleeper's victims. The most compelling evidence came from saliva recovered from the victims' breasts.

While the match highlighted its strengths, the arrest revealed a critical weakness in the justice system. In 2003, Franklin was convicted of a felony and placed under supervised probation, which included DNA collection requirements. A year later, California voters approved Proposition 69, which mandated DNA samples from all individuals charged with felonies and expanded the state's DNA database. However, due to a lack of resources and procedural issues, probation officers did not collect DNA from individuals on unsupervised probation from November 2004 to August 2005. During this time, Franklin, who was on unsupervised probation, slipped through the system, and his DNA was never collected or entered into the database.

Franklin's criminal history began in 1989 and includes crimes like receiving stolen property, misdemeanor assault, and battery. Despite his record and the stricter laws targeting repeat offenders, he managed to avoid arrest for several years. In 2010, he was finally caught and faced ten murder charges, along with one for attempted murder. Held without bail, he faced the possibility of receiving the death penalty if found guilty. Authorities chose not to press charges for the death of an eleventh suspected victim, an African American man, due to a lack of sufficient DNA evidence.

In December 2010, the LAPD released a troubling statement. Investigators found over 1,000 photographs and hundreds of hours of video footage at Franklin's home. Many of these images featured African American women, from teenagers to seniors, often appearing nude or unconscious. Some were bleeding and were likely deceased. To help identify these individuals, the police distributed 180 photographs, as they were concerned that some might be further victims. "These individuals are not suspects; we cannot even confirm if they are victims," stated LAPD Chief Charlie Beck. "However, it is evident that Lonnie Franklin's long history of terror in Los Angeles, spanning more than twenty years, warrants a more thorough investigation."

On November 3, 2011, a year later, Reuters reported that police were considering Franklin a suspect in six additional murders. Among these, two might have occurred during the 14 years from 1988 to 2002, when the Grim Sleeper was believed to have been inactive. The other four cases involved two women found dead in the 1980s and two others who went missing in 2005 but were never found. Detectives linked Franklin to these further murders by meticulously reviewing old case files and following up on public tips that surfaced after photographs were made public.

After nearly three months of trial and just a day and a half of deliberation, the jury delivered a verdict. On May 5, 2016, Lonnie David Franklin Jr. was convicted of ten murder counts and one count of attempted murder.

On June 6, 2016, a jury in Los Angeles County sentenced him to death, providing legal closure to one of the city's most chilling serial murder cases.

There Might Be a Lot More Victims

After identifying the known victims, detectives began to suspect that Franklin's crimes extended far beyond those documented. During a press conference the following spring, LAPD Chief Charlie Beck remarked, "We definitely don't think we are fortunate or skilled enough to know all of his victims. We require the public's assistance."

Serial killers typically exhibit gaps between their crimes. However, the alleged 14-year gap in Franklin's situation seems questionable. While he has not been officially charged, police consider him a suspect in the murder of Thomas Steele, who is believed to have been a friend of one of Franklin's victims. Furthermore, investigators are examining his potential connection to 14 to 100 unresolved cases involving unidentified women. Franklin maintains his innocence, suggesting that the outcomes of these cases may depend heavily on DNA evidence and witness testimonies.

Detectives are still investigating, pondering if Franklin went into hiding after the failed murder attempt on Enietra Washington in 1988. Working as a sanitation worker for the City of Los Angeles, he had access to landfills, which raises alarming concerns that he might have disposed of other bodies without a trace.

Regardless of what future inquiries reveal, Franklin is one of approximately 750 inmates still on death row at San Quentin State Prison, which has not carried out executions since 2006.

His death sentence was appealed automatically, as is the right of anyone condemned to death. However, Franklin, age 67, died on March 28, 2020. He was found unresponsive in his prison cell. The cause of death is not publicly known.

CHAPTER ELEVEN
Campus Killer – Ted Bundy

Ted Bundy, originally named Theodore Robert Cowell, was born on November 24, 1946, at the Elizabeth Lund Home for Unwed Mothers in Burlington, Vermont. His mother, Eleanor Louise Cowell, was a single parent at the time, and the identity of Bundy's biological father remains uncertain. Initial records suggest that Lloyd Marshall, a salesman and U.S. Air Force veteran, may be his father. However, other official documents, including Bundy's birth certificate, leave the father's identity blank, labeling it as unknown.

Certain family members believed that Ted Bundy was the result of incest, supposedly fathered by his maternal grandfather, Samuel Cowell. Nevertheless, in the 2020 documentary *Crazy, Not Insane*, psychiatrist Dr. Dorothy Otnow Lewis disclosed that she had a blood sample from Bundy, and DNA testing conclusively refuted this theory.

Ted Bundy spent his early childhood in Philadelphia, Pennsylvania, with his mother. In 1950, they moved to Tacoma, Washington, to stay with relatives. During this time, young Ted was misled into believing that his mother, Louise Cowell, was his sister—a family secret that endured.

After the relocation, Louise changed her son's last name from Cowell to Nelson.

Just a year later, in 1951, Louise met Johnny Culpepper Bundy at a singles event held by Tacoma's First Methodist Church. The couple married in May, and shortly thereafter, Johnny legally adopted Ted, giving him the last name that would later become infamous.

Bundy harbored deep resentment for his mother because she had concealed the truth about his biological father, a secret she safeguarded throughout his upbringing. He was notably embittered by the fact that he had to uncover the details of his paternity on his own. This revelation left him feeling betrayed and emotionally adrift.

In 1969, Ted Bundy unveiled a shocking truth about his identity that severely rattled his already unstable self-image. The woman he believed to be his sister was, in fact, his biological mother. At the same time, his so-called "parents" were his grandparents. Although this discovery was somewhat anticipated, it left a deep emotional scar. Author Stephen Michaud observes that Bundy's feelings toward his mother remained unchanged after this discovery. However, he grew increasingly bitter and resentful toward his stepfather, Johnnie Bundy, exhibiting indifference, sulkiness, and contempt.

Determining whether this revelation influenced Bundy's emerging darker tendencies is challenging. Nevertheless, the revelation that his childhood was built on deception certainly complicated the identity formation of an already troubled young man.

The exact timing and site of Ted Bundy's initial murders are unclear, leading to differing views among experts. Writer Ann Rule and former King County Detective Robert D. Keppel notably suggest that Bundy's violent tendencies may have started much earlier than usually assumed, possibly during his teenage years. A theory connects him to the 1961 disappearance of 8-year-old Ann Marie Burr from her Tacoma home, where Bundy, at just 14, lived nearby. Despite the ongoing suspicions about him, Bundy consistently denied any involvement, even in the face of execution.

In his last moments, Bundy revealed to his attorney that he had attempted to kidnap a woman for the first time in 1969. He noted that he began his murders around 1972, a point he confirmed in discussions with Keppel while on death row. If accurate, this suggests that Bundy was active long before law enforcement became aware of him.

By 1973, Bundy's meticulously crafted image began to deteriorate. A friend from the Washington State Republican Party found a pair of handcuffs in Bundy's Volkswagen backseat. Around this time, he was briefly considered a suspect in the murder of Kathy Devine in December 1973. Nevertheless, DNA testing conducted decades later eliminated him and identified another individual, leading to that person's conviction in 2002.

Bundy's confirmed series of murders started in early 1974 when he was just 27 years old. By this time, he had probably honed his techniques, suggesting that his initial acts of violence may never be uncovered.

Modus Operandi

Ted Bundy maintained a chillingly consistent modus operandi throughout his killing spree, characterized by calculated charm, deceit, and escalating violence. He often targeted his victims in broad daylight, in public spaces filled with people. This bold strategy showcased both his confidence and cunning. Notably, he abducted Janice Ott and Denise Naslund in succession from Lake Sammamish

State Park and, later, Kimberly Leach from her school in Lake City, Florida.

Bundy used disturbingly effective methods to gain trust. Frequently, he feigned injuries, wearing a sling or a fake cast to create an impression of vulnerability. This tactic consistently succeeded, as shown in the cases of Georgann Hawkins, Donna Rancourt, Janice Ott, Denise Naslund, and Susan Cunningham. At times, he impersonated an authority figure to disarm his victims further. Carol DaRonch, one of the few survivors, remembered how he posed as a police officer to lure her into his car. The day before he abducted Kimberly Leach, Bundy approached another young girl in Florida, introducing himself as "Richard Burton from the Fire Department." His efforts were thwarted when the girl's older brother intervened, causing Bundy to escape.

A significant element of Bundy's skill in blending in was his appearance. While conventionally attractive, he lacked notable distinctiveness, which allowed him to navigate different social environments without drawing attention. Eventually, he gained the nickname "chameleon-like" for his ability to subtly change his appearance through slight tweaks, such as growing facial hair, altering his hairstyle, or modifying his behavior.

Emerging patterns identified Bundy's victims predominantly as White females, typically from middle-class backgrounds and aged between 15 and 25, with many being college students. Ann Rule, in her book *The Stranger Beside Me*, observed that numerous victims shared a physical trait: long, dark hair parted in the middle, reminiscent of his former fiancée, Stephanie Brooks, whose real name was Diane Edwards. She suggested that Bundy's unresolved emotions for Brooks may have influenced his victim selection. However, Bundy subsequently dismissed this notion. In a 1980 interview, he stated, "They... simply fit the broad criteria of being young and attractive... Many have fallen for the mistaken belief that all the girls looked alike—similar hair color and parting... yet, upon closer examination, nearly all were unique... Physically, they were quite diverse."

After luring victims to his car, Bundy would strike them in the head with a crowbar, often concealed beneath the vehicle or stashed inside. All the recovered skulls—except Kimberly Leach's—showed evidence of blunt force trauma, and all the recovered bodies, except Leach's, bore signs of strangulation.

Bundy typically moved his victims far from their abduction sites. For example, he took Kathy Parks over 260 miles from Oregon to Washington. Additionally, Carol DaRonch noted that he frequently drank alcohol before his attacks, as she recalled that his breath reeked of it.

FBI profiler Bill Hagmaier recounted that Bundy considered himself an "amateur" in his early years—a disorganized and impulsive killer. However, by the time he murdered Lynda Healy, Bundy claimed he had entered his "prime," evolving into a cold, calculated "predator" who selected victims he felt were worthy of his developing sense of power and control.

Victims

Linda Healy was the first confirmed victim. On January 31, 1974, she disappeared from her basement bedroom in Seattle, Washington. Her bloodied sheets were left on the bed, and her bloodstained nightgown had been unsettlingly rehung in the closet. This disturbing detail suggested the involvement of someone who was both calculating and profoundly disturbed.

Only weeks earlier, just a few blocks away, a young woman named Susan Clarke was attacked in her bed and severely beaten. Unlike Healy, Clarke survived her life-threatening injuries and eventually recovered. In stark contrast, Linda Healy vanished without a trace.

Initially, there was no conclusive evidence linking the cases or any sign of a serial predator's emergence. However, this misconception would not last long.

On March 12, Donna Gail Manson disappeared while attending a concert in Olympia. Just over a month later, on April 17, Susan Rancourt vanished en route to a foreign film screening in Ellensburg. Then, on May 6, Roberta Parks failed to return from a late-night walk near her dorm in Corvallis, Oregon. Lastly, on June 1, Brenda Ball was last observed leaving the Flame Tavern in Seattle accompanied by an unknown man.

Ten days later, Georgann Hawkins, another young woman, disappeared while walking a busy route between her boyfriend's apartment and her sorority house at the University of Washington.

By this point, detectives could no longer ignore the connections. Each missing woman was young and attractive, bearing strikingly similar features—long dark hair parted in the middle. The photos collected by investigators bore a resemblance to a family portrait; some of the women could have been sisters or twins.

No bodies were found. At this point, even the most optimistic homicide detectives had lost faith in a rescue. The victim count continued to increase, and the worst was yet to come.

On July 14, 1974, a blistering summer Sunday attracted thousands to Lake Sammamish State Park. By the end of the day, two more women—Janice Ott and Denise Naslund—had disappeared before friends and spectators.

This time, however, witnesses recalled something crucial: several had seen Janice Ott speaking to a man with his arm in a sling, who introduced himself as "Ted."

It represented a significant breakthrough.

Before long, other women shared similar accounts: a courteous, soft-spoken man requesting assistance loading a sailboat onto a light tan Volkswagen Bug. Those who refused felt discomfort. One woman followed "Ted" to his vehicle but noticed no sailboat present. Her doubts intensified when he mentioned it was at a nearby residence. She walked away without a second glance.

Detectives crafted a composite sketch based on these accounts and started disseminating information regarding the suspect and his vehicle. The name "Ted" sparked an influx of tips. One promising lead identified a well-dressed law student at the University of Utah—Theodore Bundy.

Bundy, however, did not match the expected profile. In Seattle, he was seen as a politically active, well-groomed young man. He even attracted media attention for performing a citizen's arrest during a mugging. His charm, eloquence, and seemingly genuine integrity sharply contrasted with the emerging image of a ruthless killer.

As a result, his name was quietly overlooked.

For the time being...

On September 7, two hunters made a grim discovery on a wooded hillside near Lake Sammamish: a shallow grave containing human remains. Dental records confirmed the bodies belonged to Janice Ott and Denise Naslund, both of whom had vanished from the lake area that past summer. A third skeleton, found nearby, could not be identified and was labeled only as Jane Doe.

Five weeks later, on October 12, a different hunter stumbled upon scattered bones in rural Clark County. Among these bones was a vertebra later identified as belonging to Carol Valenzuela, who had been missing from Vancouver, Washington, since August. The remaining remains were also unidentified and designated as another Jane Doe.

Even with these disturbing findings, investigators clung to a glimmer of hope. They believed that finding the victims could lead to the vital breakthrough necessary to pinpoint the murderer. However, they remained unaware that he had already departed from Washington.

The next wave of terror erupted in Utah.

On October 2, Nancy Wilcox disappeared in Salt Lake City. Just over two weeks later, on October 18, the body of 17-year-old Melissa Smith was discovered in the Wasatch Mountains—raped, beaten, and discarded. She had been missing for nine days.

Then, another young woman vanished on Halloween night: Laura Aime, last seen walking home in costume after a party in Orem. Nearly a month would pass before her body was found; she had been brutally murdered and abandoned in a wooded area.

Then came a narrow escape.

On November 8, Carol DaRonch encountered a frightening event involving a man impersonating a police officer at a Salt Lake City mall. He informed her that her car had been broken into and asked her to accompany him to his vehicle. Once inside, he attempted to handcuff her. Recognizing the danger, DaRonch escaped and ran to find help.

Later that evening, 17-year-old Debbie Kent vanished from the Viewmont High School parking lot and was never seen again.

The attempted kidnapping of Carol DaRonch represented a pivotal moment. Authorities in Utah started working with officials in Washington to notify them about a key suspect— Ted Bundy. Originating from Seattle, Bundy was a law student at the University of Utah. Although he was articulate, polite, and seemingly well-adjusted, his name raised faint alarm bells. Nevertheless, no immediate actions were taken. Bundy's file remained open yet unaddressed.

It wouldn't stay that way for long. Colorado was next in the killer's path.

On January 12, 1975, Caryn Campbell vanished from a ski lodge in Snowmass, Colorado. She had stepped out of her hotel room to retrieve a magazine from the car—and was never seen alive again. Her body was discovered over a month later in a snowbank off a remote road. She had been raped, bludgeoned, and left exposed in the cold.

Two months later, on March 15, Julie Cunningham vanished while walking from her Vail apartment to meet a friend for dinner. She never reached her destination.

On April 15, Melanie Cooley disappeared from Nederland. Eight days later, hikers discovered her body. Her skull had been fractured, and her jeans were pulled down to her ankles—a grim signature left behind.

On July 1, Shelly Robertson disappeared in Golden. For weeks, no sign of her was found—until her remains were discovered deep within an abandoned mine shaft near Berthoud Pass.

A significant breakthrough occurred just days before the shocking final discovery, although investigators were unaware of it. In Salt Lake City, police stopped a man driving erratically in an aging tan Volkswagen. He was arrested for burglary, but what they found in the car quickly raised questions. The vehicle held handcuffs, a crowbar, plastic garbage bags, and a pair of pantyhose with crude eye holes cut out—essentially serving as a makeshift mask.

Officers found gas receipts and road maps in the glove compartment, revealing Colorado destinations like Vail and Snowmass. These places have recently been linked to women who were either missing or had been found murdered.

Soon after, Carol DaRonch, a teenager who had escaped an abduction attempt in November, confidently identified the perpetrator. Her testimony played a crucial role in securing his conviction for attempted kidnapping.

Law enforcement in several states began to grasp the broader context. The driver of the tan Volkswagen was not an ordinary criminal; he was Ted Bundy, and the probe was still active.

In January 1977, Bundy was sent to Colorado for the trial related to the 1975 murder of Caryn Campbell, who had vanished from a hotel in Snowmass. Anticipating a lengthy prison term, Bundy concluded that escaping offered better opportunities than facing a guilty verdict. In June, he made his first escape attempt, managing to slip out of custody and avoid law enforcement for eight days before being recaptured. Nevertheless, he was not discouraged and successfully escaped again on December 30.

Bundy traveled across the country and eventually resurfaced in Tallahassee, Florida. He rented a room in a boarding house under a false name, close to Florida State University.

Although he was a suspect in multiple murders, he continued to evade capture and was poised to attack once more.

In the early morning of January 15, 1978, Bundy infiltrated the Chi Omega sorority house. Clad in black and armed with a heavy wooden club, he launched a brutal attack.

By the time he slipped back into the night, two young women had been sexually assaulted and bludgeoned to death, while two others suffered severe injuries. Less than an hour later, he attacked a fifth woman in her nearby apartment as she slept. She survived.

Investigators at the Chi Omega crime scene discovered a crucial clue: a distinctive set of bite marks on one victim's body—evidence that would later prove vital.

On February 6, Bundy stole a van and drove to Jacksonville, where he was spotted attempting to abduct a schoolgirl. Just days later, 12-year-old Kimberly Leach disappeared from her middle school in Lake City. Her body was found in April, discarded in a pigsty near Suwannee State Park— violently assaulted and left to decompose.

On February 15, Bundy's escapade concluded in Pensacola when police apprehended him for driving a car with stolen license plates. He attempted to escape but was swiftly restrained. After being taken into custody, forensic specialists collected dental impressions that matched the bite marks discovered on one of the Chi Omega victims. This evidence became the cornerstone of the prosecution's case.

In July 1979, Bundy was found guilty of two murders and received a death sentence by electric chair in Florida. After being convicted of the murder of Kimberly Leach, he faced a second death sentence. During the following decade, he submitted many appeals, but on January 24, 1989, justice finally reached him.

In the final days before his execution in the electric chair at Florida State Prison in Raiford, Bundy admitted to murdering 28 women. However, investigators suspect the actual count could be significantly greater.

CHAPTER TWELVE

Coast-to-Coast Killer – Tommy Lynn Sells

On May 13, 1992, 19-year-old Fabienne Witherspoon cared for a friend's cat in Charleston, West Virginia. She was thrilled about her upcoming interview with Clinique Cosmetics and eagerly anticipated the opportunity. Later that day, she visited the local health department for a pregnancy test, which yielded negative results.

She returned to her friend's apartment on Grove Avenue and spotted a young homeless man seeking assistance beneath a bridge. He was clutching a makeshift sign that said, "*I will work for food.*"

She did not realize that the man was Tommy Lynn Sells, a remorseless sociopath who frequently took advantage of people's kindness. His sign served as a calculated trap to attract potential victims.

Unbeknownst to her, she was about to be his tenth victim.

Growing up as an Air Force brat, Fabienne had led a sheltered childhood and had never seen a homeless person before. To her, he didn't seem like a threat; instead, he appeared to be in dire circumstances.

"Are you part of a family? Do you need food?" she inquired.

He showed a picture of a woman with three children. He softly stated, "We're homeless, living under a bridge, and we're all hungry."

Fabienne showed her concern and proposed, "Why not come with me? I can get you food from my friend's place."

After receiving some extra snacks from her friend, she shared them. While on their way, they stopped at Go-Mart, where she picked up a newspaper for the man to browse the Help Wanted ads.

When they arrived, she instructed him, "Stay outside while I grab a few items from the pantry."

He nodded and asked, "Is anyone else in the apartment?"

Fabienne rejected the question by shaking her head.

Just as she reached the fridge for a Coke, he unexpectedly showed up at the front door. His sudden appearance made her uneasy, but she still asked, "Do you need anything else?"

"My wife needs some new underwear."

Even though the request felt odd, she yearned for freedom from him. She headed to the bedroom to grab a few belongings from her suitcase.

That was the pivotal moment she turned into his tenth victim.

Sells locked the front door, took a steak knife from the kitchen, and went to the bedroom. "If you obey my commands, you won't get hurt," he warned her.

He overpowered Fabienne, trapping her in the bathroom, where he brutally raped her multiple times. He then dragged her into the shower and assaulted her again.

At that pivotal moment, Fabienne decided to stand her ground.

As she was pushed against the toilet, her gaze fell on a ceramic duck perched on the tank. Seizing it, she struck it violently against his head until only the beak remained in her hand.

Then she seized his knife and stabbed him over and over, slicing his kidney, liver, and even a testicle. She tried to escape, but didn't make it to the front door before he tackled her and threw her into another bedroom. As she landed, the knife sliced her hand open.

Regaining control, Sells restrained her hands and feet with tape and pressed the blade to her throat.

"Just go," she pleaded. "I swear I won't say a word. My husband will be back shortly."

"Fine, whatever," he mocked. "Nice attempt with the husband nonsense. Now be quiet."

He covered her head with a quilt and made a weak effort to smother her. Then he hit her on the head with a stool before abruptly running away.

As he exited, Fabienne heard him muttering, "I can't believe I'm still alive."

She questioned, "Him? What about me?"

The next thing she recalled was waking up on the front steps, feeling vulnerable, injured, and shaking uncontrollably.

Paramedics arrived promptly and transported her to the hospital, where she underwent hand surgery and received stitches for her head. Afterward, a rape counselor met with her.

During this time, Sells, who had suffered 18 stab wounds, spent a week in the hospital before being transferred to the county jail.

At that moment, Fabienne was unaware that she had just evaded a serial killer; all she knew was that she had fought for her survival.

"All I wanted was to escape," she later shared. "I didn't realize I had stabbed him so many times. Accepting that I could inflict such harm was difficult for me."

How Tommy Lynn Sells ended up in Charleston in the spring of 1992 remains unclear. The inveterate drifter, who had roamed the country since the age of 14, may have hitchhiked, hopped a train, or stolen a car. By the time he arrived in West Virginia, he had already murdered at least 15 people, including five children.

After the attack, Fabienne recuperated at her fiancé's mother's home, isolating herself in a dimly lit bedroom and replaying the traumatic experience in her mind.

"I felt so foolish," Fabienne told her fiancé's mother. "It was so humiliating that I wished I could disappear."

Like many survivors of sexual assault, she took responsibility for herself.

Ultimately, she moved to Alabama with her fiancé, and they married. "In hindsight, we might have hurried into marriage," she said. "Perhaps we believed it would assist me in coping with my problems. I felt like no other man would ever desire me."

The marriage lasted less than a year.

Fabienne, now a mother of three, resides in Danville, Illinois, and treasures her moments with her grandchildren. She is a certified nurse practitioner and health coach and also teaches at a local community college.

Sells endured a troubled childhood. By the age of seven, he had already started drinking alcohol from his maternal grandfather's supply. At eight, he began spending time with a man named Willis Clark from a neighboring city, who was later identified as a child molester. Sells admitted in an interview, "I would relive those experiences while committing my crimes."

From 1978 to 1999, Sells experienced homelessness, relying on hitchhiking and train travel across the United States for over 20 years. He survived through working various odd jobs, panhandling, and scavenging for accessible resources.

Sells later claimed that his first murder occurred after he witnessed a man performing a brutal sexual act on a young boy in a house he had broken into. In a fit of rage, he killed the man. The following day, he allegedly killed another man with an ice pick at a nearby Chinese restaurant.

Tommy Lynn Sells lived a violent and nomadic lifestyle, establishing himself as one of America's most dangerous and elusive serial killers, as he targeted victims nationwide for more than twenty years.

Victims

July 5, 1979 – Port Gibson, Mississippi
John Cade, 39, died after being shot with a .32 caliber pistol during a home invasion. Witnesses reported a man similar to Tommy Lynn Sells in the area, leading investigators to explore his potential involvement.

April 27, 1982 – St. Louis, Missouri
JoAnne Tate, age 35, was murdered in her residence, while her 7-year-old daughter, Melissa DeBoer, was attacked but

survived. DeBoer identified Rodney Lincoln as the attacker, leading to his conviction. However, after viewing a 2015 episode of *Crime Watch Daily that highlighted* Sells, DeBoer became convinced Sells was the true culprit. Her efforts led Governor Eric Greitens to commute the sentence in 2018.

July 31, 1983 – St. Louis, Missouri
Tiffany Gill, 4, and her mother, Colleen Gill, 33, were bludgeoned to death inside their Washington Terrace home. A man matching Sells's description was seen fleeing the area. At the time, Sells lived near Breckenridge Hills and had family in that area.

July 26, 1985 – Springfield, Missouri
While working at a carnival in Forsyth, Sells met Ena Cordt, 28, and her son Rory, 4. He later claimed that after having sex with Ena, he awoke to find her stealing from him and beat her to death with her son's baseball bat. He then murdered the boy to eliminate a witness. The bodies were found three days later.

May 1, 1987 – Lockport, New York
Suzanne Korcz, 27, vanished after leaving a nightclub. Her decomposed body was found over eight years later near Niagara Falls. In 2004, Sells confessed to the killing and demonstrated detailed knowledge of the case but was never prosecuted due to his existing death sentence.

October 15, 1987 – Lovelock, Nevada
Stefanie Stroh, 21, was last seen at a truck stop in Wells. Sells later confessed to strangling her after they took LSD together, then disposing of her body in a hot spring encased in concrete. Her remains were never recovered.

November 17, 1987 – Ina, Illinois
Sells murdered the Dardeen family after being offered a meal and shelter by Keith Dardeen, 29. Sells shot and mutilated Keith, then bludgeoned 3-year-old Peter Dardeen

and Keith's pregnant wife, Elaine. The assault was so severe that Elaine gave birth during the attack; Sells killed the newborn as well.

December 18, 1988 – Tucson, Arizona
Kent Alan Lauten, 51, was stabbed and buried near a transient camp. His body was found two days later. Sells admitted to killing Lauten over a drug dispute.

December 9, 1991 – Marianna, Florida
Teresa Hall, 25, and her daughter Tiffany, 5, were bludgeoned to death with a table leg. The intruder broke in by kicking down the door. Initially suspected to be the work of Ángel Maturino Reséndiz, the murders were later linked to Sells through his confession.

October 13, 1997 – Lawrenceville, Illinois
Joel Kirkpatrick, 10, was fatally stabbed in his sleep. His mother, Julie Rea-Harper, confronted a masked intruder at their home and was unjustly convicted. Years later, Sells admitted to the murder, leading to Rea-Harper's complete exoneration.

October 15, 1997 – Springfield, Missouri
Stephanie Mahaney, 13, was abducted from her home, injected with cocaine, raped, and strangled. Her body was found in a nearby farm pond. Sells later provided a detailed confession.

December 14, 1997 – Las Vegas, Nevada
Yvette Sophia Mueller, age 19, vanished from an RV park. Sells claimed to have raped and dismembered a blonde woman in the area, disposing of her remains near the Snake River. While the body was never found, authorities believe he was referring to Mueller.

April 15, 1998 – San Antonio, Texas
Thomas Brose, 40, a carnival worker, was found shot dead in his motorhome. Sells confessed but later recanted. Authorities noted his presence in the area and the strong circumstantial evidence.

April 4, 1999 – Gibson, Tennessee
Debra Harris, 31, was raped and fatally stabbed with her kitchen knife. Her daughter, Ambria Halliburton, 8, was also stabbed after witnessing her mother's murder. The crime bore Sells's signature brutality and was later confirmed through his confession.

April 18, 1999 – San Antonio, Texas
Mary Beatrice Perez, age 9, was abducted from a market festival, raped, and strangled. Her body was found in a creek ten days later. Sells was convicted in 2003 and sentenced to life in prison.

May 23, 1999 – Lexington, Kentucky
Haley McHone, 13, was abducted from a swing set, raped, and strangled in a wooded area. Her body was discovered ten days later. Sells was in the area at the time and later confessed

July 5, 1999 – Kingfisher, Oklahoma
Bobbie Lynn Wofford, 14, was picked up from a convenience store and sexually assaulted. She was bludgeoned with a hatchet and shot in the head after attempting to flee. Sells kept her earrings as trophies.

December 31, 1999 – Del Rio, Texas
Kaylene Harris, 13, was raped, stabbed sixteen times, and had her throat slashed. Her friend, Krystal Surles, 10, was also attacked but survived and later provided testimony that led to Sells's arrest and eventual conviction.

On January 2, 2000, Tommy Lynn Sells was arrested after the deadly stabbing of Kaylene Harris.

While in custody, Sells confessed to the Texas Rangers that he had killed between 20 and 50 individuals across multiple states over the past twenty years.

On January 3, 2014, a judge in Del Rio, Texas, set Tommy Lynn Sells's execution date for April 3, 2014. As the day approached, Sells claimed to have found God. His mother and girlfriend visited him regularly. When a prison official asked about his views on the afterlife, Sells replied, *"Where am I going? I'm going to heaven. Society has judged me, and I must accept that. Now, it's between me and my maker."*

On April 3, 2014, at the Texas State Penitentiary in Huntsville, Sells was strapped to a gurney. When asked if he had any last words, the prolific murderer simply muttered, *"No."* As the lethal dose of pentobarbital was administered, he smiled at his witnesses, took a few deep breaths, closed his eyes, and began to snore. Within a minute, he stopped moving.

Thirteen minutes later, at 6:27 p.m. CDT, he was declared dead.

He was 49 years old.

CHAPTER THIRTEEN
Toy Box Killer – David Parker Ray

After enduring a childhood marked by abuse and molestation, Cynthia Vigil-Jaramillo turned to the streets of Albuquerque, New Mexico, at just 13 years old. Initially selling drugs to survive, she eventually turned to prostitution, unknowingly placing herself on a path that would lead her into the clutches of one of the most sadistic criminals in modern history.

Cynthia was on the verge of transforming into a woman who conquered death and achieved the remarkable in a captivating, true story of survival.

On March 19, 1999, she was working in a parking lot when she was approached by a man posing as an undercover police officer. Displaying a badge, he handcuffed her, claiming she was being arrested for solicitation, and then compelled her into the back seat of his vehicle. This man was 62-year-old David Parker Ray, "The Toy Box Killer."

After kidnapping Cynthia Vigil-Jaramillo, Ray transported her to Elephant Butte, New Mexico—a serene, sun-drenched town near the reservoir and lake it is named after. The harsh, remote desert landscape provided ideal cover for the subsequent atrocities.

However, Cynthia was far from an ordinary victim.

She refused to allow David Parker Ray to dictate the final chapter of her life.

As Cynthia approached Ray's torture chamber, a flicker of hope sparked within her. Concealed in the trailer's shadows, she discovered an abandoned or cleverly positioned screwdriver. Her heart pounded like a war drum as she twisted and pried at the screws holding the cabinet to which her hands were bound. Each turn heightened her desperation, her breathing quick and shallow.

One screw after another, her wrists throbbing, she pressed on. At last, the final screw was released with a satisfying click. The cabinet shifted a bit; she was almost liberated.

She remained alert, watching Ray's speed closely. When he slowed down, and it felt right, she tensed, prepared to react.

But then, tires screamed. He slammed on the brakes.

The abrupt jolt sent her sprawling onto the cold metal floor. Dazed and disoriented, she fought to rise, but just as she began to lift her head, a mocking laugh shattered the silence.

Cindy Hendy, Ray's girlfriend who was with them in the car, acted promptly.

Wearing a chilling, joyful smile, she pressed the cattle prod into Cynthia's side. Pain surged through her like flames racing along her nerves, causing her body to convulse violently. The world faded; the trailer spun, and then— silence—pure darkness.

Cynthia's mind teetered on the edge of oblivion. Ray wasted no time. He tasered her with clinical precision, sending violent jolts through her already dimming senses. Then came the injection, something fast-acting and disorienting.

Unable to see, she felt the cold grip of metal around her neck—a heavy dog collar that tightened with a sharp click.

She ceased to be an individual, transforming instead into an asset.

Ray chained her to a cold, medical-style table—steel restraints biting into her wrists and ankles—preparing her like a specimen for dissection.

When Cynthia finally opened her eyes, everything seemed blurred and disorienting. A dull ache pulsed in her head, and she found her limbs unresponsive. Suddenly, a voice emerged, calm and steady yet tinged with a threat.

It wasn't Ray, it was merely a recording of a dark ritual he had perfected, with his voice coming through concealed speakers, designed to psychologically break down his victims long before the actual torture began.

"Okay, bitch. We both know what you've been brought here for. I'm going to use you as a sex slave. And it's going to be painful as hell. That's the way I want it to be.

"I thrive on psychological games. Once we finish with you, you'll be heavily sedated. You'll remain under sedation for several days while I toy with your mind.

"By the time I finish brainwashing you, you won't remember a thing about this little adventure. You will always refer to me as 'Master' and the woman with me as 'Mistress,' speaking only when spoken to first."

For three agonizing days, Cynthia endured unspeakable horrors. With Cindy Hendy's eager assistance and even the participation of Ray's daughter from his third marriage, Glenda "Jesse" Ray, he subjected her to relentless torture, rape, and psychological torment. Each moment blurred into the next—a nightmare of pain, control, and despair.

Nevertheless, Cynthia would not accept being just another victim.

Ray treated his victims like animals, forcing them to eat from a bowl on the floor while tethered to a leash. He bathed Cynthia like a dog, stripping her of dignity before forcing her to perform unspeakable sexual acts for his accomplices and him. As they guzzled beer after beer, their drunken stupor only fueled their depravity.

Later that afternoon, Ray committed his most shocking and revolting act.

He stripped Cynthia naked and chained her to a chair, zip-tying her hands behind her back. He sprayed perfume in her hair, smeared bright red lipstick across her trembling lips, and pried her mouth open with small plastic sticks. Tears streamed down her face as her body quivered with terror.

Then, in an act of pure evil, Ray heated a thick gravy and forcefully inserted it into Cynthia's vagina. His dog, drawn by the scent, eagerly slurped the warm liquid from her body. Ray roared with laughter, capturing the monstrous scene on video with one hand while pleasuring himself with the other.

As his dog lapped up every drop, Ray's excitement escalated. When the animal had finished and wandered off, he continued stroking himself until he reached a climax, ejaculating into Cynthia's forced-open mouth.

Satisfied with his torture, Ray unchained her, yanked off the zip ties, and shoved her back into her coffin-like box. He didn't allow her to clean herself—her body remained sticky with saliva, sweat, and filth, her mouth still tainted by his release.

"The more pain I displayed, the more I suffered, the more he enjoyed it," Cynthia later recalled. "I knew that wasn't his first time, given how he spoke and acted. He understood what he was doing. He told me I would never see my family again."

An earlier victim, Kelli Garrett, was identified by her ex-mother-in-law after case details were made public. Garrett, a close friend of Ray's daughter and associate of Jesse, unwittingly fell into the Toy Box Killer's trap on July 24, 1996.

Following a dispute with her husband, Garrett had gone to a local bar to relax and play pool with Jesse. Unbeknownst to her, Jesse had spiked her beer with a potent sedative. Once she was incapacitated, Jesse placed a dog collar around Garrett's neck, attached a leash, and took her to the Toy Box Killer's trailer.

For two days, Ray subjected Garrett to relentless rape and torture. When he was finished with her, he slashed her throat and dumped her along the roadside, assuming she was dead.

Despite everything, Garrett endured.

She was finally found in Colorado, identified only by a small tattoo on her ankle. Unfortunately, the ordeal persisted. Both the police and her husband examined her account closely. Suspecting infidelity that evening, her husband quickly filed for divorce.

Due to the lingering effects of the drugs, Garrett's memory of those two days was fragmented. But one thing she remembered with certainty—she had been tortured and raped by The Toy Box Killer.

Years later, when police searched Ray's trailer, they uncovered a videotape from 1996 showing Garrett bound and helpless, being assaulted and brutalized. It was undeniable proof of the horrors she had endured, a chilling testament to the nightmare that many of Ray's victims never lived to recount.

Angelica Montano, an acquaintance of David Parker Ray, had the misfortune of visiting his home one day to borrow some cake mix. Instead of a simple favor, she endured a horrifying ordeal—drugged, raped, and subjected to days of brutal torture. After four days, Ray abandoned her on the side of a desert highway, expecting her to die.

Montano's circumstances shifted dramatically when an off-duty police officer spotted her and extended a ride. Overcome with trauma, she shared her harrowing ordeal. Rather than receiving empathy, she faced skepticism. The officer dismissed her story and left her at a bus stop. Holding onto her desire for justice, Montano subsequently reached out to the police again, yet they remained unresponsive.

Meanwhile, Ray persisted in his violent rampage. On March 22, 1999, he departed for work, leaving his latest victim, Cynthia Vigil-Jaramillo, in the care of his girlfriend and accomplice, Cindy Hendy. Unlike Ray, Hendy was negligent—she had left the keys to Cynthia's restraints on a nearby table. Seizing the chance, Cynthia cautiously inched the table closer with her feet, her heart racing as she strained to reach the keys.

Just as she began unlocking her chains, Hendy reentered the room. Enraged, she attacked Cynthia, brutally beating her. During the struggle, she smashed a lamp over Cynthia's head. But the pain and blood did not deter Cynthia. With a surge of desperation, she managed to free herself and grabbed an icepick, stabbing Hendy in the neck.

Now unshackled but still in danger, Cynthia searched for a phone. Finding none, she continued her assault, stabbing Hendy multiple times before fleeing.

Barefoot, naked, and wearing only an iron slave collar with padlocked chains, Cynthia sprinted into the streets of Elephant Butte. Terrified, she tried to flag down passing cars, prompting a flood of 9-1-1 calls from alarmed residents.

Cynthia understood she couldn't rely on Ray's neighbors; a disturbing video he had shared with her during her confinement suggested their involvement and possible complicity in her mistreatment. In search of safety, she fled to a nearby mobile home, where an elderly couple, whom she later called her "guardian angels," welcomed her and promptly contacted the authorities.

Law enforcement quickly descended on Ray and Hendy, who spun a web of lies, claiming Cynthia had a heroin addiction they were merely trying to rehabilitate. However, their deceit unraveled as officers searched the trailer, uncovering a nightmarish collection of torture devices, grim evidence that confirmed Cynthia's harrowing story.

Beneath the surface of his seemingly everyday life, David Parker Ray harbored monstrous desires that turned his isolated trailer in Elephant Butte into a site of unimaginable horrors.

On a tape recorded by David Parker Ray on July 23, 1993, he chillingly claimed, "I've been rapin' bitches ever since I was old enough to jerk off and tie little girls' hands behind their back."

Ray met 37-year-old Cindy Hendy in 1997 in Truth or Consequences, New Mexico. She was evading law enforcement on grand theft and drug charges in Washington State. Not long after their meeting, they became romantically involved, bonding over their shared violent sexual fantasies. Hendy was not just a willing participant; she was fully committed to Ray's sadistic acts of sexual torture and potential murders.

Hendy left school at 15 and became a mother at 16. By her late 20s, she had two more children from different fathers. When her youngest turned ten, feeling overwhelmed, she chose to have them stay with their grandparents.

Ultimately, Hendy was found guilty of kidnapping and criminal sexual penetration. In a plea bargain, she agreed to testify against Ray in exchange for a reduced sentence, ultimately receiving 36 years in prison.

During the trial, Hendy provided harrowing details of how Ray's victims were dismembered and disposed of, either buried or dumped in Elephant Butte Lake or nearby ravines.

Having served nearly two-thirds of her sentence, Hendy was granted parole and released in 2019. By March 2022, she was reportedly residing in Hamilton, Montana.

Ray's daughter, Glenda "Jesse" Ray, and his associate, Dennis Roy Yancy, played key roles in hiding his crimes. Their present whereabouts remain largely unknown.

Yancy admitted to participating in the 1997 murder of Marie Parker, a woman whom David Parker Ray and Jesse Ray had abducted, drugged, and tortured for days before Yancy ultimately strangled her to death. Both Jesse Ray and Yancy confessed to assisting Ray in disposing of multiple bodies.

In 1986, Jesse Ray attempted to alert authorities about her father's activities. FBI Agent Doug Beldon recalled her allegations, stating, "David Parker Ray was abducting and torturing women and either killing them or selling them to buyers in Mexico." However, the vague accusations prevented the FBI from taking action against Ray at the time.

Before their arrests, the Albuquerque Police Department had suspicions about David Parker Ray and Glenda "Jesse" Ray, regarding the 1995 disappearance of Jill Troia, who was 22 years old and had previously dated Jesse Ray.

Troia was last spotted at the Frontier Restaurant on East Central's 2400 block in Albuquerque, New Mexico, late September 30 or early October 1, 1995. Earlier that evening, she had gone to a bar with friends before heading to the restaurant with Glenda Ray.

Witnesses later indicated that Glenda and Jill Troia had argued at the restaurant. When questioned by the police, Glenda said, "I left Jill at the Frontier Restaurant with her father, David Parker Ray, and then David and I went to the Elephant Butte Reservoir in southern New Mexico." Troia has since been unaccounted for, leading her mother, who resides in Michigan, to file a missing persons report.

Ray's crime spree spanned decades. He evaded capture for so long because he deliberately targeted women from marginalized backgrounds, often drugging them to impair their memories, which made it nearly impossible for the few survivors to recall what he had done.

The full extent of Ray's crimes remains unknown, including how many victims he may have killed. Most of the evidence pointing to his high body count comes from a diary he kept, detailing his actions against each victim, but it never revealed where he disposed of their bodies. His reign of terror ended on the day his last victim managed to escape.

During the trial, FBI Agent Mary Ellen O'Toole, a prominent authority on criminal sexual sadism, provided testimony regarding the alarming evidence discovered in Ray's residence and the trailer he had transformed into his notorious "toy box."

She recounted the sexual paraphernalia, illustrations, and torture devices found inside, labeling Ray as a "criminal sexual sadist." O'Toole additionally claimed that no therapy exists for his disorder, emphasizing that the only solution to his behavior is imprisonment.

Before sentencing, numerous victims of Ray and their families spoke in court. Kelly Garrett, holding hands with Cynthia Vigil-Jaramillo, stated, "I want Ray to experience a long, suffering life in prison. Trust me, that demented individual will have no friends there. I hope he is confined and treated just like me and his other victims. I don't see myself as a victim; rather, I consider myself a survivor."

Loretta Romero, the mother of Angie Montano, discussed the deep impact of Ray's behavior: "My daughter was kind-hearted, but she lost her self-esteem, her smile, and everything else due to David Ray. I stood by Angie and her two young sons, whose lives he wrecked. I truly feel compassion for David Ray."

Others were much less understanding. Bertha Vigil, Cynthia Vigil-Jaramillo's grandmother, shot a fierce look at Ray and declared, "You're a disgrace to humanity. How would you feel if I treated your daughter the way you treat my Cynthia? I pray you endure suffering every single day for the rest of your miserable life. Satan has a spot reserved for you. I hope you burn in hell forever."

Finally, Cynthia stood before the court, her voice shaking with emotion. "I carry scars, both seen and unseen, that will last forever. No punishment can match the suffering I have endured. I am terrified of feeling trapped and powerless, afraid of the dark, and too frightened to venture out alone." Tears streamed down her face as she continued, "I want David Ray to spend his life in prison and to suffer the same anguish he inflicted on me."

Ray's first trial in 2001 resulted in a hung jury in Tierra Amarilla, New Mexico. His case was transferred to a small town where he had been raised decades earlier. He was convicted of crimes against Angie Montano and later admitted to the brutal kidnapping and torture of Cynthia Vigil-Jaramillo as part of a plea deal for a reduced sentence.

Cindy Hendy, his accomplice, testified in exchange for a reduced sentence, ultimately receiving 36 years for her involvement in the crimes. His daughter, Glenda "Jesse" Ray, agreed to a plea deal arranged by her father, resulting in a two-year prison sentence along with five years of probation.

Even amid these circumstances, justice was not achieved. In May 2002, David Parker Ray passed away from a heart attack before finishing his sentence, leaving many victims without the closure they needed.

Despite his death, authorities have continued to investigate the case. In 2011, law enforcement conducted another search for remains near Elephant Butte Lake, but once again, they found nothing. The true extent of Ray's atrocities—and the number of lives he destroyed—may never be fully understood.

While investigating David Parker Ray's infamous "Toy Box" trailer, authorities uncovered chilling evidence of numerous murders. Among the most damning discoveries were Ray's handwritten diaries, which detailed the brutal torture and deaths of several women. The FBI also found hundreds of pieces of jewelry, clothing, and other personal effects believed to have belonged to his victims.

Ray's meticulous efforts in constructing his torture chamber, coupled with the overwhelming physical evidence, strongly suggested a horrifyingly high number of murder victims.

Despite these findings, law enforcement encountered difficulties in building additional cases. Both Cindy Hendy and Dennis Yancy pointed out locations where they believed Ray had left bodies, but extensive searches found no human remains.

Criminal profilers identify distinct patterns among serial killers. For instance, Jeffrey Dahmer targeted young men at a specific gay bar in Milwaukee; John Wayne Gacy lured teenage boys from bus stops in Chicago, and David Parker Ray hunted his victims at the Blue Waters Saloon, a rough and unassuming bar in Elephant Butte that attracted both drifters and locals alike.

Years after Ray's arrest, investigators pursued additional leads. FBI spokesperson Frank Fisher stated, "We're still receiving promising leads. As long as these leads keep coming in and media coverage sustains interest in the case, we will continue our investigation."

Cynthia Vigil-Jaramillo, one of the rare known survivors associated with Ray, would not allow her traumatic past to control her life. Instead, she transformed her anguish into constructive efforts by establishing Street Safe New Mexico, a nonprofit aimed at aiding at-risk women escaping perilous circumstances. Along with her partner, Christine Barber, she offers secure housing and essential resources. Cynthia also provides testimony in court for assault victims, ensuring that survivors have an opportunity to confront their abusers.

David Parker Ray was born in 1939 in Belen, New Mexico, to Cecil Leland Ray, a native of Oregon, and Nettie Opal Parker from Texas. He and his younger sister, Peggie Pearl Ray, were raised on a small ranch by their strict grandparents, Russell and Dolly Parker.

Their grandfather presided over the household strictly, serving as a harsh disciplinarian who permitted minimal warmth or affection. The unpredictable visits from their father further disrupted family life, as his struggles with alcoholism and frequent violent outbursts created a profound, traumatic impact.

Cecil Ray not only failed as a protector but also actively harmed his son, introducing him to sadomasochistic pornography at an impressionable age. This act profoundly warped the boy's emerging sense of identity and sexuality.

From an early age, Ray felt like an outcast. Bullied at Mountainair High School, mistreated at home, and battling loneliness, he turned to drugs and alcohol for comfort. While still a teenager, his troubling fantasies of torture and murder began to emerge.

When he was just 14, his sister stumbled upon his sadomasochistic drawings and a stash of bondage pornography—an eerie foreshadowing of the horrors he would later unleash.

Ray found scant solace at Mountainair High School in Mountainair, New Mexico. The classrooms, hallways, and rows of lockers offered no escape from his peers' harsh treatment. He faced relentless bullying, including taunts about his awkward posture, soft voice, and intense shyness around girls. The jeers reverberated even at home, haunting his thoughts long after school was over.

Feeling isolated and worthless, Ray turned to cheap alcohol and any drugs he could find to numb his pain. Initially, casual use soon turned into addiction, which not only dulled his suffering but also warped his perception of reality. As he transitioned into adulthood, these substances served as both a shield and a prison.

Despite a complicated past, Ray served in the U.S. Army and was honorably discharged. He married four times and had two children, including Glenda "Jesse" Jean Ray, who eventually became one of his accomplices.

Ray earned his ominous nickname from the chilling "Toy Box," a soundproof trailer he meticulously converted into a harsh torture chamber, where he imprisoned, mistreated, and presumably murdered numerous women.

Beneath the surface of his seemingly normal life, David Parker Ray harbored monstrous desires that turned his isolated trailer in Elephant Butte into a site of unimaginable horrors.

Dubbed "Satan's Den," the chamber housed over $100,000 worth of custom-built equipment designed for sexual torture. Inside, an arsenal of implements awaited: whips, chains, spreader bars, and ceiling-mounted pulleys used to suspend victims in the air.

Surgical tools and electric shock devices were meticulously organized beside a makeshift generator designed to emit painful jolts. In a corner, a coffin-shaped box—sealed and soundproof—was used to confine, confuse, and mentally break those trapped within.

A skull-shaped candelabra floated overhead, its flickering flames casting grotesque shadows on the walls, each adorned with unsettling and intricate illustrations of ancient torture techniques.

At the center of the chamber stood a cold and clinical gynecological exam table, its stirrups gleaming under the dim light. Suspended above it, a ceiling-mounted mirror ensured that no victim could look away, condemned to witness every unspeakable violation committed in that room of calculated horror.

To keep his captives submissive, disoriented, and utterly powerless, David Parker Ray used a dangerous combination of drugs, particularly sodium pentothal and phenobarbital. These potent sedatives are known for their ability to disrupt memory, change perception, and induce a surreal state that blurs the line between reality and nightmares.

Under their influence, victims were often left unable to recall the full extent of their ordeal, even if they managed to escape with their lives. Throughout the 1990s, authorities believe Ray—dubbed the "Toy Box Killer"—abducted, raped, tortured, and possibly murdered as many as 60 to 100 women across Arizona and New Mexico, his crimes hidden behind the desolate backdrop of the Southwest.

Despite the unsettling testimonies, chilling audio recordings, and extensive physical evidence indicating his sadistic crimes, David Parker Ray was never formally charged with murder.

He spent his last years at the privately operated Lea County Correctional Facility in Hobbs, New Mexico. This medium-security prison held more than 1,200 male inmates. His reign of terror concluded definitively on May 28, 2002, when he died from a heart attack while in custody.

Cynthia Vigil-Jaramillo's survival is the real story. She was a victim, but even more so, she was a fighter. What she experienced in Ray's torture chamber defies comprehension. Nevertheless, her indomitable spirit allowed her to break free from the grasp of a sadistic serial predator.

Cynthia's bravery halted Ray's vicious actions, likely preventing many women from sharing the same fate. Her escape signified the end of the line for one of America's most savage murderers.

CHAPTER FOURTEEN

Classified Ad Rapist –
Bobby Joe Long

In 1984, 17-year-old Lisa McVey concluded that death was her sole escape. After enduring years of unyielding sexual abuse at the hands of her grandmother's boyfriend, she felt entirely hopeless. She even penned a suicide note, believing that ending her life was her only option. Yet, fate plunged her into an unimaginable nightmare instead.

On the morning of November 3, 1984, Lisa finished a challenging double shift at Krispy Kreme in Tampa, Florida.

She rode her bike home through the dark, empty streets, unaware that a predator lurked in the shadows. As she pedaled past a church at around 2:00 a.m., Bobby Joe Long—a sadistic serial rapist and murderer—sprang from the darkness. He grabbed Lisa from behind, yanking her off her bike.

Lisa screamed, her voice shattering the silence.

"Shut up, or I'll blow your damn brains out," Long growled, pressing a gun to her head. In that instant, Lisa had a chilling realization.

Just hours earlier, she had contemplated ending her life. Now, she was determined to live.

Lisa had grown up in a perilous environment filled with violence. Following her abandonment by a drug-addicted mother, she was taken in by her grandmother, who overlooked the abuse happening in their household.

For three years, Lisa had suffered in silence as her grandmother's boyfriend molested her, often at gunpoint. "You should be grateful you have a roof over your head," her grandmother had told her.

With Long's gun against her head, Lisa was resolute in her will to survive. He bound her hands, covered her eyes with a blindfold, and tossed her into his red Dodge Magnum.

Despite her apprehension, Lisa observed every detail possible: the texture of the fabric, the sounds from outside, and their current route. She recorded each moment, convinced this information would aid her escape.

After driving for about 20 minutes, they stopped in a wooded area. Lisa felt leaves on her face beneath her blindfold. Long briefly made her exit the car before abruptly shoving her back inside.

Then she took an unexpected step. She begged, saying, "I'll do whatever you want. Just don't kill me." Long responded with laughter. Lisa realized she had to go along with it.

Having observed crime shows on TV, she instinctively understood survival strategies. By making herself relatable, she believed she could improve her chances.

Enduring the horror at Long's apartment, Lisa remembered unimaginable abuse. He forced her to strip, blindfolded her, and sexually assaulted her repeatedly. He even forced her to shower, scrubbing her like she was nothing more than an object.

Despite her terror, Lisa remained alert. She intentionally left fingerprints in his bathroom and memorized as many details as possible about his appearance. When she overheard a news report about her disappearance, she felt a surge of panic. If Long thought the police were closing in, he would kill her.

Lisa feigned sympathy for her captor, claiming to relate to his pain from a recent breakup. She even proposed the idea of being his girlfriend. At one moment, Long allowed her to caress his face, and she meticulously traced his features, ensuring his likeness was firmly imprinted in her memory.

Her plan worked effectively. A shift occurred with Long. The brutal killer, who had taken the lives of at least ten women, unexpectedly hesitated. Lisa achieved what no one else could; she succeeded in making him lower his guard. Before long, she would utilize that to her advantage.

Over time, Lisa aimed to appear more relatable to her captor. She fabricated stories, especially claiming that her father was gravely ill and that she was his sole caregiver, in hopes of eliciting his sympathy.

"Put this on," Long instructed, tossing her a shirt that belonged to another woman. Once she wore it, he inquired, "Where do you live?"

"Why?" Lisa shot back, her voice tinged with fear.

"Because I'm taking you home."

However, the ordeal was far from over. Long subjected her to more torture, then shoved her into his car, binding her with ligatures, gagging her, and blindfolding her. Back inside his vehicle, he demanded she strip again and queried her age. Lisa lied, saying she was 19.

"As long as you do what I want, I won't kill you," he declared, leaning back. He then forced her to perform oral sex on him again.

Resigned after years of sexual abuse, Lisa thought to herself, "What is one more instance?"

After he climaxed, he coldly instructed, "Get dressed, I'm taking you home." Long drove her to an ATM and a gas station, eventually leaving her behind a business around 4:30 a.m. "Wait five minutes before taking off your blindfold so I can drive away," he instructed as he prepared to leave. Just before driving off, he added chillingly, "Tell your father he's the reason I didn't kill you."

After Long left, Lisa returned to her grandmother's house early in the morning. Upon her arrival, her grandmother's boyfriend brutally attacked her, accusing her of infidelity.

Both Lisa's boyfriend and her grandmother dismissed her troubling story. Her grandmother even informed the Tampa police that Lisa had fabricated the kidnapping allegation.

A few days later, following a news report on a local murder victim, Lisa grew convinced that Long was the culprit. She quickly contacted the police. "Come get me. I have more information to share with you," she told Sergeant Larry Pinkerton.

In her interview, Pinkerton proposed using hypnosis to uncover repressed memories. Despite opposition from her grandmother's boyfriend, Lisa bravely decided to move forward, disclosing his abusive behavior. This led to his arrest. Lisa was transferred to a secure home for teens to ensure her safety.

With her abuser incarcerated, Lisa was resolved to protect others from similar experiences. In a photo lineup, her short tactile interaction with Long and brief views through her blindfold allowed her to recognize him, leading to his apprehension.

Bobby Joe Long was born on October 14, 1953, in Kenova, West Virginia, to Louella and Joe Long. He experienced a difficult childhood, which foreshadowed a bleak future. An additional X chromosome led to breast development during puberty, subjecting him to relentless teasing. Academically, he struggled, failing first grade, and this fueled a growing resentment toward women, starting with his mother.

Louella bartended frequently, usually in revealing clothing, and brought various men home. Bobby Joe's increasing resentment was exacerbated by the unsettling fact that he shared a bed with his mother until he turned 12. These formative experiences amplified his anger and warped his perception of women, laying the groundwork for the violence that would ultimately characterize his life.

At 13, Bobby Joe Long met his future wife, Cynthia. The two married in 1974 and had two children. According to Cynthia, not long after their wedding, Long was involved in a serious motorcycle accident when a vehicle struck him. He was hospitalized for several weeks, and during his recovery, he developed an obsessive habit—masturbating up to five times a day.

Cynthia later told investigators, "After the accident, Bobby became physically violent with me and impatient with our children. His sex drive became disturbingly compulsive and, at times, dangerous. I came to realize I was likely married to a sexual sadist."

Cynthia filed for divorce in 1980. Shortly afterward, Long began cohabiting with his close friend Sharon Richards.

Their relationship turned abusive. That resulted in Richards accusing Long of rape and battery.

Then, in 1983, Long was convicted of sending an explicit letter and inappropriate photographs to a 12-year-old girl in Florida. As a result, he received a brief jail sentence followed by probation. However, probation did little to curb his escalating criminal behavior. Instead, Long took a more sinister turn, evolving from a predator lurking through letters to a full-fledged rapist.

His approach was disturbingly methodical. He searched neighborhoods for *"For Sale"* signs and meticulously reviewed classified ads in Fort Lauderdale, Ocala, Miami, and Dade County for furniture and household items.

This tactic gave him an easy way to enter the homes of unsuspecting women. Once inside, under the pretense of making a purchase, he would ask to use the bathroom—where he retrieved his so-called "rape kit." Armed and prepared, he then overpowered, raped, and robbed his victims before vanishing without a trace.

Amid the rising number of attacks, officials named him "The Classified Ad Rapist." However, despite the increasing assaults and the palpable fear in Florida communities, these crimes went unprosecuted for reasons that are still unclear.

Long relocated to the Tampa region in 1983. During that period, Hillsborough County experienced an annual average of 30 to 35 homicides in the early 1980s. Nonetheless, the murder rate saw a sharp rise in 1984.

A killer terrorized the region over eight months, striking with disturbing regularity—nearly one murder every other week. His victims were bound, raped, and murdered, their bodies discarded in eerie, staged positions. The pattern was unmistakable, yet the brutality of his methods set him apart, leaving law enforcement scrambling to catch a predator who seemed to kill without hesitation.

In May 1984, authorities discovered the body of the first victim, a nude woman, at a crime scene in Hillsborough County.

As the investigation progressed, authorities linked the crime to a series of abductions, sexual assaults, and murders spanning multiple counties in the Tampa Bay area. Court records later confirmed that Bobby Joe Long had kidnapped, raped, and killed at least ten women across Hillsborough, Pasco, and Pinellas counties.

The magnitude and severity of the killings prompted an investigation involving several agencies, including the Hillsborough County Sheriff's Office, Tampa Police Department, Pasco County Sheriff's Office, Florida Department of Law Enforcement, and the FBI. As fresh evidence surfaced, law enforcement ramped up their efforts to locate the murderer, slowly uncovering a pattern of predation that led to Long's arrest.

Typically, the victims' bodies were discovered in an advanced state of decomposition, often long after their murders. Police noted that the bodies were usually dumped near rural roadsides or dragged into wooded areas, making them difficult to find.

Long targeted vulnerable women, preying on those walking alone and those working as sex workers. He lured them into his car under false pretenses, subjecting them to brutal acts of rape and torture before ultimately killing them.

Among Long's ten confirmed victims, five were recognized as sex workers, two were exotic dancers, and the other three comprised a factory worker, a student, and one individual whose job is still unidentified.

After assaulting and torturing multiple women, Long escalated to murder in the spring of 1984, leaving a trail of victims behind.

Court records disclosed these specifics:

On March 27, 1984, Bobby Joe Long picked up 20-year-old Artiss Wick, a prostitute, under the pretense of seeking her services. After brutally assaulting and raping her, Long found himself unsatisfied. In a final act of violence, he strangled Wick to death.

Weeks later, on May 13, 1984, Long prowled Nebraska Avenue in Tampa, where he encountered 19-year-old Nguen "Lana" Long. Pulling up beside her, he offered her a ride. Lana accepted, unaware of the predator she had just stepped into a car with. Moments after she got in, Long veered off the road and brandished a knife. Panicked, Lana screamed and fought back, but Long quickly subdued her, binding her hands before driving to a secluded area. There, he raped and strangled her.

Lana Long's lifeless body was discovered days later, lying face down. Her hands were tied behind her back, and her legs were grotesquely positioned—spread apart, with a five-foot distance from heel to heel. The crime scene bore the unmistakable signature of a sadistic killer.

On May 27, 1984, Bobby Joe Long lured 22-year-old Michelle Denise Simms, a prostitute, into his car. He brutally beat and raped her before repeatedly slashing her throat in a vicious attack.

Investigators found identical red nylon fibers on both Simms and Lana Long, establishing a connection between the two murders and revealing a pattern in the killer's methods.

On June 8, 1984, police discovered Long's fourth known victim, 22-year-old Elizabeth Loudenback. By the time detectives found her, her body was severely decomposed, lying on her back, and still fully clothed. Unlike Long's previous victims, who were primarily prostitutes, drug users, or strippers, Loudenback stood apart. She had no known ties to sex work or substance abuse, making her an outlier in Long's growing body count.

Chanel Devon Williams, an 18-year-old sex worker, became Bobby Joe Long's fifth confirmed victim. On the evening of October 7, 1984, while walking along a Tampa street, Williams accepted a ride from Long, unaware that she would never return.

Long initially attempted to rape and strangle her. Still, for reasons unknown, he failed to kill her as he had his previous victims. Frustrated, he resorted to his firearm, shooting Williams in the neck and leaving her for dead.

In the weeks that followed, his killing spree continued. Authorities soon discovered the bodies of 21-year-old Kim Swann, 18-year-old Virginia Johnson, 22-year-old Kimberly Hopps, and 28-year-old Karen Dinsfriend—all brutally murdered in a similar fashion.

Long's reign of terror extended far beyond Tampa. Investigators estimated that before his killing spree, he had committed more than 50 rapes across Florida, spanning Miami, Ocala, and Fort Lauderdale. His violent rampage left a trail of victims, ultimately marking him as one of the state's most prolific predators.

Long was pursued in three jurisdictions across the Tampa Bay area, where investigators collected various forensic evidence, including clothing, carpet fibers, semen, ligature marks, and rope knots.

On November 16, 1984, law enforcement began monitoring a movie theater, believing Bobby Joe Long was present.

As Long exited the theater, officers approached and arrested him without incident. He was promptly charged with the sexual battery and kidnapping of Lisa McVey.

After being taken into custody, Long signed a Miranda waiver and consented to speak with investigators. Initially, detectives sought to obtain his confession regarding McVey's case. However, once he confessed to the assault, the interrogation shifted its focus. Detectives then pressed him for details about a series of unresolved sexual battery homicides that had affected the Tampa Bay area, seeking to compile a comprehensive confession related to his purported killing spree.

While the detectives questioned Long about the murders, he demonstrated evasiveness, often replying, "I'd prefer not to answer that." As the interrogation progressed, they showed him photos of the victims.

Gazing at the pictures, his expression changed. After a lengthy silence, he murmured, "The state of affairs has transformed. I require a lawyer."

Despite his request, he did not receive an attorney. After hours of grueling interrogation, Long ultimately broke down and confessed to the brutal murders of eight women in Hillsborough County.

For years, the sadistic serial killer had targeted women, instilling widespread fear. Yet, even as his violence intensified, he managed to escape apprehension—until now.

The FBI's study of fiber evidence played a key role in connecting Bobby Joe Long's vehicle to multiple victims. Forensic examinations showed that fibers from the victims corresponded with those discovered in Long's car, bolstering the case against him. This scientific evidence and other investigation results provided law enforcement with the essential proof needed for convictions.

In April 1985, Long was found guilty of eight murders in Hillsborough County, along with multiple other offenses, such as armed burglary, aggravated assault, kidnapping, robbery, and sexual battery. The ample evidence in his trial and confessions left little room for doubt regarding his guilt.

Long was given multiple life sentences, and in the summer of 1986, he received the death penalty for the murder of Michelle Simms. Although Long officially confessed to ten murders, he hinted during police interviews that the actual number of victims might be higher, suggesting his total could exceed the confirmed figures provided by law enforcement.

The Hillsborough County State Attorney's Office and the Public Defender's Office agreed on a plea bargain. On September 24, 1985, Long admitted guilt to eight homicides and the abduction and rape of Lisa McVey. This plea deal required Long to spend the remainder of his life in prison.

Long received a sentence of 26 life terms without the possibility of parole, out of which 24 were to be served concurrently and two consecutively. He was also given seven extra life sentences, with the possibility of parole after 25 years. In addition, the State retained the option to pursue the death penalty for the murder of Michelle Simms, eventually leading to a death sentence.

In July 1986, Robert Joe Long was sentenced to death at Florida's State Prison.

On April 23, 2019, Florida Governor Ron DeSantis signed the death warrant for Long, marking the first such action since he took office in January. The execution was scheduled for Thursday, May 29, 2019.

Nevertheless, Long's attorney contested the warrant, asserting it should be invalidated since it used the name "Robert Joe Long" instead of the legal name "Bobby Joe Long." The lawyer emphasized, "If the state plans to enforce harsh penalties, accuracy is essential."

The effort to halt Long's execution was rejected despite the legal challenge.

Bobby Joe Long repeatedly challenged Florida's lethal injection procedures, claiming that the drugs could cause unnecessary suffering—an assertion that medical professionals reportedly contested. However, Long's later appeals were denied, sealing his fate.

On May 23, 2019, Long was executed through lethal injection at Florida State Prison, years after being convicted. That morning, at 9:30 a.m. local time, he savored his final meal, which included roast beef, bacon, French fries, and soda.

Before his execution, Long was offered the opportunity to speak his last words but opted for silence instead.

At 6:47 p.m., the lethal injection was administered. His breathing turned irregular almost immediately, and his mouth twisted as he struggled for air. A state official pressed down on his shoulders as his breath grew more labored. By 6:48 p.m., it appeared he had stopped breathing entirely.

His eyelids turned pale before his face took on an unnatural shade of white. At 6:54 p.m., a doctor assessed him. Just six minutes later, at precisely 7:00 p.m., Bobby Joe Long was pronounced dead.

Florida State Prison (FSP) is the sole facility in Florida officially designated a "prison"; all other sites are referred to as "Correctional Institutions."

FSP contains one of Florida's two male death row cell blocks and the state's execution chamber. Male death row inmates are also held at Union Correctional Institution, while female death row inmates reside at Lowell Annex.

It is important to note that FSP is the location where Ted Bundy was executed in the electric chair.

A few select media representatives and the families of his victims attended to witness justice fulfilled.

Lisa McVey, Long's last victim, demonstrated remarkable bravery that resulted in his apprehension. She sat in the front row, donning a shirt that proclaimed, "Long… Overdue." Reflecting on that moment, she expressed, "I wanted to be the first person he saw."

For numerous people, the execution symbolized a long-awaited sense of justice. "We thank God this day has finally arrived," McVey remarked. "After 35 years, we can achieve peace of mind knowing that justice has been served."

Lisa Avery Rich, Kim Swann's cousin, commented, "While this won't restore our loved ones, it will offer us some closure."

Bobby Joe Long's case highlights the crucial importance of forensic evidence in criminal investigations. The FBI's fiber analysis played a key role in linking him to his crimes, showcasing the significance of forensic science in contemporary law enforcement. His conviction and sentencing brought justice to his victims and their families, guaranteeing that he would no longer inflict harm on anyone.

After her abduction, Lisa McVey's life changed dramatically. Two years later, she married a police officer and gave birth to a daughter. However, their marriage ended after five years, profoundly impacting her life.

Motivated to progress in her career, Lisa started her role at the Hillsborough County Parks and Recreation Department. Following a break-in at her office, the deputy who responded caught her off guard by remarking, "You have the qualities of a police officer. Have you ever thought about pursuing that path?"

Inspired by her motivation, Lisa embarked on a career in law enforcement. She became a dispatcher at the Hillsborough County Sheriff's Office in 1999. She went to the police academy, obtained her deputy designation, and became a reserve deputy in 2004.

In an extraordinary full-circle moment, Lisa was in the department that had previously detained her captor. Specializing in sex crimes, she devoted her career to safeguarding children and preventing others from facing the same traumas she once did. Additionally, she took on the role of a middle school resource officer, leveraging her experiences to educate students on identifying and reacting to perilous situations.

Now a grandmother, Lisa is officially known as Lisa McVey Noland. She openly recounts her journey, transforming her past trauma into a powerful source of strength and inspiration.

CHAPTER FIFTEEN
Amazon Review Killer – Todd Kohlhepp

On August 21, 2016, Kala Brown and her boyfriend, Charles Carver, went to a remote property near Woodruff, South Carolina, for a cleaning job. What appeared to be a routine assignment would alter their lives forever.

Kala had known Todd Kohlhepp, a 45-year-old real estate owner, for five years through her cleaning work. Their acquaintance gave her no cause for concern regarding their meeting. Tragically, she could never have foreseen the horrific events that were about to unfold.

Kohlhepp confronted the couple when they arrived at his expansive estate, surrounded by a sturdy $80,000 chain-link fence. Brandishing a gun, he took them hostage. Their sudden disappearance ignited a frantic search, but Kala and Charles remained unaccounted for over three months.

This traumatic event triggered a series of incidents that led to Kohlhepp's downfall. Identified as a registered sex offender, Kohlhepp was revealed to be a ruthless serial killer responsible for seven murders. Kala was his last victim, the sole survivor whose courageous resolve directed authorities right to her captor, effectively putting an end to his reign of terror.

Many thought the couple had eloped, but some feared something was amiss. Leah Miller, a close friend of Kala, felt worried enough to file a missing person report just two days after they vanished.

A few days after Kala and Charlie visited Kohlhepp's property, Charlie's mother, Joanne Shiflet, became increasingly concerned. At first, she thought his lack of communication was due to fatigue from his 12-hour shifts, which were particularly demanding. However, as days passed without any word from him, she began to feel that something was seriously amiss.

On September 3, 2016, Joanne reported Charlie as missing, stating to the police, "I haven't heard from my son in days." Following her conversation with law enforcement, Joanne contacted the apartment complex manager to request permission for herself and Bonnie Newsom, Kala's mother, to enter the couple's apartment.

When the manager knocked on the apartment door, there was silence. After unlocking the door and stepping inside, they encountered a disturbing sight.

Bonnie Newsom later reflected, "It appeared that no one had come by for quite a while. We found a distressing situation— Romeo, Kala's beloved Pomeranian, had been left alone without food or water. To her, that dog felt like a member of her family. She would never have chosen to leave him in such a dire state."

Meanwhile, Leah Miller's anxiety intensified due to the prolonged silence. She began articulating her concerns clearly, seeking answers, but ultimately found them empty.

Unexpectedly, unusual posts began appearing on Kala and Charles's social media. These updates suggested that the couple had married, acquired a new house, and were happily cohabiting. Nevertheless, the timing and nature of these announcements raised skepticism among family members. They struggled to trust the authenticity of this abrupt surge of happiness following several days of unexplained quiet.

Family members doubted the legitimacy of the claims: "If they are genuinely fine, then why are they not answering our calls or replying to texts? How could they suddenly afford to purchase a house?"

Confronted with growing uncertainties and concerns, Joanne Shiflet took action. She filed a missing person's report, prompting the police to begin their investigation for answers.

The police initiated their investigation by reviewing Kala and Charlie's cell phone and social media records. Data from Kala's phone showed that it had last connected to a tower in Spartanburg County, but the precise location was still uncertain.

Detectives investigating Kala's case found Facebook messages between her and Todd Kohlhepp regarding her work at his property. Kohlhepp's land, close to where Kala's phone had pinged, emerged as crucial evidence. As a result, law enforcement secured a search warrant for the 100-acre estate owned by the prominent South Carolina realtor.

On November 3, 2016, investigators reached Kohlhepp's property and quickly heard frantic banging and screams emanating from a large metal shipping container.

The chilling reality became apparent when they opened the container: Kala was inside, handcuffed and shackled with heavy chains measuring two and a half to three feet around her neck and ankles, leaving her no possibility of escape.

Sheriff Chuck Wright of Spartanburg County characterized the scene as "quite emotional, to say the least."

As detectives hurried to save Kala using bolt cutters, they stumbled upon another concerning discovery—Charles Carver was gone.

Kala provided an accurate account of the events to the detectives.

"When we arrived, we entered, grabbed the hedge clippers, and went back outside. Out of nowhere, Todd showed up with a gun and shot three times into Charlie's chest without any warning. Charlie collapsed instantly, dead on the spot. I was paralyzed with shock, unable to speak or move. That's when Todd grabbed me from behind, dragged me into the building, threw me to the ground, and cuffed my wrists. Afterward, he wrapped Charlie's body in a blue tarp and placed him in the tractor bucket. That was the last time I ever saw him.

"For three months, Todd repeatedly raped me. Most of my captivity was spent locked inside a shipping container, except for brief moments when Todd would take me outside, walking me like an animal. I tried to distract myself during my confinement with books and a DVD player, which Todd provided. At night, I slept on two thin dog beds. My daily diet consisted of one meal, usually crackers and peanut butter, around 6:00 p.m. I was permitted just one toilet break per day. To stay alive, I did and said whatever I thought Todd wanted to hear.

"Todd often mentioned that by keeping me alive, he was violating all his rules. He hadn't made up his mind yet about whether he would eventually kill me or sell me.

"Every afternoon, Todd would untie me, forcing me into brutal and degrading sexual acts. I believe Todd wanted me to develop Stockholm syndrome—a psychological reaction where abuse victims bond emotionally with their captors—in hopes I'd fall in love with him or at least become submissive enough to stop resisting."

Following Kala's interview, authorities discovered Carver's vehicle concealed in a ravine, obscured by brush, spray-painted brown, and left deep in the woods. Kohlhepp's mother subsequently revealed to investigators, "I think Carver was killed for having a 'really smart mouth,' something Todd despised."

Unfortunately, this discovery marked only the beginning of more horrific revelations.

Todd Kohlhepp was apprehended shortly after Kala's rescue on December 25, 2003. Following his arrest, authorities uncovered Carver's body on Kohlhepp's property, next to a freshly dug grave. Investigators surmised that Kohlhepp had intended to murder Kala as well, burying her beside Carver.

Further searches of Kohlhepp's property revealed various firearms, such as 9mm handguns equipped with suppressors, semi-automatic rifles, and a large stock of ammunition. Officials suspected these weapons were acquired illegally.

After his arrest, Kohlhepp consented to collaborate with investigators to fulfill three specific requests.

He intended to send his mother a photo, transfer money for his friend's daughter's college fees, and contact her directly. After fulfilling these needs, he provided the authorities with detailed information regarding his offenses.

Police records show that Todd Kohlhepp was charged with kidnapping and was facing a forthcoming murder charge, along with four murder counts related to the 2003 deaths of Scott Ponder, Brian Lucas, Chris Sherbert, and Beverly Guy.

Investigators discovered that Kohlhepp, armed with a pistol, entered the Superbike Motorsports motorcycle shop through the rear door and fatally shot Chris Sherbert, age 26, while he was working.

Kohlhepp entered the showroom, shooting Beverly Guy, 52, before targeting Brian Lucas, age 30, at the central doorway. Ultimately, he fatally shot Scott Ponder, 29, in the parking lot while Ponder attempted to flee.

In subsequent interrogations, Kohlhepp openly admitted, "I shot each of them once in the forehead."

This information remained hidden from the public, highlighting Kohlhepp's role as the perpetrator since only the murderer would possess such vital details.

Scott Ponder's wife noted that Kohlhepp frequently expressed dissatisfaction as a customer at Superbike Motorsports. Furthermore, Kohlhepp's mother shared that he had attempted to return a motorcycle purchased from the shop. Instead of assistance, he faced ridicule from the employees. They refused to grant his refund request and reportedly mocked his riding abilities, possibly intensifying his drive for the murders.

Only a few months before Kala and Charles disappeared, Todd Kohlhepp hired Johnny Coxie, age 29, and his wife, Meagan Leigh McCraw-Coxie, 26, to assist with projects on his estate. Unfortunately, Kohlhepp shot and killed Johnny with a single bullet to the chest.

He then carried out repeated attacks on Meagan during the week before brutally shooting her and burying their bodies in shallow graves, which he would subsequently disclose to Kala.

The county coroner verified the Coxies' identities using their distinctive tattoos.

Kohlhepp distinctly represented the bleakest aspects of human nature. Police documents reveal that his violent crime spree extended over nearly 30 years—from November 25, 1986, to November 7, 2003, concluding on August 31, 2016.

Following his arrest, Kohlhepp chillingly hinted to his mother that there were numerous other victims beyond those killed at the Superbike Motorsports motorcycle shop. When pressed by his mother on how many lives he had taken, Kohlhepp ominously replied, "You do not have enough fingers."

During a subsequent police interrogation, Kohlhepp confessed to murdering an additional victim in Arizona, revealing the severity of his heinous acts.

On November 18, 2016, the Tempe Police Department announced an investigation into Todd Kohlhepp's alarming assertions of more murders. Officials stated that the primary focus would initially be on cold cases from 1983 to 1986, which coincided with Kohlhepp's residency with his father in Arizona, as well as the timeframe from August to November 2001, after his release from prison for kidnapping and before his return to South Carolina.

Throughout the distressing three months of Kala Brown's captivity, Kohlhepp often discussed his previous crimes, including several that law enforcement had not associated with him.

He boasted to Kala, "I killed nearly 100 people, and I want to murder even more because I have dreams of my body count being in the mid-three digits." Kala later stated, "He liked to brag like hell that he was a serial killer and a mass murderer."

Kohlhepp took Kala around his property on a chilling day, deliberately pointing out three graves. He warned her, "Kala, if you attempt to escape, you'll go straight into one of those."

A particularly unsettling discovery from the investigation involved Kohlhepp's alarming product reviews on Amazon, earning him the nickname "Amazon Review Killer."

In his padlock review, Kohlhepp ominously remarked, "Strong locks... feature five on a shipping container... won't completely deter them... but will delay them until they lose interest."

Another review noted a chilling remark about a folding shovel: "Keep it in the car for when you need to hide the bodies, and you forgot the full-size shovel at home... it doesn't come with a midget, which would have been convenient."

These concerning reviews were connected to Kohlhepp via his Amazon account and wish list.

Todd Kohlhepp was born in Florida on March 7, 1971, to William Sampsell and Regina Tague. His parents divorced when he was just two years old, after which his mother obtained custody. Not long after, she remarried, and her new husband adopted Todd. Reports suggest that Kohlhepp felt significant resentment and anger toward his stepfather, contributing to a challenging home life. Subsequent psychological evaluations uncovered a complex and unhealthy relationship between Kohlhepp and his stepfather, which intensified his longing to connect with his biological father.

In 1983, Kohlhepp moved to Arizona to stay with his biological father following his mother and stepfather's separation. While living there, he held various local jobs and developed an interest in his father's hobbies, especially weapon collecting. His father also exposed him to perilous activities, including the creation and detonation of explosives.

Kohlhepp's father noted his son's demeanor, tagging him as emotionally restricted, showing only "anger and madness." From a young age, Kohlhepp exhibited notable psychological difficulties; even in nursery school, he demonstrated aggression toward other children and purposely damaged their belongings.

At the age of nine, psychological counseling revealed he was notably volatile, exhibited early inappropriate sexual preoccupations, and engaged in animal cruelty, including shooting his dog with a BB gun and killing his goldfish by pouring bleach into the bowl.

Kohlhepp was hospitalized for three and a half months in a psychiatric facility in Georgia due to escalating behavioral problems and difficulties relating to peers. During his stay, he received a diagnosis of borderline personality disorder, highlighting the significant psychological challenges he faced.

Kohlhepp began his initial prison term while still a teenager.

In October 1986, 15-year-old Kohlhepp kidnapped 14-year-old Kristie Granado in Tempe, Arizona. After taking her to his house, he threatened her with a .22-caliber revolver, tied her up, taped her mouth shut, and repeatedly raped her.

Before she was released, he threatened to kill her entire family if she disclosed what had happened. Kohlhepp was subsequently charged with kidnapping, sexual assault, and serious crimes against minors.

In 1987, he admitted guilt to the kidnapping charge, leading to the dropping of the other charges. He received a 15-year prison sentence and was registered as a sex offender.

Court records indicate that Todd Kohlhepp had a diagnosis of borderline personality disorder and an IQ of 118, which is regarded as above average. The judge remarked that he was "very bright and should excel academically," yet characterized him as "behaviorally and emotionally dangerous," ultimately concluding that his chances for rehabilitation were limited. In court documents, his probation officer supported this evaluation, stressing that Kohlhepp "believed the world owed him something."

Despite these cautions, Kohlhepp's lawyer later remarked, "During my defense, I didn't believe he would threaten others in the future."

While in prison, Kohlhepp faced disciplinary actions for multiple offenses, such as violent behavior. Nonetheless, after he turned 20, he kept a clean record and was given a 15-year sentence.

In August 2001, Todd Kohlhepp completed his 14-year prison sentence and moved to South Carolina to be near his mother

From January 2002 to November 2003, Kohlhepp was a graphic designer at a Spartanburg company. In 2003, he started his studies at Greenville Technical College, and the following year, he transferred to the University of South Carolina Upstate. He earned his Bachelor of Science in business administration and marketing in 2008.

On June 30, 2006, Kohlhepp acquired a real estate license by submitting false information despite being a registered sex offender with a felony conviction. He later established a thriving real estate business with more than a dozen agents. He earned recognition as one of the top-selling agents in the Carolinas. The firm was closed after his arrest.

In addition to his real estate career, Kohlhepp obtained a private pilot license and invested in several out-of-state properties.

A previous client who sold her house to Todd Kohlhepp portrayed him as friendly and professional. Nonetheless, she remembered that he often talked about his guns and sometimes made suggestive remarks during their discussions.

Conversely, a woman who helped one of Kohlhepp's employees characterized him as aggressive and condescending, especially toward her partner. A banker who collaborated with him noted that Kohlhepp frequently viewed pornographic videos while on the job.

Kohlhepp frequented the Waffle House in Roebuck, but his actions caused discomfort among the waitresses, leading the male cook to take over his orders. Among those waitresses was Meagan Leigh McCraw-Coxie, who would eventually become one of his victims.

Despite his disturbing tendencies, Kohlhepp managed to avoid legal trouble for years. That changed on November 3, 2016, when police discovered Kala Brown chained like a dog inside a metal shipping container on his property.

Kohlhepp faced a kidnapping charge for abducting Kala Brown, which ultimately revealed the full extent of his crimes.

On May 26, 2017, Todd Kohlhepp confessed to seven counts of murder, two counts of kidnapping, and one count of criminal sexual assault. He accepted a plea deal that allowed him to avoid the death penalty, resulting in seven consecutive life sentences without the possibility of parole.

At his sentencing, Kohlhepp chillingly confessed to the judge, "There were more victims, but I won't reveal their identities."

After his conviction, many of Kohlhepp's items were sold at auction in August 2020, with the funds going to the victims' families. He is presently serving a life sentence at the Broad River Correctional Institution in Columbia, South Carolina.

Postscript

Kala Brown, the only survivor of Kohlhepp's horrific actions, would not let her captor dictate her identity. When questioned about her message for him, she replied, "He attempted to break me, yet I remain unbroken. He cannot erase who I am... I triumphed."

During the trial, a psychiatrist testified that Kala would need ongoing medication and therapy to manage her enduring trauma. Despite all she went through, Kala discovered strength in her survival. She built her life in Anderson, South Carolina, alongside her partner and their daughter, determined to reclaim her life.

In August 2018, a court awarded Kala $6.3 million in damages from Kohlhepp's estate.

Unfortunately, Kala's life following her traumatic ordeal and rescue has proven to be quite complicated. Her 2019 arrest for domestic violence underscores the enduring psychological impacts that survivors frequently encounter, influencing their relationships and decisions long after the initial trauma has passed.

The disagreement between Kala and her boyfriend, James Devon Moore, illustrates the common and often volatile nature of domestic conflicts. While police reports detail the altercation that led to both of their arrests, this incident hints at more profound issues that Kala may be grappling with after her widely recognized survival experience. A comment from her representative indicates that she was not taking her medication during the incident, highlighting her persistent mental health struggles—an unfortunate yet expected consequence of the trauma she has faced.

The timing of the legal problems is particularly notable, occurring just as Kala was about to receive a financial settlement from her civil suit against Todd Kohlhepp. The court's ruling on distributing Kohlhepp's assets to his victims, including Kala, highlights a broader initiative to pursue justice even though the financial restitution may seem insufficient in light of their suffering.

The families of victims who perished at Superbike Motorsports in 2003 bear their own profound grief and loss, even after receiving compensation. Though financial settlements cannot erase the devastation caused by Kohlhepp's actions, they act as legal recognitions of the lasting effects of his crimes.

Since her rescue, Kala has faced both significant triumphs and challenges. Her remarkable survival against a serial killer highlights her resilience. Yet, her challenges after rescue underscore the complicated reality of life after trauma. Ongoing legal battles, mental health struggles, and personal relationships greatly influence her journey, demonstrating that survival often initiates a lengthy and complex fight.

David Wyatt, Kala's attorney responsible for crafting the proposed payout and securing agreements from the recipients, remarked, "Around $353,000 was set for distribution. However, authorities were finalizing the total value of Kohlhepp's assets."

Furthermore, media reports reveal that the mother of one of Todd Kohlhepp's homicide victims has initiated a lawsuit against Dustan Lawson. Lawson is accused of buying guns and silencers for the murderer, as well as against the store that reportedly sold the firearm used in her son's murder.

From 2012 to 2016, Lawson admitted to purchasing at least 12 firearms and five silencers, claiming falsely that they were for personal use. In 2018, he entered a guilty plea to 36 federal firearm charges.

CHAPTER SIXTEEN

International Serial Killer –
Harold David Haulman III

Erica Gene Shultz was born on November 21, 1994, at Geisinger Medical Center in Danville, Pennsylvania. She was the daughter of Neil A. Shultz from Orangeville and Brenda Shultz Adams from Bloomsburg. At 26, Erica was reported missing on December 4, 2020. Her body was found two days later, on December 6, in the woods of Luzerne County, Pennsylvania.

Erica exuded vibrant energy. She delighted in singing and dancing, lifting the spirits of everyone nearby. Her lively character, genuine smile, and compassionate heart brought joy to others. She valued her achievements, her family, and the life she built. No matter where she was, she made the world a bit brighter.

Medical records reveal that Erica was diagnosed with both diabetes and autism, exhibiting a cognitive level similar to that of a 13- or 14-year-old. Despite these obstacles, she maintained independence in Bloomsburg. She depended on family for transportation to and from work, as she lacked a car and driver's license.

Erica graduated from Columbia-Montour Area Vocational Technical School in 2013. She then continued her education at Luzerne County Community College. Erica gained experience as a sales associate at Weis Markets in Bloomsburg and as a monitor for the Advocacy Alliance of Bloomsburg. Her background included positions at Bon Ton in the Columbia Mall, the Bloomsburg Children's Museum, Danville Children's Day Care Center, and she served as an activities aide at the Emmanuel Center for Nursing in Danville.

Beyond her professional life, Erica actively engaged with the Special Olympics, where she earned a gold medal and acted as a Global Messenger. Additionally, she was a member of the Go MAD Players Drama Club in Bloomsburg.

On December 2, 2020, Erica shared her online conversations with a man named Dave with a friend. He encouraged her to "gather everything and go away with him." In response to her friend's concerns, Erica stated, "I'll see how it unfolds. I plan to meet him in a few days."

This choice triggered a series of horrific incidents. Erica was the last acknowledged victim of a 42-year-old American serial killer, the same person responsible for the brutal slayings of Joseph Lawrence "Jay" Whitehurst in 1999, Ashley Marie Parlier in 2005, and Tianna Ann Phillips in 2018.

Investigators later discovered that Erica frequently used dating apps such as MeetMe, Skout, and Facebook, despite her sister Emily Corbin's ongoing warnings about the risks associated with online interactions.

When Erica didn't show up for work and left her emotional support cat without sufficient food or water, as well as her crucial medications, her family became concerned that something was seriously wrong. On December 6, 2020,

Erica was reported missing, leading authorities to swiftly categorize her disappearance as suspicious.

Just two days later, the search for Erica concluded in heartbreak.

What started as a standard missing persons case soon turned into a chilling investigation that lasted two decades and crossed two continents, ultimately connecting multiple murders to one suspect.

Soon after Erica Shultz went missing, her sister voiced her worries on Facebook, saying, "Erica is 5'4", weighs 220 pounds, has blond hair and blue eyes. She has diabetes and is without her medication. She does not drive and does not possess a driver's license. She would never leave without informing us, nor would she abandon Luna, her emotional support cat. Our family is offering a reward for any information about her location."

Authorities quickly identified Harold David Haulman III as a person of interest. A search warrant showed that his cell phone was next to Erica's in her apartment on December 4, 2020. Both phones traveled together along Interstate 80 until Erica's phone ceased transmitting.

The final signal from Erica's phone was detected in Pennsylvania in the early hours of December 6, after which it was either switched off or destroyed.

Investigators tracked Haulman's movements and discovered that, during the early hours of December 6, he brought Erica to a remote wooded area between I-80 and I-81 in Butler Township.

There, he forced her out of the vehicle, physically assaulted her, and bludgeoned her with a mallet-like hammer. When she remained alive, he slashed her throat and stabbed her twelve times, ensuring her death.

What came next was even more unsettling. Haulman took photographs of Erica's lifeless body and disturbingly shared these images with his wife, who opted not to inform the authorities about the crime.

Following the murder, Haulman disposed of his bloody clothes and drove to the nearby Susquehanna River in Sunbury, where he carelessly tossed the weapons into the water, hurling both the hammer and knife away.

On December 23, 2020, FBI agents interviewed Haulman regarding Erica's disappearance. Still, they did not have sufficient evidence to arrest in the absence of a body.

Amid mounting pressure, Haulman resorted to extreme measures. The next day, he severed all communications and vanished. On December 26, officials tracking a GPS device discreetly affixed to his van located him near Duncannon, Pennsylvania.

In a frantic effort to evade justice, he attempted to take his own life by cutting his arm with a box cutter next to some railroad tracks.

A railroad worker subsequently reported to Norfolk Southern Railway police, "Haulman injured his arm and said, 'I want to end my life. I must atone for my sins.'"

The worker promptly transported Haulman to Geisinger Holy Spirit Hospital in Camp Hill, Pennsylvania.

After he received medical treatment, FBI agents questioned him again. During this interrogation, he ultimately confessed to the brutal murder of Erica Shultz.

Yet, his confession marked only the start. As investigators probed further into his past, they discovered a disturbing pattern of violence, connecting Haulman to numerous murders spanning two continents. This unveiled a longstanding legacy of death that had been hidden for decades.

On December 27, 2020, Harold David Haulman III was apprehended in Butler Township, Pennsylvania, on allegations of killing Erica G. Shultz. He was subsequently processed into the Luzerne County Jail, where he would await his trial.

Details about Haulman's early life are limited. Born in Michigan on November 28, 1978, he moved to Ramstein-Miesenbach, Germany, in the mid-1990s when his father took a job as a civilian technician at Ramstein Air Base.

In the late 1990s, Haulman encountered a substantial conflict with his father. After their disagreement, his father left the air base, moved away from Germany, and relocated to Turkey. During his father's absence, Haulman stayed at his girlfriend's house. However, when their relationship concluded in early 1999, he needed to gather his things and find a new place to stay.

Struggling with homelessness, Haulman lived for months in the woods located between the city and the air base. He built a makeshift shelter for rest and depended on irregular jobs and occasional thefts to get by.

On June 5, 1999, Haulman faced charges of petty theft. During questioning, he surprised investigators by admitting to the murder of 21-year-old Joseph Lawrence "Jay" Whitehurst, the son of an Air Force colonel, committed on May 30, 1999.

Haulman acknowledged that he and Whitehurst had frequented local bars in Ramstein-Miesenbach on several occasions. On May 29, they spent hours enjoying drinks together, and the next day, they went to a nearby park to set up a campfire. As the evening went on and the drinks continued to flow, a drunken Whitehurst started running around and dancing with enthusiasm. In response to this, Haulman suddenly struck him on the head with a club.

Whitehurst succumbed to his head injury, and Haulman buried his body beneath leaves. His remains were discovered three days later near the air base.

Haulman was later charged with manslaughter. During his trial, he made a chilling statement to the court: "I murdered because I wanted to see what it was like to kill someone." He paused, smiled, then added, "Killing people was a pleasure that made me feel a way that no drug ever could."

His attorneys sought a forensic psychiatric evaluation, which concluded he was sane despite early signs of schizophrenia.

In late 1999, Haulman confessed to all charges that could have resulted in a maximum ten-year prison term—the harshest penalty for juvenile offenders in Germany. However, the judges opted for a more lenient sentence, placing him in a German reform school for six years. He was paroled after three years and subsequently returned to the United States.

After returning, Haulman moved to Battle Creek, Michigan, where some relatives lived. He promptly secured housing and started working as a truck driver. However, in 2009, he departed Battle Creek and traveled across the country, residing in Pennsylvania, California, Illinois, and Maryland until 2020.

In 2010, Haulman married Anne. Still, their relationship ended in 2013 when she refused to participate in his brutal bondage fantasies. Following their split, he pursued relationships with multiple women he met through online dating sites.

In an unexpected turn of events in May 2021, Haulman admitted to a murder that took place in 2018.

Twenty-five-year-old Tianna Ann Phillips was last seen on June 13, 2018, following a dispute with her boyfriend. Around 11:00 p.m., she departed from a friend's residence on the 400 block of East 9th Street in Berwick, Pennsylvania. At that time, Tianna was unemployed and did not possess a driver's license; notably, she left her phone behind. Before her disappearance, she had told her friend that a man named Dave, whom she had met online, was en route to pick her up.

She vanished without a trace.

Even though she was in a relationship, Tianna sometimes met with a man named Dave. Investigators eventually uncovered that Haulman was the enigmatic Dave who intended to meet her that evening.

According to his ex-wife, Anne Frances Haulman, she knew that her husband was not only seeing other women but was also capable of murder. She recalled that after Phillips's boyfriend confronted Haulman about the affair, he became enraged, threatening to kill either Phillips or her boyfriend.

Anne further revealed that months after Tianna's disappearance, Haulman took her to the crime scene to help remove evidence. She stated, "He took some black trash bags and filled them with clothing and some parts of Phillips' body. He put the bags in some dumpsters behind the AMC Theaters in Scott Township, Pennsylvania."

In May 2021, authorities charged Harold David Haulman III with murdering Erica Shultz, even though her remains were never recovered. Haulman subsequently confessed to the crime, providing investigators with unsettling details.

He told police, "I picked up Shultz and took her to a wooded area near Hobbie Road, stabbed her multiple times, and took photographs of the corpse."

A few days later, Haulman confessed to another murder: the June 12, 2005, death of 21-year-old Ashley Marie Parlier in Battle Creek, Michigan. Family members shared that Parlier had left home after an argument with her parents and never returned. Upon discovering her pregnancy, her parents expressed their concerns and urged her to seek prenatal care, which prompted her departure.

Ashley had graduated from Battle Creek Central High School and worked at a Taco Bell on Capital Avenue Northeast, saving money for a car. After her disappearance, no activity was connected to her Social Security number.

She lacked a driver's license, a vehicle or access to one, a cellphone, and credit cards; however, she had about $700 in cash. Investigators received tips that she could be camping near Houghton Lake, but none were verified.

Shy and reserved with only a small circle of close friends, Ashley vanished under mysterious circumstances. Authorities looked into her ex-boyfriend, whom they suspect might be the father of her unborn child. Still, they did not exclude him as a potential suspect. While her father passed a polygraph test, her mother, who chose not to participate in one, had since passed away.

Haulman subsequently gave a chilling account of Ashley's murder.

"On the day Ashley was murdered, I drove her to a secluded spot in Newton Township, just south of Battle Creek. After a brief argument, I struck her on the head with a large log.

"Two months after abandoning her body in the woods, I came back to check if it had been found. Just a skeleton was left."

After his confession, Haulman was extradited to Michigan to face murder charges related to Ashley. In July 2021, he was officially indicted in her case.

During police interviews, Haulman requested the combination of the cases involving Shultz, Phillips, and Parlier, stating he was not interested in going to trial. To avoid the death penalty, he pleaded guilty to the murders of Erica Shultz and Cynthia Phillips in September 2021.

When Haulman appeared before Judge Michael T. Vough of Luzerne County to enter his guilty pleas, the judge showed his contempt openly.

"Having spent 30 years in this courthouse, I thought I had witnessed everything. Then you came along, bringing a new form of malice. You are truly evil."

Judge Vough imposed two consecutive life sentences without parole on Harold David Haulman. Throughout the sentencing, Haulman was composed and showed no remorse for his actions, choosing not to address the court. Afterward, he was moved to Calhoun County, Michigan, to face trial for the murder of Ashley Marie Parlier.

Haulman's trial for the murder of Ashley Parlier began on December 14, 2022, and he entered a guilty plea on February 1, 2023. Nicole Campen, Ashley's sister, felt this plea gave her much-needed clarity. "Hearing that it was a multiple-victim case was overwhelming, especially since it had dragged on for years... but it's comforting to finally connect a face to what occurred. I don't recall seeing Haulman when my sister went missing, yet something about him resonates with me."

Attempting to maintain her composure, she added, "Ashley had the mental capacity of a 12- to 14-year-old. She could be easily manipulated. He had a type and was taking advantage of women who didn't know any better. Ashley wasn't aware of such evil."

Campen stopped to dry her tears. "I'm thrilled that we finally have answers, and I'm glad that these other families got theirs without enduring a wait of 10, 15, or even 16 years."

Haulman was sentenced to 60 years in prison, with the possibility of parole after 37 years and six months.

Similar to numerous serial killers, Haulman displayed no apparent motive or red flags. Following the murders, he exhibited no feelings of remorse.

What prompted him to choose these women? They exhibited compassion, trust, and a willingness to see the best in others—traits that someone like Haulman would seek to exploit. At this point, he has yet to reveal his true motivations for the murders.

Harold David Haulman III is incarcerated at the Calhoun County Correctional Facility in Battle Creek, Michigan. This facility employs a Direct Supervision model, which involves correctional officers stationed within the inmate living areas. It has a rated capacity of 630 inmates and operates with a staffing of about 120 members. The local inmate population typically fluctuates between 275 and 325 individuals. To help cover expenses and generate income, the facility leases extra beds to other municipalities, counties, and the federal government.

In the wake of Erica Shultz's untimely death, Special Olympics Pennsylvania issued a touching statement: "We at Special Olympics Pennsylvania are deeply saddened by the news of Erica Shultz's tragic circumstances. We hope her involvement with our organization brought her joy, pride in her accomplishments, and many friendships. Our heartfelt condolences and prayers are with her family, friends, and fellow athletes during this difficult time."

CHAPTER SEVENTEEN

Charlottesville Bogeyman – Jesse L. Matthew Jr.

On October 17, 2009, Morgan Dana Harrington, a 20-year-old student from Virginia Tech, attended a Metallica concert at the University of Virginia's John Paul Jones Arena with three friends.

During the opening act, Morgan left her friends to visit the restroom. After 20 minutes had gone by without her return, one friend called her cell phone at 8:48 p.m. Morgan, born on July 24, 1989, to Dan and Gil Harrington, replied, "I'm locked out of the arena due to the 'no re-entry' policy, but I'll arrange for my ride home, so don't worry."

That was the final instance in which anyone interacted with her.

Witnesses reported that two of Morgan's friends saw her alone and likely injured around 9:30 p.m. hitchhiking on Copley Bridge. She looked disoriented, had a facial injury with visible bleeding, and seemed oblivious to three strangers lurking in the nearby shadows. Despite several witnesses acknowledging her distress, no one assisted her.

Following her disappearance, investigators found Morgan's cell phone—battery taken out—and her purse, which held her identification, left behind in the RV lot at the University of Virginia Athletic Field.

Several concerning questions remain. Why did no one help Morgan when she was hurt? How could a modern venue with advanced video surveillance not record any footage of her inside or outside the arena?

A surprising question emerged at that time: Could Morgan's 2009 disappearance be resolved five years later, just like the murder of Hannah Elizabeth Graham, which ultimately resulted in Jesse L. Matthew Jr.'s arrest?

On January 26, 2010, a farmer in Albemarle County, Virginia, discovered Morgan Harrington's remains while inspecting his fences on an abandoned 742-acre farm. This isolated land was ten miles from the concert venue where she had vanished and over a mile from the nearest road.

Virginia police stated, "The individual who killed Morgan and left her body on a remote farm was aware of the significant 'obstacles' to reach that location."

During a press conference, Virginia State Police Lieutenant Joe Rader called on local residents to share any information about people who knew the pathways and terrain around Anchorage Farm, where Morgan's body was found.

Investigators suspected that those responsible for Morgan's murder might possess relevant expertise. "Residents are familiar with the area and its history," Rader noted. "They can recognize regular visitors to the neighborhood; even if they are not fully aware, they may have vital information. We urge anyone with knowledge to reach out to us."

Rader highlighted the strategic importance of the crime scene, aiming to elicit a response from the community. He noted that accessing the area where Morgan's remains were discovered presented unique challenges—obstacles that a person unfamiliar with the location would probably find difficult to navigate.

Rader pointed out that choosing that specific location differed from selecting a public highway or its shoulder. "That area presents a considerable risk unless you know it well," he stated.

Authorities shared a few details about Morgan's death. However, her parents, both medical professionals, confirmed that she was murdered.

Morgan's mother, Gil Harrington, an oncology nurse, described the horrific violence her daughter had faced. "He opts to kill with savagery, breaking her bones before ultimately taking her life. Morgan's remains displayed severe injuries."

The family also asserted that Morgan had been raped and suspected that her killer was familiar with the area.

While they did not disclose which of Morgan's bones were broken, pending the official autopsy report, they were confident that the assailant was a talented criminal, possibly a convicted sex offender.

"This isn't his first offense," Gil Harrington stated emphatically. "His actions have deteriorated notably. A monster walks among us. The man responsible for my daughter's death is violent, sadistic, and incredibly dangerous."

Morgan's father, Dan Harrington, reflected on the day that changed everything. "Morgan had come to visit us for the weekend, which was typical, and she was thrilled about attending the Metallica concert. Then, on Sunday morning around 11:00, I got a call from the University of Virginia police. They told me they had found Morgan's purse in a parking lot. At that moment, I realized something horrific had occurred. And Morgan, she was gone."

As tears streamed down her face, her mother stated, "Morgan brought immense joy, you know? We had finally reached a point where our relationship with her felt like that of adults. It was a thrilling and deeply satisfying time."

On January 31, a haunting blog post was published on a site devoted to Morgan.

Dan Harrington asked, "How could anyone have erased so much of what Morgan was, leaving behind only a disordered pile of bones? Who could have imagined I would see every image of Morgan's life from the first faint shadows on her fetal ultrasound to the deep hollows in her skull? It's a horror to witness this conclusion."

Morgan's murder garnered significant national attention, leading the Virginia General Assembly to commemorate the deceased student with a special resolution.

Crimestoppers provided a $100,000 reward for tips that could lead to an arrest. At the same time, Metallica, the band Morgan was so excited to see that evening, added another $50,000. They also took part in the hunt for her murderer. In a public service announcement, Metallica's lead vocalist, James Hetfield, earnestly called on the community for help.

"If you know the person in this sketch or have information about this case, please reach out to your local police or share your info online," Hetfield urged. "Keep in mind that every detail, even if it seems trivial, could be the key element that investigators require to resolve the case."

Morgan's murder sparked concern among her family and the community about a possible serial killer in Virginia. Her parents, Dan and Gil Harrington, worked relentlessly to promote enhanced campus safety, engaging in events like the University of Virginia's annual "Take Back the Night" rally. They urged university authorities to implement stronger protections for students.

Morgan was often described as vibrant and loving. As a dedicated music enthusiast and a passionate advocate for children's rights, she was a junior at Virginia Tech, gearing up for a career in education.

In a heartfelt message, Morgan's parents shared a family photograph and conveyed their gratitude.

"Gil and I genuinely appreciate each of you for your support throughout this challenging journey. The extraordinary love and encouragement you have shown our family have genuinely humbled us. We are grateful for your kindness, compassion, and prayers, which have been crucial to our resilience."

Lindsay Crisp, a long-time friend of Morgan from elementary school, felt profoundly impacted. She happened to be in Europe when Morgan went missing and returned home to the heartbreaking news.

"My parents led me to the den and said, 'We need to inform you that Morgan is gone. She has been missing for ten days.' At that moment, everything felt completely hopeless. I dashed upstairs and cried," she shared with the police.

The inquiry then took an unexpected direction.

The Pantera T-shirt worn by Morgan Harrington on the night of her disappearance was found near an apartment complex about a mile and a half from the arena where she had last been seen. A breakthrough happened in April 2010 when forensic tests showed that the DNA on the shirt matched that of 32-year-old Jesse L. Matthew Jr.

Investigators quickly learned that Matthew was operating a taxi in Charlottesville the night Morgan went missing. DMV records showed he received a permit to drive a cab in the region in 2007. However, what police would later find out was much more troubling: Matthew was a predator concealed in plain sight, indulging in a personal crime spree without feeling any guilt.

On Saturday, September 13, 2014, 18-year-old Hannah Elizabeth Graham vanished from the University of Virginia. A second-year student known for her vibrant personality, athletic prowess, and creativity, she left a lasting impression on everyone she met.

Hannah was last seen in the early morning near Charlottesville's Downtown Mall. Her last message to friends, sent at 1:20 a.m., indicated that she was lost while trying to find a party. Some friends verified that she had attended an off-campus gathering earlier that evening but did not return home afterward.

Surveillance footage and witness accounts painted a troubling picture. On that evening, Hannah was seen at Tempo Restaurant in Alexandria, Virginia, accompanied by Jesse L. Matthew Jr. One witness noted that Matthew had his arm around Hannah, who appeared to be quite intoxicated. Another observer commented that the man with her looked unwelcoming.

Hannah was last seen near a 1998 orange Chrysler Sebring owned by Jesse L. Matthew. A witness claimed she said, "I'm not getting in that car with you."

In an instant, she vanished without a trace.

Five weeks later, the somber quest for answers concluded with the discovery of Hannah's remains on a deserted property in Albemarle County. The connection between Morgan Harrington and Hannah Graham became unmistakable. What started as two distinct tragedies transformed into a haunting realization—one that exposed the unsettling truth of a predator who had eluded detection for years.

Hannah Graham was born in Reading, England, to Sue and John Graham on February 25, 1996. At the age of five, she relocated to Virginia with her parents.

Her friend, Leila Nasser, said, "She's brilliant, musically gifted, with a dry sense of humor. She genuinely comprehends herself. A real go-getter. She exudes confidence and resolve."

"Hannah possessed a sharp wit and was far more intelligent than any coach on the field," stated her high school coach, Craig Maniglia.

Hannah attended West Potomac High School in Northern Virginia. Those close to her characterized her as a responsible and resilient young woman. She excelled in her studies, had a deep passion for skiing, loved Starburst candy, and played the alto saxophone.

"Hannah consistently showed outstanding commitment in her endeavors and adhered strictly to the rules," stated Stephen Rice, the band director at West Potomac. "She isn't the kind of student who would take an impulsive road trip and vanish."

On September 19, local authorities identified a man from surveillance footage who left a bar with Hannah. They classified him as a "person of interest" and suspected she may have entered a vehicle with him.

The individual in question was Jesse L. Matthew Jr.

Authorities subsequently examined Matthew's car and apartment but initially chose not to arrest him.

On September 20, 2014, more than 1,000 volunteers participated in the most extensive search operation in Virginia's history in Charlottesville. The substantial turnout necessitated detailed organization, with search teams scheduled to start at staggered times for maximum city coverage. Even after covering 85 percent of Charlottesville, Hannah was still missing. Nevertheless, search coordinator Mark Eggeman remained hopeful, asserting, "The effort yielded more leads, and in the coming days, we will focus our search further."

During a news conference, Hannah's father, John Graham, thanked the volunteers for their commitment while appealing to the public for more assistance. "Who has seen Hannah?" he implored. "Someone must know what happened to her."

On September 22, police searched Matthew's apartment a second time, confiscating clothing without disclosing how it related to the case. Authorities characterized the searches as a significant step forward in the investigation. They introduced a $100,000 reward for any information leading to Hannah's whereabouts.

On September 21, an arrest warrant was issued for Jesse L. Matthew Jr., accusing him of reckless driving.

On September 23, Police Chief Timothy Longo revealed that Matthew faced abduction charges aimed at violating Hannah Graham's chastity.

At a joint press conference with the FBI on September 24, Chief Longo announced that Matthew had been apprehended in a secluded part of Galveston County, Texas, after being recognized by a woman at a beach.

As of September 29, 2014, forensic reports indicated that evidence from the investigation into Morgan Harrington's 2009 murder corresponded with evidence linked to Matthew. Additionally, sources connected to the Graham investigation revealed that Morgan had contacted Matthew the night she went missing.

On October 18, 2014, search teams from the Chesterfield County Sheriff's Office discovered human remains at an abandoned site in Albemarle County. During a press conference that day, Chief Longo remarked, "The remains have not yet been definitively identified as Hannah Graham." The remains were later sent to the Chief Medical Examiner's office in Richmond, which confirmed on October 24 that they belonged to Hannah Graham. On the same day, Graham's parents visited the location where their daughter was found.

On November 14, 2014, Matthew entered a not guilty plea to the charges against him. Just four days afterward, on November 18, authorities announced that they had determined the cause of death. Still, they kept the details confidential at the request of law enforcement. Later that same day, the Albemarle County Police Department disclosed that the cause of death was categorized as a homicide with an "undetermined etiology."

On February 10, 2015, Denise Lunsford, the Commonwealth's Attorney for Albemarle County, announced that Matthew had been indicted for the first-degree murder of Hannah Graham, in addition to facing abduction charges. Eight days later, on February 18, Matthew appeared in court, where Judge Cheryl Higgins of the Albemarle County Circuit scheduled the jury trial on June 29.

On May 5, 2015, prosecutors upgraded Matthew's charges to capital murder, which could lead to the death penalty if he was convicted. The trial was set to begin on July 5, 2016.

During the trial, Morgan Harrington's father, Dan Harrington, described his daughter as "beautiful, intelligent, and talented."

In a heartfelt statement, he conveyed the deep sorrow his family has experienced since her murder, stating, "Matthew took Morgan from us and stole our joy. He robbed my daughter of her future, her opportunities to learn, marry, become a parent, and age gracefully. Jesse Matthew took our daughter's life. How can this be real? The brutal and deliberate nature of Morgan's murder haunts us daily, and it will persist until we are reunited with her." Struggling with his emotions, he asked, "How could he commit such an act? What was his motive? The surveillance footage of Matthew with our daughter will be etched in our family's memory forever."

On February 29, 2016, prosecutors announced that Matthew intended to plead guilty. Two days later, on March 2, 2016, Matthew formally admitted to his crimes, detailing how he snapped the bones of both Morgan Harrington and Hannah Graham before discarding their bodies.

According to the plea agreement, Matthew forfeited his right to appeal and was therefore ineligible for senior release. That same day, newly surfaced evidence revealed that Matthew's cell phone had registered a signal near the location where Morgan Harrington's remains were found.

Following his guilty plea to the 2009 murder of Morgan Harrington and the 2014 murder of Hannah Graham, a judge sentenced Matthew to four consecutive life sentences.

Soon after, Matthew unexpectedly entered an "Alford" plea, which allows a defendant to assert their innocence while recognizing that the prosecution's evidence could lead to a conviction. Ultimately, he was found guilty on all counts.

In March 2016, Matthew was transferred from Red Onion State Prison in Wise County, Virginia, to Sussex I State Prison in Waverly, Virginia. This facility is designated as a level-five institution, just under maximum security. It includes a "Secure Care Unit" for inmates requiring medical care, such as chemotherapy. The families of Morgan Harrington and Hannah Graham were notified of his transfer. As of this writing, he is still alive.

Jesse L. Matthew Jr. grew up on the outskirts of Charlottesville with a close circle of four friends. In his junior years, he earned the nickname "LJ." As a child, he endured bullying due to his family's financial difficulties, a speech impediment, and pronounced learning disabilities. His father, battling alcoholism, was often absent, occasionally dragging him into adventures with different mistresses. When Matthew turned 16, his parents divorced.

Matthew discovered peace through sports, excelling in football and wrestling. He earned MVP honors in high school and captured a state wrestling championship during his senior year in 2000. His exceptional athletic skills earned him a full football scholarship to Liberty University in Lynchburg, Virginia.

During his time at Liberty University, Matthew began dating Diana, who later confided in him about her trust issues stemming from his childhood sexual abuse. His sister, Latasha Matthew, described him as a devoted figure in her son's life, frequently taking him fishing, hiking, and to the beach. In a touching letter, she reminisced about the time Matthew carried her for over a mile to get help after she injured her foot on broken glass. She highlighted his financial assistance, remarking, "I still can't comprehend how someone so loving, generous, and outgoing could commit such acts. I am left speechless."

Gil Harrington, Morgan's mother, shared how Albemarle County Commonwealth's Attorney Robert Tracci informed her of Matthew's stage four colon cancer diagnosis and treatment options. Reflecting on this situation, she said, "Whatever justice may signify, perhaps this initiates the next chapter of his justice. Maybe this is his karma. Although I feel uneasy, I remain hopeful for what lies ahead." Struggling with her emotions, she added, "Our daughters didn't ascend to heaven on a pink cloud. They suffered, cried, and bled. They were not shown any mercy."

Gil Harrington has committed herself to Help Save the Next Girl, a nonprofit she founded in memory of her daughter. The organization aims to educate young women about the dangers posed by predatory individuals.

Following the discovery of Hannah Graham's remains, students at the University of Virginia created a memorial to honor her. In 2021, they launched the Hannah E. Graham Memorial Scholarship to recognize her commitment to and involvement in softball leagues across Northern Virginia.

CHAPTER EIGHTEEN

University Students Rapist – Brian Lee Golsby

On February 8, 2017, 21-year-old Reagan Delaney Tokes, a student from Ohio State University, had just finished her shift at Bodega, a bar and restaurant in downtown Columbus, Ohio. Horrifically, as she made her way to her car, she encountered a brutal and persistent assailant.

Brian Lee Golsby walked through downtown Columbus that evening, unbeknownst to Reagan, looking for a victim. GPS data later showed him circling the OSU campus and North High Street before catching a Central Ohio Transit Authority bus downtown. He lingered near the Bodega restaurant and a bar in the Columbus Short North area for almost an hour, biding his time for the ideal moment to act.

At 9:45 p.m., Golsby stepped out from the shadows and attacked Reagan. He brandished a gun to threaten her, compelling her to get into her vehicle while taking her captive. To ease her anxiety, he stated that his only demand was money and assured her that he would let her go afterward.

However, that statement was not accurate.

Golsby advised Reagan to investigate two ATMs for cash. At 10:02 p.m., they first visited Chase Bank but were unable to withdraw $500. At 10:14 p.m., they attempted Huntington Bank, but once more, they could not access any funds.

At approximately 10:18 p.m., Golsby led Reagan to an alley, where they stayed for twenty minutes. During this time, he robbed and sexually assaulted her on two occasions.

A subsequent rape kit confirmed that he had assaulted her.

Following the assault, Golsby forced Reagan to go back to the Chase Bank ATM, where she withdrew $60 for him. He then ordered her to stop at two gas stations: a Sunoco at 11:12 p.m. and a Turkey Hill at 11:41 p.m. in continued attempts to obtain cash, but neither attempt was successful.

Golsby understood that Reagan could identify him and made a firm decision that she must die. During subsequent police questioning, he confessed that she begged for her life, stating, "All I want is to live."

Confronted with the choice between defiance or compliance for her safety, Reagan opted to comply. Following Golsby's orders, she drove to Scioto Grove Metro Park in Grove City, Ohio, where he instructed her to undress, including taking off her shoes.

After sexually assaulting her again shortly before midnight, he led her into a field and, without hesitation, executed her with two gunshots from a handgun—one to the back of her head and the other to the left side of her face.

Following the tragic crime, Golsby took Reagan's silver Acura TL to his girlfriend's house. At 1:45 a.m., they visited a McDonald's, acting as if everything was normal. Golsby even handed his girlfriend Reagan's black Kate Spade purse and a white wallet, both of which he had stolen from the victim.

He tossed the gun and shell casings into a sewer to eliminate evidence, but he couldn't ignite Reagan's car.

Before her shift ended, Reagan had texted her father, Toby Tokes, earlier in the evening to let him know she would call later. When the call didn't happen, her parents became increasingly worried. They anxiously tried to reach her throughout the night through messages and calls, but Reagan never replied.

On February 9, 2017, Lisa became worried when Reagan did not return home and missed class the next day without a word. As a result, she contacted the police to report her daughter missing.

Lisa stated, "I quickly contacted the police but could not file a missing person report since I wasn't the last person who saw her. Her coworkers at the restaurant had to handle that."

Reagan's father, Toby, told the police, "I started feeling uneasy around ten o'clock, suspecting something was wrong... I tried to contact her for four hours that night. Her phone went unresponsive around 2:00 a.m. Reagan didn't have any enemies or risky behaviors that could have put her in danger. We were puzzled."

He conveyed deep feelings, stating, "I always felt fortunate that she took the time to talk with me daily. Therefore, it was surprising when Reagan stopped answering my calls or returning to her apartment after work."

The day after Reagan's murder, a passerby discovered her lifeless body at Scioto Grove Metro Park and notified the authorities. Detectives identified her through a tattoo and a necklace, and her uncle, who was nearby, ultimately confirmed her identity.

At trial, a forensic pathologist testified that two bullets were recovered from Reagan's head during an autopsy. The pathologist said, "The gunshot wounds she had suffered were fired at close range, once to the back of her head and the other through the left side of her face."

His report was supported by another forensic pathologist's testimony that her DNA was inside the barrel of the gun. A rape kit confirmed she had been brutally raped and murdered. The forensic team was able to retrieve a semen sample from her body.

Following the report of Reagan's missing car, the police believed that finding it could help in identifying her killer. Detective Rick Forney from the Grove City Police Department later stated, "Given that the car was absent from both the crime scene and its vicinity, we were quite confident that the suspect had driven her vehicle away."

The detectives got a lead when a digital reader on a commercial vehicle recorded the front license plate of Reagan's car after Golsby left it behind. This data was logged into a database that law enforcement accessed later.

Using that information, detectives found the car on Columbus's southeast side, approximately ten miles from Scioto Grove Metro Park. The suspect had tried to set the vehicle on fire but failed. At the scene, detectives uncovered cigarette butts and a gas can linked to Golsby's DNA.

Further investigations revealed that a similar gas can was purchased on the night of Reagan's murder. While executing a search warrant at the gas can seller's store, police recovered surveillance footage of Golsby making the purchase.

Golsby was already a registered sex offender, and his DNA was in the system. He had a long history of violent crimes dating back to his youth and an extensive juvenile record. In 2010, after becoming an adult, he abducted a pregnant woman and her 2-year-old son at knifepoint.

He threatened both their lives before orally raping the woman in front of her child. Golsby then forced the woman to take him to her home, where he robbed her, brutally raped her again, and stole some of her belongings.

In the short time that Golsby had been out of jail, he violated parole multiple times. Between January 24 and February 7, he committed several robberies and physical assaults. Despite wearing a GPS tracking device, he was not actively monitored. As a result, he was able to abduct, rape, and murder Reagan Tokes.

Brian Golsby's circumstances changed when law enforcement analyzed his recent whereabouts. The GPS ankle monitor indicated that he had visited several crucial locations associated with Reagan Tokes, including her car's parking site, the ATMs for cash withdrawals, and Scioto Grove Metro Park.

On February 11, 2017, around 4:00 a.m., SWAT officers arrested Golsby without incident. He was booked and subsequently interrogated by Detective Rick Forney. During this questioning, Golsby admitted to coercing Reagan into driving to various ATMs to withdraw money and later forcing her to Scioto Grove Metro Park.

While describing the incident, Golsby told Detective Forney, "Upon arriving at the park, I instructed Reagan to exit the car and remove her clothing, after which I departed." At first, he denied any sexual engagement with Reagan or having a firearm. However, the detectives employed a tactical method, proposing that he might have had an accomplice in the crime.

Golsby took the bait. He fabricated a story about a man named "T.J.," claiming that T.J. had demanded money from him and threatened to harm his children if he did not comply. Golsby alleged that T.J. forced him to assault Reagan at gunpoint. "I wanted just to run and call the cops, for real. I could have, but at the same time, I didn't want to put my babies in jeopardy," he told Detective Forney. He further claimed that at the park, T.J. forced Reagan to strip before mercilessly shooting her in the head.

Detectives, recognizing the falsehoods in his story, played along. Soon after, police formally charged Golsby with Reagan's murder. A rape kit confirmed his DNA inside her body, and forensic analysis revealed gunshot residue on his clothing. GPS data from his ankle monitor placed him precisely at the location of Reagan's abduction on February 8.

In court, Golsby faced convictions for aggravated murder, kidnapping, and rape, along with seven counts of aggravated robbery and two counts of tampering with evidence. Despite the serious nature of these offenses, the jury was unable to reach a unanimous decision on sentencing. Consequently, the judge imposed a life sentence without the possibility of parole.

During his time in prison, Golsby confessed to the murder of Reagan Tokes. This case garnered significant media attention, ranking among the top ten news stories in Central Ohio in 2017, and was also featured on national and federal news broadcasts.

Reagan's tragic death ignited conversations about criminal justice reform in Ohio. In 2018, Governor John Kasich introduced parts of the Reagan Tokes Act to improve the state's parole and sentencing systems.

The Reagan Tokes Act highlighted four essential aspects of Ohio's criminal justice system aimed at boosting public safety and enhancing supervision of violent offenders:

1. Indeterminate Sentencing for Certain Felonies: The law stipulates indeterminate sentencing for first- and second-degree felonies and third-degree violent felonies. This adjustment grants judges greater flexibility in determining suitable sentences for offenders.

2. Reentry Program for Violent Offenders: The Ohio Department of Rehabilitation and Correction (DRC) needs to develop a program specifically tailored for violent and high-risk felons who are ineligible for current reentry options like Alvis House or Oriana House.

3. Parole Officer Supervision: The law requires the DRC to establish explicit guidelines for parole officers, detailing the minimum supervision hours needed for each parolee. This initiative aims to ensure that parolees receive proper oversight and that any potential violations are promptly addressed.

4. Enhanced GPS Monitoring Policy: New legislation mandates establishing a system for tracking offenders via GPS. This system will allow authorities to track parolees' movements and detect suspicious activities based on location.

State Representative Kristin Boggs highlighted the significance of this legislation, asserting, "Reagan's case is a tragedy, and it's regrettable that it takes such a grievous incident to motivate the crucial changes necessary to safeguard our communities. I aspire that the Reagan Tokes Act not only addresses the shortcomings in our criminal justice system but also lays the groundwork for continuous assessment and improvement of our policies to avert another senseless tragedy."

The family of Reagan Tokes has initiated legal action against the Ohio Department of Rehabilitation and Correction (ODRC) and NISRE Inc., the facility housing Brian Golsby, claiming their negligence resulted in their daughter's murder.

In September 2018, Judge Patrick McGrath dismissed the lawsuit against the ODRC, concluding that the agency had no legal duty to protect Reagan Tokes. He stated, "The ODRC was not required to stop Golsby from harming Reagan Tokes since there existed no special relationship with her."

The lawsuit revealed significant shortcomings in the GPS monitoring system. Although Golsby was mandated to wear an ankle monitor, the system failed to alert parole officers about curfew violations or geographical restrictions. Court documents indicated that Golsby had a prior history of violent crimes in the German Village area leading up to Reagan's murder, with numerous incidents occurring between 10:00 p.m. and 6:00 a.m., the hours he was required to remain at his assigned residence according to curfew regulations. These violations of the curfew went unreported to parole officers, allowing Golsby to continue his criminal activities without intervention.

The trial jury for Brian Golsby was chosen on February 23, 2018, and hearings commenced on March 5, 2018, presided over by Judge Mark Serrott.

Defense lawyers sought a venue change because of extensive media coverage, but Judge Mark Serrott rejected the request.

In his opening statement, Franklin County District Attorney Ron O'Brien described Reagan's horror: "Reagan Tokes experienced a night of terror. She was a psychology major who never reached graduation because she was executed at point-blank range by Golsby's handgun."

During the trial, jurors visited significant sites linked to the case, such as Bodega, where Reagan had been earlier that evening, and Scioto Grove Metro Park, where her body was found. They also examined crime scene photographs and heard testimony from the witness who found Reagan's body.

Three of Reagan's roommates testified about the night she vanished. Golsby's ex-girlfriend, who received Reagan's purse from him, an agent from the Ohio Bureau of Criminal Investigation, and a representative from the Adult Parole Authority also provided testimony.

On the last day of the trial, forensic specialists provided key evidence indicating that Golsby's sperm was present in Reagan's body, along with her DNA being found on the barrel of the murder weapon that was found during an investigation.

The trial and resulting legislation highlight the systemic failures that led to Reagan's tragic murder and the pressing necessity for ongoing reforms in Ohio's criminal justice system.

On March 13, 2018, Reagan Tokes would have celebrated her 23rd birthday; on that same day, Brian Lee Golsby was found guilty on all counts. During sentencing, the jury had mixed opinions: eight jurors favored the death penalty, while four preferred life in prison. As the jury could not come to a unanimous decision, the ultimate sentencing choice was assigned to Judge Mark Serrott.

On March 21, 2018, Judge Serrott sentenced Golsby to life imprisonment without the chance of parole. Following his sentencing, he confessed to six more robberies that had occurred in the days before Reagan's murder.

Remembering Reagan Delaney Tokes

Reagan was born on March 13, 1995, in Edgewood, Kentucky, to Toby Tokes and Lisa McCrary-Tokes. She grew up with her younger sister, Makenzie, in Maumee, Ohio, specifically in Monclova Township. Growing up in a Christian household, Reagan cultivated a strong compassion and a desire to help those in need.

Dedicated to her studies, she graduated from Anthony Wayne High School with a 4.5 GPA. She thrived as a varsity athlete in lacrosse and tennis. When she commenced her journey at Ohio State University, her family relocated to Florida, allowing Reagan to embark on her new chapter in Ohio independently. She resided off campus with her four friends: Jackie, Madison, Kirsten, and Stephanie.

Reagan began her college path as a pre-med student but eventually switched to psychology, intending to work at the Cleveland Clinic after graduation. Just days before her untimely death in early February 2017, she shared her enthusiasm on social media about selecting a frame for her diploma.

Reagan's funeral took place on February 15, 2017, at the Maumee United Methodist Church, with her burial at Fort Meigs Cemetery in Perrysburg, Ohio. Subsequently, on May 7, Ohio State University awarded her a posthumous degree in psychology. During the commencement ceremony, her parents and sister received their degrees from then-President Michael V. Drake.

In response to their profound loss, Reagan's family created the Reagan Tokes Memorial Foundation. This organization provides scholarships, promotes self-defense education, and advocates for legislative reforms to decrease violent crime.

The Criminal History of Brian Lee Golsby

Brian Lee Golsby was born on January 26, 1988. While he alleged experiencing childhood abuse, including sexual assault, prosecutors found inconsistencies in his statements. Golsby's criminal record started early, featuring offenses such as criminal trespassing, theft, shoplifting, and threatening his mother with a knife.

A review conducted by the Ohio Department of Youth Services found that Golsby had a history of sexual violence, including the rape of young children. Furthermore, he was associated with the Crips street gang during his adolescence.

Despite his history of violent crime, Golsby was released from prison in 2016, just months before Reagan's murder, after serving six years for the 2010 abduction, sexual assault, and robbery of a pregnant woman and her 2-year-old son at knifepoint.

DNA from Reagan's rape kit and gunshot residue on his clothing directly linked him to her murder.

Furthermore, GPS data from the ankle monitor he was required to wear indicated that he was at the exact locations where Reagan was abducted, assaulted, and murdered on the night of February 8, 2017.

Before Reagan's murder, Golsby committed several robberies, assaults, and kidnappings. He is a violent repeat offender who exhibits no remorse and is presently incarcerated for life at the Ohio State Penitentiary, a supermax facility located in Youngstown, Ohio.

Without Reagan Tokes, justice for Golsby's previous crimes, including the 2010 assault on a mother and her child, may never have been realized.

CHAPTER NINETEEN

Human Hunter – Brandon Scott Lavergne

Michaela "Mickey" Shunick, a 21-year-old anthropology student at the University of Louisiana, disappeared during the early hours of May 19, 2012. The night prior, she had gone to a concert with friends at Artmosphere Bistro, a popular local music venue in Lafayette, Louisiana.

Later, clad in a brown leather jacket and jeans and with a backpack purse, Mickey pedaled her black Schwinn bike, featuring gold handlebar grips, back to her best friend Brettly Wilson's place. Around 1:45 a.m., she left Brettly's house, cycling home in anticipation of her younger brother's graduation ceremony. Mickey's ride home was habitual, as she was a dedicated cyclist.

The Shunick family was on the brink of a dramatic and tragic transformation.

Mickey enjoyed socializing, but she was also dependable and had strong family ties. Her family was perplexed when she was late for their graduation departure. At first, they assumed she might have lost track of time at a friend's house. However, Mickey didn't show up for the ceremony either.

After it ended, her family rushed home to search for her, yet she was nowhere to be found. Mickey never returned, leaving her family uncertain about her location.

Her family didn't realize that Mickey had become Brandon Scott Lavergne's last victim, marking the end of a monstrous figure accountable for abduction, murder, sexual assault, and robbery.

When Mickey didn't answer their calls, her parents contacted a few friends. They learned she had been out with friends on Friday night, but had left to go with Brettly Wilson to get food and Brettly lived approximately four miles away on Ryan Street. He informed Mickey's family, "She left my house at about 1:45 a.m. Saturday and mentioned she was going home."

After failing to reach her, Mickey's parents, Tom Shunick and Nancy Rowe, reported her missing. In the police investigation, Brettly stated, "I went to the Artmosphere Bistro with

Mickey on Friday night around 10:15 p.m. for drinks and live music. After that, we biked to my house, picked up my car, and went through the Taco Bell drive-thru. We then returned to my place to eat the takeout. Some friends were expected to join us, but Mickey went home before they arrived because she felt tired."

Police analyzed the bar's security footage and identified Mickey and Brettly. The two were there for about two and a half hours, appearing to enjoy themselves. When they departed, neither seemed to be intoxicated. Additional footage from Taco Bell captured Brettly placing an order at the drive-thru. Authorities also secured video of the likely route Mickey took while biking home.

Police noticed Mickey multiple times in the footage as she cycled by, allowing them to identify the street where she vanished. Additional footage showed a white Chevy pickup truck trailing behind her. The police searched the area for Mickey's bicycle, hoping to determine if a hit-and-run occurred, but found nothing.

"If she has been taken, where might she be? What could be happening to her?" inquired Tom Shunick, Mickey's father. "The video footage was not reviewed over the weekend since the managers were unavailable, resulting in a two-day delay. If she has been kidnapped and is currently on the Interstate, that gives them a two-day advantage."

The Shunick family clung to the hope that Mickey remained alive. They could not celebrate Mickey's 22nd birthday or her brother's graduation, focusing solely on the search for her, directed by her sister, Charlene "Charlie."

Charlie enlisted volunteers to assist in the search and participated in multiple interviews with local radio and television stations, all aimed at keeping Mickey's story in the public eye. As time passed, the harsh reality of her potential death became increasingly evident. Nevertheless, Charlie and the family remained resolute in their hope.

On May 28, a momentous event occurred with the discovery of Mickey's bike under a bridge at Whiskey Bay, set in a secluded, marshy region next to the Atchafalaya River, 25 miles from her last confirmed location. The bike's condition suggested it had been hit from behind by a vehicle, heightening fears of foul play. At that moment, it became clear that someone had intentionally taken her—this wasn't merely an accident. The person holding her is considering these factors."

By July 2012, with no solutions in sight, Charlie faced a brutal truth, yet she remained hopeful. "The odds don't seem to favor us, but as I've stated before, until I'm standing over the casket at the funeral, I will hold onto the hope that she might still be out there. We want that person, whoever is responsible or involved, to tell us where Mickey is so we can take her home."

Several days later, the Lafayette police received a significant lead: a white truck had been discovered burned in Jacinto County, Texas. Investigators inspected the vehicle and observed that it closely matched the one seen in surveillance footage from the night Mickey disappeared.

This lead became the crucial breakthrough the authorities needed. They traced the truck to its owner, 33-year-old registered sex offender Brandon Scott Lavergne. In 2000, Lavergne was arrested and charged with oral sexual battery but was released in 2008. Investigators discovered that on the night Mickey went missing, he was roaming the streets looking for his next victim.

Lavergne quickly raised suspicions due to his recent stab wounds, which aligned with Mickey's disappearance timeline. When police interrogated him, he asserted, "They resulted from a mugging at a gas station in New Orleans, Louisiana."

On June 4, 2012, a used car dealership employee gave the police a crucial tip: "Lavergne bought a truck from me and wanted it to resemble his old one. When I inquired why, he mentioned that his previous truck had burned in Texas but didn't explain further."

Investigators quickly positioned Lavergne near the area where Mickey disappeared and where her bicycle was found. Their concern intensified upon discovering that just a day after Mickey went missing, Lavergne admitted himself to a hospital in New Orleans with stab wounds.

On July 5, 2012, police arrested Lavergne on charges of aggravated kidnapping, murder, and failure to re-register as a sex offender.

Shortly after his arrest, on August 7, officials announced that they had found Mickey's body based on a credible tip. Her remains were discovered in a remote wooded area adjacent to a cemetery along Route 10 in Evangeline Parish, approximately 45 miles from the last sighting location.

Officials from the Lafayette Parish Coroner's Office stated, "The body believed to be Mickey Shunick was in a significant state of decay, requiring us to send it to a facial identification specialist at Louisiana State University."

Confident in their evidence, prosecutors disclosed to Lavergne their intention to pursue the death penalty. Aware that escape was hopeless, Lavergne admitted to the crime.

"In the early hours of Saturday morning, May 19, I was driving around Lafayette when I saw Mickey. I followed her in my truck and deliberately struck her bicycle with my vehicle. She fell, and I forced her into my truck, throwing her bicycle into the bed. I had a knife and a semi-automatic handgun with me.

"As Mickey tried to call for help while reaching for her phone, I threatened her with a knife. At that moment, she fought back—spraying pepper spray in my face and managing to grab my knife.

"She stabbed me repeatedly. While I fought to take the knife from her, my hands were severely injured, cutting through tendons.

"Then I stabbed Mickey four times. She collapsed and lay still. I checked for a pulse, but there was none.

"I drove for forty minutes, searching for a secluded place to bury her. But Mickey wasn't dead. Suddenly, she sprang up, seized my knife, and stabbed me in the chest. Instinct took over—I grabbed my handgun and shot her in the head. She died instantly.

"I was in critical condition. My injuries were later termed life-threatening. Instead of burying her body, I drove home with her lifeless body in the passenger seat. "I stripped off my clothes, disposed of the knife and handgun, cleaned my injuries as best I could, and devised a plan. I went to an old cemetery in Evangeline Parish to bury her.

"Nonetheless, I was too pained to excavate. So, I positioned Mickey's body along a nearby tree line, and covered her with branches and debris.

"Later, I visited New Orleans and stayed with a friend. Before returning to Lafayette, I received medical treatment at a hospital. A few days later, I went back to the cemetery and buried Mickey's body in a nearby sugar cane field. Afterward, I disposed of her bike in the river beneath a bridge in Whiskey Bay.

"Mission accomplished. I got back home, tidied up, got rid of evidence, including Mickey's backpack and iPod, and refined my strategy. To conceal my whereabouts, I drove to San Jacinto, Texas, ignited my truck, and reported it as stolen. I purchased a nearly identical truck to lessen any suspicion.

"To escape the death penalty, I admitted guilt for Mickey's murder.

"But my confession didn't end there. I also admitted guilt for a second murder."

In June 1999, 35-year-old Lisa Ann Pate, a mother of three from Youngsville, Louisiana, disappeared. Months later, her body was found. Investigators learned she had met Brandon Lavergne in Lafayette. Reports indicate that they stayed together at a hotel for several days until Lavergne prevented her from visiting her children. When Lisa tried to escape, he held her back.

One night, while Lavergne was asleep, Lisa attempted to steal his car keys and wallet in order to flee. He awoke and attacked her. Later, Lavergne admitted to police that he had suffocated a woman to death using a plastic bag. Authorities believed he was referring to Lisa.

Lisa's skeletal remains were discovered in September 1999 in the Church Point area. Evidence suggested that a plastic bag had been placed around her skull. Her body was concealed under three large boards in a remote area northwest of Church Point, and dental records were used to confirm her identity.

During the investigation, Sheriff Kenneth Goss of Acadia Parish emphasized his commitment to collaborating with Lafayette officials to obtain more information about Lisa's murder. He mentioned, "In cases like this, there's a risk they could become cold cases. Nevertheless, the determination to find answers remains, regardless of whether it takes two years or two decades. Hope never fully fades. While addressing other matters is important, there's always a chance that new evidence could surface to aid in resolving the case."

Early in the investigation of Lisa's disappearance and murder, Lavergne was noted. Yet, it took more than ten years for law enforcement to make an arrest. On July 18, 2012, Lavergne faced two charges of first-degree murder—

one for Lisa Ann Pate and another for Mickey Shunick, who vanished in 2012.

In August 2012, Lavergne received two consecutive life sentences without parole. A psychological assessment by Lafayette criminal psychologist Larry Benoit on August 8, 2012, revealed essential details about Lavergne's history and mental condition. He informed Benoit that, after leading investigators to Mickey Shunick's remains to negotiate for his own life, he had experienced ongoing physical abuse from his adoptive father. He had several encounters with molestation by a teenage babysitter during his early years.

According to Benoit's report, Lavergne had undergone treatment for anger and depression by the age of 15, which included a 30-day inpatient stay at Central State Hospital in 1995. Furthermore, he participated in outpatient counseling for several months in 2011.

Benoit noted in his assessment, "He sometimes drinks, but he often binge drinks when he does."

He acknowledged a history of aggressive tendencies, further complicated by a family background marked by substance abuse and mental health challenges. Lavergne's adoptive father experienced paranoid schizophrenia.

The report determined that Lavergne had the mental capacity to proceed with his plea agreement. Nonetheless, it highlighted troubling characteristics: He showed extroverted, impulsive, and self-indulgent behaviors, along with a lack of moral maturity and questionable judgment. His actions demonstrated hostility, emotional outbursts, and an inability to learn from previous errors.

Following Lavergne's sentencing, Nancy Anne Rowe, the mother of Mickey Shunick, expressed her reflections on her daughter's bravery: "She does not see herself as a victim.

My brave daughter faced a monster. Now, I believe I can confront monsters too. And so can you."

Mickey's sister, Charlie, echoed those sentiments: "My sister was a fighter. Without her, our community would never have successfully confronted a dangerous man who hurt many people."

Motivated by her family's harrowing experience, Charlie Shunick established the Resource Association for Missing People in September 2013 to support and aid families of missing persons.

In February 2022, the court rejected Brandon Scott Lavergne's appeal for post-conviction relief, guaranteeing his ongoing imprisonment at the notorious Louisiana State Penitentiary in Angola, West Feliciana Parish.

Commonly known as the "Alcatraz of the South," Angola is a vast, isolated maximum-security prison with a contentious past. Originally a slave plantation, it was named after the African country from which a significant number of enslaved individuals were transported. Warden Burl Cain managed the facility for many years, establishing the record as the longest-serving warden in Angola's history.

Charlene "Charlie" Shunick shared a devastating truth. "My lovely 21-year-old sister was the last victim of Brandon Scott Lavergne."

CHAPTER TWENTY

Tagged Killer – Khalil Wheeler-Weaver

Tiffany Taylor grew up in public housing in Jersey City, New Jersey, where she endured a harsh environment marked by violence, drugs, and neglect. From an early age, she faced more trauma than many. As a teenager, she witnessed sexual assaults and, devastatingly, the murders of several individuals, including two of her boyfriends, right before her eyes.

During difficult times, Tiffany envisioned a life away from the streets. At 18, she started her college journey in Orlando, focusing on music and psychology. Unfortunately, after two years, she got pregnant and moved back to New Jersey, struggling to find stable employment. To support herself, she turned to sex work, navigating the dangers of an underground world where her survival often depended on outsmarting those looking to exploit her.

In 2016, a mutual friend introduced Tiffany to Khalil Wheeler-Weaver. At 25, he was five years her junior. While their initial encounters seemed innocent, her connection with Wheeler-Weaver led to a chain of events that would profoundly change her life. Tiffany was not his last victim;

that tragic distinction would go to Sarah Butler later that year.

Reflecting on their beginnings: "With my best friend, we played video games and spent time at his house. Khalil appeared to be fun."

Tiffany later admitted that she had become weary of being viewed as an object. She started robbing the men she met for sex, justifying her actions as a form of retribution. Strange but true, as a Jehovah's Witness, she would not have sex with a married man, but she would certainly rob him if she had the chance.

Before long, Wheeler-Weaver began to pressure Tiffany for sex, persistently asking her until she ultimately relented. Yet, her real aim was not to please him. She planned to rob him instead.

Tiffany arrived at his house, collected $200, and entered his childhood room. Just as the session was about to start, she paused and mentioned that she had left something in her car before heading outside.

Tiffany drove away in her car, leaving Wheeler-Weaver behind.

In October 2016, Tiffany was pregnant with her second child and working odd jobs for a friend at the Ritz Motel in Elizabeth, New Jersey, to make ends meet. She began receiving persistent text messages from an unknown number during this time. The man on the other end was relentless, continually begging for sex. Frustrated, Tiffany told him to leave her alone and even changed her number to escape his harassment.

Despite the ongoing messages, the man discovered her new number and contacted her nearly daily. Worn out and eager to stop the relentless harassment, Tiffany consented to meet him at the Ritz Motel.

Upon meeting the stranger, she noticed his tall and thin frame, concealed by a ski mask, black gloves, and an oversized sweatshirt that seemed appropriate for the chilly weather. Eager to resolve the situation quickly, she offered him a ride in a friend's car so she could move on.

While driving, the man abruptly ordered her to stop, claiming he needed a bathroom break. As soon as she obliged, he struck her violently on the back of her head, causing her to lose consciousness immediately.

When Tiffany regained awareness, she found her head wrapped in duct tape, which restricted her breathing. Her wrists were bound in handcuffs, and she was in the back seat of the car, trapped in a chokehold as the stranger mercilessly sexually assaulted her.

Overcome by shock, she felt trapped in the horrifying situation. As he reached his climax, he took off his ski mask, exposing himself as Khalil Wheeler-Weaver.

A chill rushed over Tiffany. In her desperation, she screamed and pleaded for mercy, exclaiming, "I'm pregnant," while sobbing.

Wheeler-Weaver grinned, his eyes shining with wicked pleasure. "I know," he stated.

At that moment, Tiffany understood he intended to kill her.

Motivated by her survival instinct, she quickly devised a plan. In hindsight, she thought, "If he intended to kill me, then he had to die too. I refused to be conquered."

With tears shining in her eyes, she begged him to loosen the handcuffs, portraying herself as a shattered victim. When he agreed, she saw an opportunity to trick him. She began to speak.

"I recorded our entire conversation at the Ritz Motel on my phone," she feigned. "That talk could connect you to my murder."

Her words struck a chord with him. Wheeler-Weaver took a moment before climbing into the front seat and igniting the engine. During the ride back to the motel, he adopted a victim mentality, complaining, "No one values me. Why must I pay for a girl to notice me?"

Tiffany concentrated on her escape, subtly releasing her double-jointed hand from the loosened cuffs as she prepared to break free at the right moment.

They returned to the motel, and Wheeler-Weaver tore the duct tape off her face as they approached her room. Still playing her role, Tiffany let the handcuffs hang from her wrist, concealing her ability to remove them. As they reached the door, she seized her opportunity—kicked it open, dashed inside, and firmly closed it behind her. The deadbolt clicked shut immediately, locking him out.

She pulled back the curtain, showing she had escaped from the cuffs. In a panic, Wheeler-Weaver hurried away from the scene.

Eager to pursue justice, Tiffany contacted him shortly after, firmly stating she would avoid involving the police if he returned the car keys. Nevertheless, she had already dialed 9-1-1.

Before escaping, he was tricked into leaving the keys on the stairs near the security cameras.

Shortly after, police officers from Elizabeth arrived, and Tiffany recounted her ordeal. "He sexually assaulted me, kidnapped me, and attempted to kill me," she stated, presenting her phone records and the handcuffs as evidence.

Instead of providing help, the officers dismissed her allegations. They charged her with prostitution and left her handcuffed for over an hour. Despite Tiffany's strong evidence, they chose to disbelieve her.

"I felt stripped of my humanity by the officers," she recalled.

After surviving Wheeler-Weaver's assault, she faced a fresh challenge—the indifference of the system meant to protect her.

A week later, on November 22, 2016, 20-year-old Sarah Butler was at home celebrating Thanksgiving when she connected with Khalil Wheeler-Weaver via the social media platform Tagged. Although they had planned to meet, Butler ultimately chose not to go through with it.

In the end, she accepted Wheeler-Weaver's offer of $500 for sex. Before their encounter, she playfully texted him, *"You're not a serial killer, are you?"*

Sarah told her mother she planned to meet a friend and asked to borrow the van. Trusting her judgment, her mother gave her the keys and said goodbye. This was the last time anyone saw Sarah Butler alive.

Later that day, December 1, 2016, Sarah was found dead. Her body was located in the 400-acre Eagle Rock Reservation in West Orange, New Jersey.

Driven by their pursuit of justice, Sarah Butler's family and friends acted rapidly. Her sister accessed Sarah's social media accounts, including Tagged, with her passwords. Alongside two friends, they pinpointed one of the last individuals she had interacted with: Khalil Wheeler-Weaver.

A plan was created to capture him. Butler's sister set up a fake profile on Tagged and collaborated with the Montclair police to conduct a sting operation. Posing as a potential date, they arranged a meeting with Wheeler-Weaver at a restaurant in Glen Ridge.

On December 6, Wheeler-Weaver arrived at the arranged meeting location, where he met undercover police officers and was arrested without incident.

A search at Wheeler-Weaver's home uncovered three cell phones holding crucial evidence. Investigators found questionable searches on these devices that conflicted with his claims about his whereabouts when his victims went missing. His browsing history included alarming queries, such as:

How to make homemade poisons to kill humans.

What chemical could you put on a rag and hold to someone's face to make them go to sleep immediately?

Additionally, authorities discovered that Wheeler-Weaver searched for a "Police entrance exam practice test," suggesting he might have considered pursuing a career in law enforcement.

Wheeler-Weaver was born on April 20, 1996, in the wealthy Seven Oaks area of Orange, New Jersey. His stepfather, a detective in East Orange, came from a law enforcement background, and his uncle was a retired officer in Newark. After graduating from Orange High School in 2014, he was viewed as a loner with few friends and no involvement in extracurricular activities or relationships. Classmates described him as nerdy, noting his habit of wearing tucked-in shirts, khaki pants, and plain white shoes.

Police later determined that Wheeler-Weaver targeted Black sex workers, using dating apps to find his victims. He either strangled or asphyxiated them, executing a calculated killing spree between April and November 2016. His reliance on dating apps ultimately led to his downfall.

While committing his crimes, Wheeler-Weaver was employed as a security guard at Sterling Securities in Newark, New Jersey. It is disturbing to note the irony in his aspiration to become a police officer in light of his heinous actions.

The Crimes of Khalil Wheeler-Weaver

Khalil Wheeler-Weaver reportedly first struck on August 31, 2016, when he picked up 19-year-old Robin West in his car. He strangled her to death before setting fire to her remains.

At first, Robin's parents remained composed. Her mother, Anita Mason, observed, "Robin has done this. She may disappear for a day or two but hardly for longer." Residing with a friend in West Philadelphia, Robin was a lively teenager who brought happiness and sadness to her family.

Concerned, her family sent messages and made numerous calls but received no reply. After a week, they officially reported her missing.

Authorities later tracked Wheeler-Weaver's cell phone, placing him at an abandoned house in September 2016— the same house where Robin West's burned, unrecognizable remains were discovered. Robin lay unidentified in the morgue for nearly two weeks before dental records confirmed her identity.

Additional examination of Wheeler-Weaver's phone location data revealed that he initially left the burning house but subsequently returned to observe the flames consume it.

Just under two months later, on October 22, 2016, Wheeler-Weaver took the life of 33-year-old Joanne Brown from Newark, New Jersey. Weeks later, on December 5, her body was discovered in an abandoned house in Orange, New Jersey.

Authorities confirmed that Brown had been killed at the scene. "The murder occurred in that location, and her body was left there. It was a concealed location within an abandoned residence," Acting Essex County Prosecutor Carolyn Murray later stated.

In October 2016, Wheeler-Weaver committed another crime against 15-year-old Mawa Doumbia. She was reported missing on October 7, and her remains were discovered on April 19, 2019—two and a half years later—in an abandoned house in Orange, New Jersey. For years, Doumbia's body remained unidentified. However, investigators eventually obtained sufficient digital evidence to confirm that Wheeler-Weaver had solicited her for sex shortly before her disappearance.

By February 2017, Wheeler-Weaver was indicted on three counts of murder, as well as charges of attempted murder, aggravated arson, desecration of human remains, aggravated sexual assault, and kidnapping. He pleaded not guilty to all three murders and the attempted murder charge.

In December 2019, Khalil Wheeler-Weaver, known as "The Tagged Killer," finally received justice in court.

As the lone survivor of Wheeler-Weaver's brutal attacks, Tiffany Taylor played a pivotal role in exposing his calculated methods. Her testimony outlined his signature pattern: luring women with promises of payment for sex, the use of duct tape to restrain his victims, ambushing them in their cars, and the final act of strangulation. For an entire day in court, Tiffany relived the night she narrowly escaped death, detailing every harrowing moment.

She frowned as she addressed the courtroom, saying, "If the Elizabeth Police Department had believed me, Sarah Butler would still be alive."

Wheeler-Weaver continued to assert his innocence, despite strong evidence and a direct witness. Nevertheless, DNA evidence firmly linked him to the murders of Robin West, Joanne Browne, and Sarah Butler.

A prosecutor revealed the unsettling rationale behind Wheeler-Weaver's behavior: "He targeted prostitutes, thinking their disappearances would go unnoticed. To him, they were expendable people."

Wheeler-Weaver was convicted of three murders, two counts of aggravated sexual assault, three counts of desecrating human remains, plus additional charges of kidnapping, arson, and attempted murder, supported by strong forensic and testimonial evidence.

Wheeler-Weaver maintained his innocence, claiming that he had been framed.

During the October 6, 2021, sentencing, the victim's family members were allowed to speak.

"I will forever cherish her smile, her expressions, her walk, and her willingness to help the homeless," stated Anita Mason, mother of Robin West. "Although many focus on the last month of her life, she truly lived a meaningful life before passing."

"She will always hold the title of my middle child," she continued. "Her passion for music, love of dance, enjoyment of singing, deep devotion to family, adoration for children, care for the elderly, and special affection for dogs all stood out."

The next witness called was Tiffany Taylor. "My life has completely changed. I am always looking over my shoulder and battling numerous inner demons. I've stopped wearing makeup and lost all my friends. I remain in a state of constant high alert. Still, I am grateful to be alive." She then turned to the judge. "I request that you show him no mercy, as he has shown none."

While addressing the court, Sarah Butler's father fixed his gaze on his daughter's killer. "I hope you experience pain, young man," he declared, "night after night."

Despite Wheeler-Weaver's assertions of innocence, Superior Court Judge Mark Ali stood resolute. He sentenced "The Tagged Killer" to 160 years in prison, with no possibility of parole for 140 years, ensuring that he would remain behind bars for life.

Assistant Essex County Prosecutor Adam Wells summed up the gravity of the case: "The defendant believed those victims were disposable. After he killed them, he went on about his day as if nothing had ever happened. But each of those women's lives mattered."

In the Newark courtroom, Sarah Butler's mother, Lavern, leaned on her husband, Victor, while their oldest daughter, Bassania Daley, approached the stand. Almost whispering, she recounted how she lured her sister's murderer into the open. Although she was terrified to testify, she believed it was her responsibility to her family.

"He picked the wrong girl to confront," Lavern Butler later told the judge. "I promise you, everyone loved Sarah."

The case highlighted contrasting perspectives on victims. The other three women, two of whom were killed and one who barely escaped, were sex workers—marginalized individuals often ignored by society and routinely disregarded by law enforcement. In stark contrast, Sarah Butler hailed from a secure two-parent family in Montclair, prompting her community to organize efforts when she disappeared swiftly.

Wheeler-Weaver committed a grave mistake by selecting women he viewed as vulnerable. However, the families of the victims ensured that he was held accountable.

Assistant Essex County Prosecutor Adam Wells stated during the trial that the killer's actions regarding his last victim, Sarah Butler, were his "fatal mistake."

The jury found Khalil Wheeler-Weaver guilty of three murder charges related to Sarah Butler, Robin West, and Joanne Brown in less than three hours.

For the Butler family, moving to Montclair represented an exciting new beginning. They had chosen this area in search of improved opportunities for their three daughters, departing from the challenges of their previous neighborhood. Their home, a modest house in Montclair's 4th Ward, mirrored the working-class community of Orange, primarily African American, where Wheeler-Weaver grew up.

Although the polished mansions and well-kept lawns of Upper Montclair might seem distant, the South End remained connected to the town's elite school district. As gentrification progressed, the neighborhood underwent notable changes. A new train service to Manhattan shortened commute times to just 30 minutes. Trendy coffee shops and upscale apartment buildings featuring rooftop lounges began to emerge. Despite the rent increase, the Butlers continued to support their church and the lively community they had fostered.

Victor and Lavern Butler were dedicated to ensuring their daughters lead fulfilling lives. While Lavern devoted her days to caring for children from affluent families, Victor balanced family responsibilities with his bartending role at the Glen Ridge Country Club, where he crafted cocktails for Wall Street professionals unwinding after work. In his spare time, he practiced his golf swing at a public course in Belleville.

Sarah Butler, the middle sibling, exuded passion and resolve. She headed the dance team at Montclair High School. She distinguished herself as a performer in the touring group at Premiere Dance Theatre. Additionally, she won the school's scholarship and achieved third place at Amateur Night at the Apollo Theater in Harlem.

Sarah's dear friend, Sophia Nigro, now 18, reminisces about the enjoyable sleepovers at the Butler house, which were filled with laughter, spontaneous dance lessons, and makeup tutorials.

Nigro remarked, "She was always dancing. Even during our downtime, Sarah would twirl in the corner."

However, Sarah's passion for dance extended far beyond that. Despite being too young to work in a bar, she worked as a lifeguard, took various babysitting jobs, and even enrolled in bartending classes.

Shirlise McKinley-Wiggins, the founder of Premiere Dance Theatre, reminisced, "I questioned, 'How can you bartend if you're not even 21?' Sarah answered, 'I'll be ready, Miss Shirley.'"

Sarah Butler possessed extraordinary potential—an ambitious young woman brimming with talent and relentless resolve. Tragically, in November 2016, her life was abruptly taken by a predator lurking in plain view.

In the autumn of 2016, Sarah Butler, a second-year New Jersey City University student, was the first in her family to attend college.

Yasmeen Chism, a professor at Butler, remarked, "I can close my eyes and distinctly recall the brightness of her smile. Her joy seemed limitless, and her energy was infectious."

However, the circumstances beyond the classroom seemed bleak.

Butler now resides in the Jersey City dorms. Enthusiastic about participating in campus life, she struggled to form friendships and was unhappy with her roommates. This sense of isolation began impacting her well-being. In search of connection, she created a profile on Tagged, a social media platform aimed at facilitating friendships, romantic ties, or casual interactions..

On Tagged, she encountered a young man using the screen name LilYachtRock. He offered Sarah, whose screen name was Sara Smile, $500 for sex. After some hesitation, she agreed.

Friends and family would later describe this choice as unusual for Sarah.

On November 22, 2016, she drove the family minivan to meet Lil Yachty Rock. Nine days later, her body was found concealed beneath leaves, twigs, rusted pipes, and debris in a county park.

"She was a charming girl," recalled Lavern Butler. "I understand my daughter well and see the love and care she received during her upbringing. She adored dancing, relished swimming, and cherished her moments with children. It's heartbreaking that you never got the chance to know her."

At Sarah's funeral, dancers from Premiere Dance Theatre, dressed in white, performed "Rise Up" by Andra Day. A video showcased Sarah, also in white, dancing beautifully to the same piece. The heartfelt performance deeply impacted the dancers, moving them to tears and leaving them unsteady as they observed Sarah's graceful movements on the screen above them.

A horse-drawn carriage transported her to her final resting place.

Sarah's Jamaican relatives cooked goat head soup in the church basement reception, a beloved family recipe. Lavern Butler warmly welcomed each guest, ensuring they felt nourished and at ease.

Sarah's friend Sophia Nigro still visits the Butler home, but it feels different now. The house is significantly quieter these days.

Nigro noted, "Lavern talks about Sarah every day, but there's a pause since no one knows how to react."

Sarah's mother believes her daughter remains spiritually connected.

"Sometimes, I see her," Lavern said. "In the mornings, she twirls in the kitchen, asking, 'Mommy, what's for breakfast?' That's my Sarah—always dancing around the house."

Recently, Aliyah, Sarah's younger sister, performed her senior dance at the Premiere Club in Atlantic City. Her touching tribute to Sarah featured the Hall & Oates song *Sara Smile*: "Smile awhile, oh, won't you smile awhile for me, Sara."

Yet, doubts regarding Sarah's last moments persist.

Before her disappearance, did Khalil Wheeler-Weaver have any prior acquaintance with her? Prosecutors contend that while they did not share a romantic relationship, they assert that they met several times on the night she went missing.

Essex County Prosecutor Carolyn Murray remarked, "Ms. Butler, a student from New Jersey City University, appears to have been acquainted with the defendant, as their interaction occurred in Orange, New Jersey, on November 22."

That news took Sarah's family aback.

Lavern Butler stated, "I've never met or heard of him. None of us are familiar with him."

Only hours before Sarah's disappearance, she began receiving unusual phone calls that her sister, Aliyah, remembers vividly.

"I felt unsure," Aliyah said. "I wish I had inquired about their identities."

Forensic evidence later linked Wheeler-Weaver to Sarah's murder. A forensic scientist from Newark reported that DNA matching Wheeler-Weaver was found under Sarah's fingernails.

A detective stated, "DNA and blood samples connected the suspect to the victims in the NJ serial killer case. Despite the limited DNA evidence caused by Wheeler-Weaver wearing gloves and using condoms, a small trace of his DNA was found underneath one victim's fingernails."

His phone's geolocation tracked his movements, revealing where he encountered his victims and where their bodies were later found.

During the interview, investigators observed a new scratch on Wheeler-Weaver's arm after Sarah's disappearance. However, his lawyers challenged the DNA evidence's validity, claiming the timeline and the collection method were ambiguous. Additionally, his DNA was absent from the samples of the other three alleged victims.

One of those victims, Joanne Brown, had been left in an abandoned home for months. Her body was too decomposed to yield DNA evidence, but medical examiners determined she had been strangled.

Currently, Khalil Wheeler-Weaver is serving a 160-year sentence in the maximum-security New Jersey State Prison in Trenton.

A profoundly tragic element of this case is that it might have been prevented. If authorities had taken Tiffany's claims seriously, as she provided crucial evidence before Sarah's death, Sarah Butler could still be alive today.

CHAPTER TWENTY-ONE
Car Burning Killer – Kylr Yust

Kara Elise Kopetsky was born on February 17, 1990, in Frankfurt, Germany, the only child of Rhonda and Michael Kopetsky. She went missing from Belton, Missouri, on May 4, 2007, 17 years later.

For almost ten years, her fate was uncertain until 2016, when her friend, Jessica Runions, tragically became the last victim of a merciless killer.

Kara's friendly smile and welcoming demeanor effortlessly attracted others. She had a profound love for music, shopping, and animals, along with a steadfast commitment to family and friends. Unfortunately, her vibrant spirit departed from this world far too soon.

On the first Friday of May, Kara called her mother to say she had forgotten her textbook. Her mother, Rhonda Beckford, took it to the front desk of Belton High School for Kara to pick up. Surveillance footage captured her walking through the hallway at 10:30 a.m.

Not long after, classmates remembered that Kara had left school early without warning. The weather was sunny and spring-like—ideal for students to skip class and for adults to leave work early. Yet, after that day, Kara was never seen or heard from again.

Neither her parents nor friends, nor even the police, understood what had happened. Her MySpace page overflowed with worried messages:

"Hey, sweetheart! I miss you immensely! The family is doing everything possible to ensure your safe return home. They're going wild for you, girl."

At home, everything indicated that this wasn't simply a case of running away. Kara had abandoned her clothes, makeup, and nearly a whole carton of Marlboro Lights. Additionally, she left behind her iPod, a Christmas gift, and the hair straightener she used every day.

Her schedule was hectic: she had an interview at QuikTrip Travel Center the next day and weekend plans with friends. Meanwhile, her bank account remained unchanged, and her debit card was still in her school locker.

Interestingly, the only item missing was her Motorola cellphone, a birthday gift that had remained untouched since the morning of May 4.

A detective shared their worry, saying, "For a child that age, it's troubling if their phone isn't on."

Reports of sightings skyrocketed nationwide. Kara was allegedly spotted in California, Florida, and even aboard a plane. One witness reported seeing her on a tram at Disney World. Another insisted they recognized her alongside a young man at a gas station in Louisburg, Kansas. A psychic claimed to have seen her somewhere in the middle of the Atlantic Ocean.

Lieutenant Brad Swanson of the Belton Police Department gathered over 400 tips and received more than 100 reported sightings.

Swanson recalled a call indicating that Kara lived just outside an Amish community in Missouri, was married, had two children named Kane and Abel, and had changed her name to Kari.

Kara's friends, referring to her as a firecracker, found it hard to believe she had run away. However, the police couldn't rule out that option.

"Currently, there are no suspects in Kara's disappearance, and we do not have evidence of any crime," Lieutenant Swanson stated. "Since Kara is 17, which is the legal age in Missouri, we cannot compel her to return home, even if she is found. She likely knows how to go missing if that was her choice. It's possible she purposely left her belongings behind."

Although some critics wondered what else could have been done, Kara's parents felt that law enforcement had done everything necessary. Lacking answers, they decided to act for themselves. They enlisted family and friends, canvassed the neighborhoods, created flyers and T-shirts, and reached out to anyone who might have information.

For nine agonizing years, Kara's family searched, hoped, and waited. Her fate was a mystery until 2016, when the disappearance of another girl led investigators to reveal a chilling truth.

One of Kara's friends was Kylr Yust, 18, who experienced a tumultuous, on-and-off relationship with Kara during the 2007 school year. Kara's social media followers were well aware of the ups and downs in their relationship.

In the days before her disappearance on April 24, Kara shared a provocative message:

"Recently, I have encountered significant challenges. For the last nine months, I dedicated myself entirely to Kylr, which led me to become distanced from friends and family. As a result, I lost touch with my true self, and now I'm starting a journey to reclaim that identity."

Court records show that approximately a week before her disappearance, Kara filed a restraining order against Yust, claiming he had choked and assaulted her. However, the order was subsequently dismissed.

Yust's violent past surpassed Kara's. An ex-girlfriend, who was pregnant, subsequently informed the police:

"One day, Kylr came home drunk and tried to kill me by choking me. He also claimed that he had killed girlfriends in the past and would do the same to me. Yust abused and killed kittens in front of me and said that he would kill my family if I went to the police. He also said that he killed out of sheer jealousy. 'I will kill you,' he told me.

"He took hold of me with both hands, pulled me into our bedroom, and locked eyes with me, grinding his teeth and licking his lips, before wrapping both hands around my neck. Then, he threatened to kill me if I screamed."

After Kara vanished on May 4, 2007, Yust became the main suspect. However, due to lack of strong evidence linking him to the incident, law enforcement could not proceed with an arrest.

This changed on September 11, when Yust was taken into custody at his brother Jessep's home and charged with intentionally setting fire to Kara's car. Following the arrest, a former roommate stepped forward, revealing to law enforcement that Yust had confessed to murdering Kara Kopetsky in a prior conversation.

Despite this concerning revelation, Kara remained missing for nine years. Throughout this period, Yust often cycled in and out of jail for various unrelated offenses, including domestic violence and animal cruelty.

Only a few days following his recent prison release on September 8, 2016, Kylr Yust, now age 27, attended a party in Grandview, Missouri. The events that followed unexpectedly revitalized the case.

Several attendees saw Kylr Yust departing a party with 21-year-old Jessica Runions. Unfortunately, Jessica did not return home that night and was quickly reported missing.

Jessica's car was discovered in flames at the intersection of 95th Street and Blue River Road at 2:00 a.m. the next morning. Consequently, Yust was apprehended and accused of intentionally igniting the vehicle.

Linda Runions, Jessica's grandmother, fondly recalled her granddaughter, stating, "She was the sweetest girl—just a typical girl: loving, independent, and caring."

Jessica began her career as a server three years earlier before moving up to baking for the residents at a nearby retirement home. Her aunt, Michele Runions, remembered, "She lived independently, was diligent, and had her car. She was responsible and loved making birthday cakes. Jessica was saving money to enroll in culinary school."

Faced with growing suspicion, Yust declined to disclose any information regarding Jessica's location. Many suspected his involvement in the 2007 case of Kara Kopetsky's disappearance, fueling concerns that Jessica might have met a similar fate. Yet, lacking the girls' remains or DNA evidence, authorities were unable to file murder charges against him.

This was updated on April 3, 2017.

A mushroom hunter discovered human remains in a quarry. Following a thorough search of the site, authorities found a second set of skeletal remains approximately 20 to 30 yards away.

Within a few days, it was confirmed that the first set of remains had been identified as Jessica's. Although many believed the second set was Kara's, official confirmation was provided on August 17, 2017. On that date, Diane C. Peterson, the chief medical examiner for Jackson County, stated, "I have received mitochondrial and nuclear DNA reports from the FBI concerning the unidentified skeleton found in Cass County. Both reports confirm that the remains belong to Kara Elise Kopetsky."

Kara's mother, Rhonda Beckford, conveyed mixed feelings of sorrow and relief. "After ten years and four months, we finally found her. She is back where she belongs, allowing us to provide her with a proper resting place finally," she stated. "The next step is to arrange a dignified burial and pursue justice."

While Rhonda struggled with her emotions, she reminisced about Kara. "Kara embraced life fervently. She cherished relationships and endeavored to connect with everyone, believing that each person deserved a genuine friendship. Even at 17, Kara displayed incredible wisdom beyond her years."

She expressed the deep challenge of progressing without clarity on Kara's fate. "My son remarked that even if we emptied it, it would always remain Kara's room. Even though we were uncertain about Kara's return, we felt trapped until everything was resolved and we could finally bring her home."

Kara's stepfather, Jim Beckford, recognized the difficulties authorities encountered in identifying her remains. "The identification of Kara was considerably delayed compared to Jessica's, as her remains had been at the site for more than ten years. We thought we would never recover her. When her remains were found, that weight was lifted. It was a relief. We just knew—this was it."

Jim recounted his memories of Kara: "She expressed her goals for advancing her education. She was transforming into a young woman and planning her future. Kara was a delightful girl with a bright future ahead. I'll always remember the last time I saw her at the Popeyes drive-thru. She had on her purple shirt and the Popeyes chicken visor, leaning out of the window with that smile and the sparkle in her eye."

On October 6, 2017, Kylr Yust was charged with the murders of Kara Kopetsky and Jessica Runions, along with two counts of abandoning corpses. He pleaded not guilty to all charges, which was an anticipated response.

Jessep Carter, Yust's half-brother, addressed the media on his family's behalf, stating, "We just want justice for the families of Kara and Jessica. If he is convicted, we hope it brings them peace knowing he will finally be behind bars. I'm not doing well, and my family struggles with his actions."

Even though Jessep confessed to being with Yust when Jessica's car was burned, he faced no charges for that event. In July 2018, he was arrested for allegedly igniting a house fire in Kansas City. A few weeks later, he was found dead in Jackson County Jail, and police reports classified his death as a suicide. His untimely passing sparked concerns since he was expected to be a crucial witness in Yust's murder trial, prompting fears of potential delays in the court process.

On October 1, 2018, Yust's trial was scheduled for December 3, 2019. Soon after, his attorneys claimed he was unfit to stand trial. The court found that Yust "cannot comprehend the murder trial proceedings," yet the judge firmly decided to keep the trial date.

The state ultimately deemed Yust fit for trial, although his defense team sought a second opinion. As a result, the judge mandated a new evaluation within 60 days, which delayed the trial. In an unexpected development, Yust's lawyers proposed to retract their request for an additional mental health assessment if the jail doctor could prescribe him medication for anxiety and depression.

On December 3, 2019, Yust appeared in court, where his attorneys requested further DNA testing on the remains of Kara and Jessica, potentially causing more delays. Two weeks afterward, a judge announced that jury selection would commence on July 22, 2020.

Months later, Yust's legal team gained approval for additional DNA testing. In April 2020, while sorting through an old desk, Belton police officers uncovered papers detailing eyewitness accounts from 2013 concerning another suspect, whose vehicle was subsequently searched by the FBI. Additionally, a recording surfaced in which a suspect admitted to several individuals that he had killed Kara. Yust's lawyers also claimed to have pinpointed witnesses who observed Kopetsky alive after her reported disappearance on May 4, 2007, a revelation that could greatly undermine a critical element of the prosecution's case against Yust.

In July 2020, a shocking event came to light when Joshua Meierer, a Kansas City police officer, faced allegations of engaging in an inappropriate sexual relationship with a witness in Yust's case. Reports suggested that this officer had privately taken on the investigation of Kopetsky's disappearance over the past decade during his off-duty time. It was alleged that he had formed a romantic relationship with a witness during this unofficial investigation. Police guidelines strictly prohibit officers from forming relationships with witnesses during ongoing criminal investigations. Yust's defense team seized upon this issue, arguing that it compromised the possibility of a fair trial for Yust.

Kylr Yust's trial commenced on April 5, 2021.

Court records show that prosecutors depicted Yust as a ruthless murderer driven by jealousy over the romantic connections of young women. Conversely, Yust's defense team asserted his innocence, seeking to undermine the police investigation by claiming that no physical evidence linked him to the murders.

Candice St. Clair, who was previously in a relationship with Yust, shared her account of their alleged abusive partnership that commenced when she was only 17.

"In 2011, after I was expelled from my home for smoking weed, I moved in with Yust, but our relationship was characterized by violence," she shared.

Reflecting on a traumatic event from July 2011, she recounted, "When I attempted to leave him, Yust returned home intoxicated, climbed on top of me, and attempted to suffocate me by pressing on my throat with both hands. He insisted that I was 'not allowed' to leave."

"As he strangled me, he said, 'I have killed other ex-girlfriends in jealousy. I will kill you before you can let another scream out of your throat.'"

During the assault, she stated that Yust hit her legs, choked her several times, drew a pentagram on her forehead, and spoke in unfamiliar languages. She ultimately lost consciousness and later awakened to find him holding her, whispering, "I love you."

"On July 25, 2011, I ended our relationship upon learning of his infidelity," she testified. "The following month, I reported the abuse to the police."

Nick Yeates, a former friend and bandmate of Yust, testified that Yust had confessed to killing Kara Kopetsky. "He told me at a Burger King after a party that he killed her because 'she didn't love him, and he didn't want anyone else to have her.'"

The following day, Kara's mother, Rhonda Beckford, took the stand to testify.

"I can confirm the tumultuous nature of Yust and Kara's relationship," she said. "While in Kara's bedroom, I found a poem that references him."

Marlene Rockwell, the family's private investigator, noted, "I suspect Yust might have a role in Kopetsky's disappearance." She highlighted the troubling similarities between Kopetsky's case and that of Jessica Runions, saying, "Both girls turned off their phones immediately. They resembled each other and were young and trusting— perfect targets for someone seeking to dominate. Each girl had hopes for the future, and both were acquainted with Yust."

Friends and acquaintances provided further testimonies, with many describing Yust as abusive toward Kara and alleging that he had admitted to her murder.

The following witness was Jaxxon Mallett, who had a relationship with Jessica at the time of her disappearance.

"I used to be friends with Kylr Yust, but I ended our relationship after discovering he was living with Jessica," he shared. "Yust would visit their home late at night, banging on the door and insisting on speaking with Jessica. He was furious and worried for her safety."

The prosecution subsequently summoned Jessica's mother, Jamie Runions.

"I was supposed to meet my daughter for a doctor's appointment on September 9, 2016," she recalled. "It was vital—she required clearance to go back to work after her appendectomy. I became worried when she didn't respond to my calls, texts, or Facebook messages. Eventually, I discovered that Jessica hadn't been seen since September 8, 2016."

Runions shared the harrowing months that followed, saying, "The seven months until my daughter's remains were found were the longest of my life. Regardless of the weather, search teams continued to look for Jessica. During this time, I grew very close to the Beckfords."

On April 12, 2021, the defense started its case, intending to attribute blame to Yust's late half-brother, Jessep Carter, who took his own life in 2018 while serving time for arson.

Defense attorney Sharon Turlington stated, "There is no hair or blood evidence linking Yust to these murders. He possesses solid alibis for the times of the crimes. On the day Kara went missing, he was with his grandparents and aunt and then attended band practice."

Turlington showed phone records indicating that Yust and Runions were apart during certain times, a point raised by prosecutors. She also named Carter as a potential suspect. "This case spans over ten years, and there is no physical evidence connecting Yust to either murder," she stated. "Kylr Yust is innocent."

Kylr Yust chose to take the stand and testify on his own behalf.

During his two-hour testimony, he claimed, "Kara asked me to pick her up from school on May 4, 2007. I brought my half-brother, Jessep, with me. I left Kara and Jessep alone together that afternoon and never saw Kara again. I only confessed to killing her when I was drunk and depressed about going to prison on unrelated charges."

In relation to Jessica's disappearance, he stated, "I was intoxicated that night. Jessica drove me to my grandfather's house, and Jessep arrived soon after. I don't recall anything else until the next morning."

He recently finished his testimony by acknowledging his past abusive behavior. He mentioned, "When Kara tried to leave me, I told her, 'If I can't have you, no one can.'"

During the trial, prosecutors Ben Butler and Julie Tolle carefully detailed Yust's pattern of abusive relationships with both victims. Tolle stated, "A severe sentence is warranted due to Yust's absence of remorse and refusal to accept responsibility. For parents, the loss of a child is a continuous nightmare. Days transformed into weeks, weeks into months, and months into years. Over 14 years, Yust had numerous chances to be honest but chose not to."

The defense sought to undermine the investigation by claiming the detectives mishandled evidence. Turlington remarked, "The suspects affected this investigation. Detectives misplaced crucial evidence, such as Yust's phone records. It seems illogical to expect Kylr to have committed two murders without leaving any trace."

However, Prosecutor Butler countered, "Yust murdered Jessica with deliberation, just as he did Kara before. He admitted to friends that he 'strangled the shit out of Kara and threw her in the middle of the damn woods.'"

In conclusion, the prosecution presented a 2011 recording in which Yust purportedly asked an ex-girlfriend, "Does it excite you that I killed a girl, huh?"

At last, the families of Kara Kopetsky and Jessica Runions got the much-anticipated verdict.

On April 15, 2021, after 13 hours of deliberation, the jury convicted Yust of voluntary manslaughter for Kara Kopetsky's death and second-degree murder regarding Jessica Runions.

Yust displayed no response when the verdict was announced.

He received a life sentence, along with an extra 15 years to be served consecutively, amounting to a total of 45 years, with the possibility of parole.

Following the sentencing, Kara's stepfather, Jim Beckford, expressed to reporters, "We are incredibly thankful for justice. We succeeded. The girls brought us together. Kara and Jessica deserved better than what happened to them."

Conversely, Kara's mother expressed her dissatisfaction: "To be precise, I don't think justice was served for Kara."

Currently, Kylr Yust is incarcerated at the Western Missouri Correctional Center, located in Cameron, Missouri, which adheres to medium to maximum security protocols.

Jessica Runions' murder provided Kara Kopetsky's family with closure nearly 14 years after her disappearance.

CHAPTER TWENTY-TWO

Butcher Baker – Robert Christian Hansen

Robert Christian Hansen, notoriously referred to as "The Butcher Baker," was an American serial killer who haunted Anchorage, Alaska, between 1972 and 1983.

He abducted, raped, and murdered at least 17 women—many of whom he released into the remote Alaskan wilderness, only to stalk and hunt them like prey.

Armed with a Ruger Mini-14 rifle and hunting knives, Hansen converted the forest into his personal hunting grounds. His violent rampage ended in 1983 when he was apprehended and sentenced to 461 years in prison, serving without the possibility of parole.

Hansen's journey began in Estherville, Iowa, where he was born on February 15, 1939, as the first of two children to Edna Margret Hansen and Christian "Chris" Hansen, a Danish immigrant and local baker. From an early age, Robert assisted his father in the bakery, although some concerning personality traits were starting to emerge.

During his youth, Hansen seemed fragile and frequently experienced feelings of isolation. His battles with severe acne and a constant stutter made him a common target for mockery. The sweet-natured girls in school rejected him, exacerbating the pain of rejection—a burden that trailed him to Alaska.

In 1942, the Hansen family moved to Richmond, California, but returned to Iowa in 1949, settling in Pocahontas. In this town, Hansen became known for his shyness, social isolation, and the difficulties arising from his strained relationship with his overbearing father. To address these issues, he developed a deep passion for hunting and archery—hobbies that would later take on a darker significance.

In 1957, Hansen joined the United States Army Reserve, serving for one year before being honorably discharged. After his service, he went back to Iowa and became an assistant drill instructor at the local police academy. During this time, he began a relationship with a younger woman, and the couple married in 1960.

On December 7 that year, Hansen was apprehended for arson after igniting a fire at a school bus garage in Pocahontas County.

This incident stemmed from lingering anger resulting from past bullying and social exclusion, culminating in a three-year prison term. Hansen served 20 months at Anamosa State Penitentiary, during which time his first wife divorced him. While incarcerated, he received a diagnosis of manic depression and encountered sporadic episodes of schizophrenia. A psychiatrist at the facility described him as possessing an "infantile personality" and having a dangerous obsession with vengeance.

Following his release, Hansen struggled to stay out of legal issues, facing several arrests for minor thefts. In 1967, he relocated to Anchorage, Alaska, with his second wife, whom he married in 1963. Together, they had two children, and

Hansen seemed to be beginning anew. He gained recognition as a friendly neighbor and an accomplished outdoorsman, even establishing several local hunting records.

However, deep down, the sharpshooter concealed a violent fury—one that was about to explode into one of the most horrifying killing sprees in Alaskan history.

His downfall started with Cindy Paulson, a 17-year-old prostitute. He paid her $200 for a blow job, then changed the rules. He took her back to his house, made her strip, and slapped handcuffs on her.

For hours, he tortured her, his excitement heightening his stutter. It felt as though one could hear him saying, "B-b-b-bitch, y-y-you t-t-take it." However, every game must come to an end.

He permitted her to dress. They were on their way to his cabin, where he brought women like her. There, he informed her that he would keep her for a week before ending her life.

He brought her to his private plane, ready to fly her into the isolated wilderness where no one could hear her screams. That's where he erred.

As he removed one handcuff and ordered her to board the plane, she saw her opportunity and fled. He pursued her, but she successfully escaped, running directly into the path of a police car while yelling, "He's going to kill me!"

The police followed her to the house she had fled. Robert Hansen, the respected local baker, owned it. They took her to the airport, where she identified his plane. All the details aligned perfectly. They had a suspect.

Hansen maintained an easy demeanor. When the police apprehended him, he remained composed, appearing anxious and stuttering, yet still convincing. He presented an alibi supported by two esteemed figures in Anchorage. Who would believe a prostitute's account over that of a reputable businessman?

The matter has been resolved.

In December 1971, Hansen had faced two arrests—first for the abduction and attempted rape of a housewife, and later for the rape of a sex worker.

He entered a no-contest plea for assault with a deadly weapon in the first case, and the rape charge was dismissed as part of a plea agreement.

He received a five-year prison sentence but was incarcerated for just six months before moving to a work-release program and subsequently to a halfway house.

In 1976, Hansen was arrested once more, this time for attempting to steal a chainsaw from a Fred Meyer store in Anchorage. He pleaded guilty to larceny and received a five-year prison sentence along with a requirement for psychiatric treatment. However, the Alaska Supreme Court subsequently commuted his sentence, allowing for his release due to time served.

Authorities suspect that Robert Hansen's first murder victim was 18-year-old Celia Van Zanten. On December 22, 1971, Van Zanten was abducted and tragically froze to death in the Alaskan wilderness after managing to escape from her captor.

Her body was discovered on December 25. The kidnapping occurred just three days after Hansen was jailed for assaulting a sex worker. While some aspects of Van Zanten's abduction align with Hansen's typical behavior, there is no conclusive evidence linking him to her murder, and he has denied any involvement.

More than a decade later, on June 13, 1983, Hansen abducted 17-year-old Cindy Paulson after offering her $200 for oral sex.

Paulson later recounted to authorities that Hansen had chained her by the neck to a post in his basement before taking a nap on a nearby couch. Upon waking, he forced her into his car. He drove to Merrill Field, where he intended to transport her to his remote hunting shack near the Knik River, accessible only by boat or bush plane.

While Hansen was preparing his Piper PA-18 Super Cub, Paulson seized the moment to flee. Though her hands were cuffed, she maneuvered out of the back seat, opened the driver's door, and dashed toward Sixth Avenue. Intentionally, she left her blue sneakers behind in the car as evidence of her escape. When Hansen noticed she was missing, he panicked and pursued her.

Officers from the Anchorage Police Department (APD) arrived at the Mush Inn, but Paulson had already traveled by taxi to the Big Timber Motel. They discovered her in Room 110, still handcuffed and alone. She was taken to APD headquarters, where she provided a detailed description of her assailant. When questioned, Hansen denied all accusations, claiming Paulson was attempting to extort him. His composed demeanor, positive reputation as a baker, and alibi from his friend John Henning led the police to rule him out as a serious suspect.

On July 21, 1980, Detective Glenn Flothe of the Alaska State Troopers was looking into a string of murders occurring in Anchorage, Seward, and the Matanuska-Susitna Valley. The initial victim, found by construction workers close to Eklutna Road, was an unidentified woman referred to as "Eklutna Annie" by investigators.

Later that year, the remains of Joanna Messina, age 24, were discovered in a gravel pit near Seward. In 1982, the body of 23-year-old Sherry Morrow was found in a shallow grave near the Knik River. Flothe suspected that all three women were victims of the same murderer.

In pursuit of deeper understanding, Flothe reached out to FBI Special Agent John Douglas, a leading expert in criminal profiling. Douglas theorized that the killer was a skilled hunter struggling with feelings of inadequacy and a background of rejection by women. He inferred that this individual probably kept items like jewelry from his victims and might have had a stutter. With this profile in mind, Flothe focused his investigation on Robert Hansen, who owned a private plane and fit the description.

With the backing of Paulson's testimony and Douglas's profile, investigators obtained a warrant to search Hansen's aircraft, vehicles, and residence.

On October 27, 1983, authorities discovered a cache of damning evidence in Hansen's attic, which included jewelry belonging to missing women and a variety of firearms.

Among the weapons was a .223-caliber Ruger Mini-14 semi-automatic rifle. More chillingly, investigators found an aeronautical chart concealed behind Hansen's headboard, marked with 37 small "X"s. Many of these locations corresponded to sites where bodies had already been discovered, and others later revealed additional remains.

Confronted with compelling evidence, Hansen first rejected all allegations. Yet, as detectives systematically revealed incriminating information, he started to shift the blame onto his victims to rationalize his behavior.

Ultimately, he confessed to a violent spree that began in 1971, targeting young women, primarily aged 16 to 19.

While his earliest victims were not sex workers, many of the women he later hunted were, a pattern that ultimately led to his capture.

Robert Hansen is confirmed to have raped and assaulted over 30 women and murdered at least 17, with victims ranging in age from 16 to 41. However, based on forensic and circumstantial evidence, law enforcement suspects the actual number of his victims could be at least 21.

He was accused of kidnapping and sexually assaulting Cindy Paulson.

Here is a list of victims known or believed to be associated with Hansen. He was officially charged with the murders of four individuals: Sherry Morrow, Joanna Messina, Eklutna Annie, and Paula Goulding.

Confirmed and Suspected Victims

Celia Beth van Zanten (18) – Disappeared in Anchorage on December 22, 1971; found deceased on December 25 in Chugach State Park. Her body showed signs of sexual assault and knife wounds before being left to die from exposure. Though an "X" on Hansen's map marked the location of her body, he denied involvement.

On July 7, 1973, 17-year-old Megan Siobhan Emerick vanished from Seward after being spotted leaving her dormitory's laundry room. Extensive searches yielded no results, and a marked "X" on Hansen's map near Seward hints at his possible connection.

Mary Kathleen Thill (22) – Last seen near a waterfall in Seward on July 5, 1975. Hansen admitted to killing her and disposing of her body in Resurrection Bay.

Eklutna Annie (Unknown) – Found on July 21, 1980, close to South Eklutna Lake Road. Hansen admitted to killing her, stating she was his first victim. Parts of her remains were eaten by wildlife.

Joanna Messina (24) – Killed on May 19, 1980, after refusing to engage in sex work. Hansen shot her and disposed of her body near Snow River, where it was found in July.

On June 28, 1980, Roxane Easland (24) vanished following a scheduled downtown meeting. Despite Hansen's confession to the murder, her body remains missing.

On September 6, 1980, 41-year-old Lisa Futrell was kidnapped and discovered buried in a shallow grave near the Knik Arm Bridge in 1984.

On November 17, 1981, Sherry Morrow (23) went missing after scheduling a photography session. Her remains, discovered in 1982, showed gunshot wounds to her back.

Andrea Mona "Fish" Altiery (24) was last spotted on December 2, 1981. Hansen confessed to abducting and killing her, yet her remains are still undiscovered.

Sue Luna (23) – Last seen on May 26, 1982, after agreeing to a photography session. Hansen admitted to hunting her like an animal before shooting her. Her body was found in 1984 near the Knik River.

At 19, Robin Pelkey was called "Horseshoe Harriet" until she was identified in 2021. In April 1984, her body was discovered near Horseshoe Lake with both stab and gunshot wounds.

DeLynne "Sugar" Renee Frey (22) was last seen in March 1983; her remains were discovered near the Knik River in August 1985.

Hansen lured and abducted Paula Goulding, 30, who was shot on April 25, 1983. Authorities found her body in September 1983 near the Knik River.

On June 13, 1983, Cindy Paulson, 17, was abducted. She managed to escape and later identified Hansen, leading to his arrest.

Malai Larsen (28) went missing on July 10, 1981, and her remains were found near the Knik Arm Bridge in 1984.

Teresa Watson (22) was last seen on March 25, 1983. Hansen left her body at Scenic Lake since he could not bury it due to the frozen ground. Her remains were uncovered in April 1984.

Angela Lynn Feddern (24) was last seen in February 1983 and reported missing in May. Her remains were found near Figure Eight Lake in April 1984.

Tamera "Tami" Pederson (20), a nightclub dancer, vanished in August 1982. Her remains were found in April 1984 after Hansen revealed where she was buried.

Following his arrest, Robert Hansen faced serious charges including assault, kidnapping, numerous weapons violations, theft, and insurance fraud. This fraud arose from a claim he filed, asserting that several of his hunting trophies had been stolen. Investigators found that Hansen had used the insurance money to purchase a small aircraft. When questioned, he asserted that he had discovered the trophies buried in his back yard, claiming he had merely forgotten to notify the insurance company.

Faced with compelling evidence, Hansen eventually accepted a plea deal, which included ballistic examinations connecting bullets found at various crime scenes to his hunting rifle. During the court proceedings, he admitted to the murders of Sherry Morrow, Andrea "Fish" Altiery, Eklutna Annie, and Paula Goulding, all of whom had substantial physical evidence. In exchange, Hansen sought to avoid media attention and to be incarcerated in a federal prison.

The plea agreement also mandated Hansen to assist law enforcement in deciphering the cryptic symbols on his aviation map, which supposedly indicated where his victims' bodies were located.

During a series of interviews, Hansen confessed to abducting women under false pretenses and supported the investigators' theory: he transported his victims to remote wilderness areas, released them, and then hunted them down like game. He stated that he sometimes spared victims if they convinced him they wouldn't report him to the police. He acknowledged that his killing spree began in the early 1970s.

Taking Hansen's suggestions into account, investigators identified 17 burial sites throughout Southcentral Alaska, including twelve previously unknown sites. Nevertheless, Hansen's map lacked clear information about specific markings, particularly three locations close to Seward in Resurrection Bay. Authorities believe that two of these sites might be associated with the remains of Mary Thill and Megan Emrick, though Hansen refutes any links to their disappearances.

A total of 12 victims have been discovered and positively identified. However, law enforcement believes that Hansen's actual victim count may range from 21 to 37.

In 1984, Robert Hansen received a sentence of 461 years in prison, with no parole. He began his incarceration at the United States Penitentiary in Lewisburg, Pennsylvania, but was relocated back to Alaska in 1988. Upon his return to Alaska, he was initially placed at the Lemon Creek Correctional Center in Juneau before being transferred to the Spring Creek Correctional Center in Seward.

In May 2014, Hansen was transferred to the Anchorage Correctional Complex for medical treatment due to his deteriorating health.

He died of natural causes at Alaska Regional Hospital in Anchorage on August 21, 2014, at the age of 75.

This case occupies a unique position in true crime history for two primary reasons. First, it is the only documented case where multiple victims were allegedly kidnapped, taken deep into the Alaskan wilderness, released, and hunted like prey. While Hansen admitted to numerous murders, the complete scope of his offenses is still ambiguous. Many presumed victims have not been located, and others might never be recognized.

Secondly, it marked a pivotal moment in forensic history. In 1983, psychological profiling was used for the first time as the primary basis for issuing a search warrant, directing investigators to Robert Hansen's property. This innovative legal precedent transformed the way law enforcement handled intricate and predatory criminal cases.

Hansen's disturbing modus operandi of abduction, sexual assault, and execution-style murders greatly affected the methods detectives employ to monitor wandering serial criminals across states and countries.

CHAPTER TWENTY-THREE

SoCal Serial Rapist – Andrew Urdiales

On September 28, 1992, Jennifer Asbenson, a 19-year-old, was abducted and brought to a secluded location in Palm Desert, California.

Jennifer's abductor, Andrew Urdiales, a 32-year-old former U.S. Marine, had already murdered several people in California before he targeted her. That night, while buying candy for disabled girls at the hospital where she worked as a nursing assistant, Jennifer missed her bus.

Feeling nervous about her 10:00 p.m. shift—an arrival time her boss had warned could jeopardize her job—she experienced a wave of relief when Urdiales pulled up in a light-colored sedan and offered her a ride. Initially hesitant, she soon saw it as a fortunate opportunity. After assessing him and reassuring herself that she could manage any potential risks, she opted to accept the ride.

Urdiales drove Jennifer to the hospital, making flirtatious remarks that she brushed off. Once she got out of his car, he invited her to have breakfast after her shift. To avoid any more contact, she provided him with a fake phone number to close the conversation.

After Jennifer completed her shift the next day, Urdiales was waiting outside for her. He greeted her with a smile and again proposed a ride. Since nothing unsettling occurred the night before, she agreed. However, just two blocks later, his attitude shifted entirely.

In a fit of rage over the fake phone number, he grabbed her by the hair and repeatedly slammed her head against the dashboard.

Blood dripped from her forehead as he tied her hands behind her back, pressed a knife to her throat, and muttered a chilling, "Damn bitch."

Urdiales subsequently took her to a secluded area of the desert, where he committed a violent assault.

He was calculated and vicious, pulling out a gun, attempting to rape her, and then retrieving a bag of blades.

He bit her neck, beat her savagely, and stuffed part of her torn underwear into her mouth. With his fist lodged in her mouth, he demanded she say she loved him. When her muffled words didn't satisfy him, he slapped her. "You're lying, bitch. Say it like you damn well mean it," he snarled.

He then forced her to perform oral sex, but when he failed to get an erection, his frustration turned deadly. Enraged, he strangled her until she passed out.

When Jennifer regained consciousness, she noticed an opportunity to escape. She took off running, but Urdiales caught her, yanking her by the hair and dragging her across rough terrain filled with rocks and cacti before throwing her into the trunk of his car.

While he accelerated away, she fought against her restraints. In her frantic state, she scratched at the inside of the trunk, ripping the carpet in a desperate attempt to find something that could help her flee. Finally, she found the lever that would unlock the trunk latch.

Barefoot and lightly dressed, she jumped from the moving vehicle, fleeing in terror while crying out. She glanced back and spotted Urdiales chasing her, wielding a machete overhead.

She waved down a truck. Noticing Urdiales pursuing her, the two Marines inside quickly helped her into their vehicle. They sped to the nearest gas station, where Jennifer immediately contacted the police.

Jennifer's courage and resolute determination enabled her to face challenges and avert a tragic outcome. She firmly confronted Andrew Urdiales in court, achieving the justice she rightfully deserved.

Initially, no one, not even Jennifer's family, believed her horrific ordeal. They viewed her story as if it were pulled from a horror novel. Unbeknownst to Jennifer, Andrew Urdiales had already murdered four women and would go on to kill four more in Illinois and California.

Five years later, when Urdiales confessed, she felt overwhelming relief and a sense of closure. Looking back on the 1990s, Jennifer recognized her naivety; having been raised without television or electricity, she was completely oblivious to the existence of serial killers, let alone someone like Urdiales.

Confined in the trunk of the car, a chilling realization struck her—he had done this unspeakable thing before. Yet, she remained unable to comprehend the depth of his heinous deeds fully.

Urdiales claims that Jennifer Asbenson was the sole woman capable of escaping him. She was the final target of a clever predator who had managed to avoid being detected.

On the night of January 18, 1986, 23-year-old Robbin Brandley served as an usher at a jazz concert held at Saddleback College in Mission Viejo, California. After the concert concluded, a routine shift in the auditorium took a dark twist. While the audience dispersed, Robbin headed toward her car, oblivious to the predator lurking in the pitch-black parking lot.

Robbin never reached her vehicle. A security guard later found her body; she had been stabbed 41 times with a knife, suffering wounds to her back, neck, chest, and hands.

The brutality of the attack stunned everyone. Initially, there were no witnesses, motives, or suspects identified, and months stretched into years.

Determined to uncover the truth, Robbin's parents worked tirelessly to keep her story alive. They hired a private investigator, pursued every lead, and even contemplated the possibility that her murderer might be a classmate. Sadly, each lead proved to be a dead end.

"It was utterly irrational, totally arbitrary, and severe," remarked Helen Moreno, a supervising investigator with the Orange County District Attorney's Office. "There was no indication of a robbery... her purse was left untouched, and her keys were located nearby. Sadly, Robbin Brandley found herself in the wrong place at the wrong time."

The murder remained unsolved for more than ten years before Andrew Urdiales became a suspect.

Cook County Prosecutor Jim McKay later commented on Urdiales, stating, "He aimed to harm someone defenseless, someone innocent. The motive for this remains ambiguous. To grasp it, we must explore the disturbed mind of Andrew Urdiales. Each stab wound unveiled deep-seated hatred and fury. He had no connection to her, and she did not provoke his actions."

Later police records would reveal the disturbing extent of Urdiales' premeditation. He meticulously planned his crimes, preparing himself not only for murder but also for avoiding capture.

Even after leaving California, he maintained a storage locker near Palm Springs, filled with the instruments of his horrific profession—his "special murder kit."

Investigators uncovered a .45 caliber pistol, ammunition, a machete, masks, Illinois license plates, shovels, twine, and duct tape. Every item, disturbingly selected, served as tools for carrying out his imminent murder.

"Urdiales had a carefully devised plan," said Orange County Deputy District Attorney Howard Gundy. "He would fly in, rent a car, assemble his murder kit, and then kidnap and kill a woman in the desert."

In his younger years, Urdiales was seen as a solitary figure and an outsider. He graduated from Thornridge High School in Dolton, Illinois, in 1982, frequently tagged as a social misfit.

At a high school reunion years later, he disclosed a shocking truth. He confided to a former classmate, "I killed two women in California, thinking they were prostitutes, believing I was helping them."

His colleague dismissed the remark as absurd. "That's ridiculous, Andrew; we're just going in circles," he replied.

However, it was not absurd; it was a frightening truth.

Andrew Urdiales was born on June 4, 1964, to Alfre and Margret Urdiales. He served in the Marine Corps from 1984 to 1991, starting his service at the Marine Corps Air Ground Combat Center in Twentynine Palms from 1987 to 1989, before being moved to Camp Pendleton.

In 1991, he served as a trained radio operator during Desert Storm, although his colleagues were oblivious to the fact that he was also a ruthless criminal.

In a humorous twist, Urdiales acquired the nickname "Corporal Urinalysis" while serving in the Marines, thanks to his quirky twitch and awkward small talk. Although he held the rank of corporal, his subordinates often brushed aside his orders, typically reacting with laughter rather than obedience.

During his military service, Urdiales developed a relationship with a 15-year-old girl, leading to her pregnancy. Worried about her parents' response and the ramifications within the military, he agreed to her request for an abortion. "I loved her and still love her," he later told Dr. Dorothy Otnow Lewis, a psychiatrist and internationally recognized expert on violence, who has spent the last quarter century studying the minds of killers. She co-authored the book *Guilty by Reason of Insanity: A Psychiatrist Explores the Minds of Killers.* She testified in his initial trial.

Dr. Lewis informed the court, "The law, the State of California, and the Marine Corps might interpret this in various ways." She also disclosed that Urdiales came from a family with a history of mental illness. He had endured both physical and emotional abuse from his parents, as well as sexual abuse from his sister and a male cousin. Moreover, he had faced persistent bullying in school and during his military service.

Despite ongoing challenges, Urdiales was honorably discharged from the Marines. He then sought psychiatric help at a veterans' hospital in Chicago. On April 12, 1996, just two days before a woman was murdered, a psychologist recommended that he be more open about his anger.

Experts confirmed that Urdiales suffered from a brain injury and lived with Tourette's Syndrome, a common neurodevelopmental disorder. He also experienced auditory hallucinations, often perceiving coded messages that prompted him to undertake violent "missions."

In his working-class Chicago neighborhood, locals recalled him as an average teenager, until he came back from the Marines and appeared to have undergone a significant transformation.

His former Bowen High School classmates in Chicago recalled having beers with him by the warm glow of bonfires near the Skyway.

At 31, Gerry Thompson recalled, "Urdiales had a relationship with my sister for several months before enlisting in the Marines."

Another acquaintance, Gary Zabala, 34, noted, "He changed significantly after returning from the Marines. I truly believe the Marines had a profound impact on his life."

Urdiales frequently visited the Casino Restaurant directly opposite his parents' house. As noted by owner Nick Pervan-Kennedy, "He consistently came alone, quietly seated in a corner, enjoying a few beers."

His disturbing crime spree began on July 17, 1988, with the disappearance of 29-year-old Julie McGhee, a sex worker last seen in a prominent sex work district in Cathedral City, California.

"I drove her to a remote construction site far out in the desert, where we had sex. A short time later, I told McGhee to get out of my car, then for no particular reason, I shot her in the head," Urdiales later confessed to investigators.

"I felt nothing after killing McGhee. The desert was quiet where it happened. Afterward, I headed to a strip club, had a few beers, and watched the dancers."

McGhee's body, stripped of identification, was left exposed to the elements. By the time authorities discovered her remains, scavenging animals had mutilated much of her corpse, making identification a challenging task.

On September 25, 1988, 31-year-old Mary Ann Wells, known for her involvement in prostitution, was picked up by Andrew Urdiales in San Diego. He transported her to a remote industrial area that he likely had surveyed beforehand.

Hours later, authorities discovered her body abandoned in an alleyway.

San Diego Police Lieutenant Jim Collins later stated, "Law enforcement officials believe Urdiales shot and killed Mary Ann Wells. She was shot in the head. Urdiales dumped her body in an alley where it was later found, along with the spent condom he had left behind."

Less than a year later, on April 16, 1989, Urdiales focused on 19-year-old Tammie Erwin, another prostitute with whom he had previously engaged at least once. That night, he picked her up and drove her to a vacant lot near Palm Springs. After she performed oral sex on him, Urdiales made a decision that would transform another casual encounter into murder.

"I don't recall having arguments with Erwin as I did with some others," he later confessed. "However, I remember shooting her while she was outside my truck, preparing to leave."

He described the execution with chilling detachment: "I was inside the pickup when I shot her. She was standing there holding her head. I shot her a second time, which brought her to the ground. Before I took off, I shot her a third time."

Years later, the cycle of violence persisted. On March 11, 1995, Urdiales roamed the streets of Riverside County and picked up 32-year-old Denise Maney, a sex worker from the Palm Springs region. He drove her deep into the desert, far from any potential witnesses. Once they arrived at a remote location, the nightmare commenced.

After forcing Maney to strip, Urdiales bound her hands behind her back and raped her. But his sadistic hunger remained unsatisfied. He yanked her by the hair and forced her to the front of his car, where he made her lie face down.

Then, with calculated cruelty, he flipped her onto her back and forced her to perform oral sex. When that no longer pleased him, he shoved her onto her knees. He violently assaulted her anally with his fingers, ignoring her screams of agony as he tore into her.

As Maney wept and bled, Urdiales executed his final act. He turned her to face him, thrust the gun's barrel into her mouth, and pulled the trigger. The blast blew apart the back of her skull, instantly killing her.

After satisfying his desire for control, Urdiales left Maney's body to rot under the desert sun—yet another unidentified victim discarded without a second thought.

On April 14, 1996, 25-year-old Lori Uylaki, who worked as a sex worker, was abducted from the street and taken to the Wolf Lake area, which borders Hammond, Indiana, and Chicago.

Once there, she was brutally attacked—stabbed and shot twice in the head and chest with a .38-caliber Smith & Wesson revolver. After she collapsed, Andrew Urdiales approached her body to confirm she was dead before callously discarding her nude remains into Wolf Lake.

At that moment, officials in Illinois did not associate Uylaki's murder with the killings happening in California.

Just months later, on July 13, 1996, Urdiales encountered 21-year-old Cassandra "Cassie" Corum, another prostitute, at a bar on Michigan Avenue in Hammond. He lured her into his vehicle and drove her back to Wolf Lake, where he engaged in sadistic sexual intercourse.

At one moment, Cassie said something that infuriated him; however, he stated during his trial that he could not remember what it was.

"I started hitting Cassie in the face with my fist and open hand," he testified. "She got scared, bit my face, and began to panic, so I took out my handcuffs and forced them on her, securing her hands behind her back. I tore her clothes off and taped her mouth shut with duct tape, then drove south on Interstate 55. About 100 miles from Chicago, I pulled off the highway into a park, turned off my truck's lights, and removed the handcuffs and duct tape. Cassie, still naked, got out of the truck."

As she walked to the back of the vehicle and turned to face him, likely about to plead for her life, Urdiales shot her in the face. His rage is still unchecked; he grabbed a knife and stabbed her repeatedly. "I don't remember how many times," he admitted in court. "The knife didn't have much blood on it, so I put it back in the truck."

Once it was over, he picked up Cassie's lifeless form and tossed her into the Vermilion River from a bridge.

The following day, July 14, 1996, Cassie's lifeless body was found floating in a river in Livingston County, Illinois, close to the town of Pontiac. An autopsy indicated she had suffered seven stab wounds to her chest and head.

On August 2, 1996, Andrew Urdiales visited Chicago's North Side, where he met 22-year-old Lynn Huber. Seeing her walking with a plastic bag of clothes, Urdiales offered her a ride, and she accepted.

An argument erupted as they traveled toward the L tracks at 1036 W. Irving Park Road. Without warning, Urdiales grabbed Huber by the hair, yanked her from the truck, and threw her to the ground. He pulled out his gun and fired multiple times, hitting her only once in the head.

The detective who secured his confession recounted, "Urdiales mentioned that he loaded her and her bag of clothes into his truck and drove south, thinking it was the right direction. He also noted his frustration as he drove with the window down."

Upon arriving at Wolf Lake, Urdiales removed Huber's clothing and, showing chilling indifference, stabbed her repeatedly before nonchalantly pushing her body into the water.

He discarded her clothes in a dumpster before heading back to his Southeast Side home, where he slept as if it were just another typical day.

Days later, Lynn Huber's body was found floating in Wolf Lake, only a few yards from where Laura Uylaki's remains had been discovered that spring.

Seven victims demonstrated the same violent patterns. Yet, investigators failed to make the connections. These cases were not linked to a serial killer by anyone.

The real question is: Why not?

On November 14, 1996, events took a turn. Urdiales was positioned outside a notorious drug house at 831 Becker Street in Hammond, Indiana, alongside a known prostitute, when Patrolman Warren Fryer approached his truck, he noticed something was amiss and called for backup.

Shortly thereafter, more officers arrived. While Urdiales nonchalantly talked about his time in the Marines, Fryer noticed a revolver and yelled, "Gun!"

An officer promptly secured the firearm—a fully loaded chrome-plated .38 Smith & Wesson snub-nosed revolver housing six bullets. A swift review of police records indicated that Urdiales did not possess the required firearm permit in Indiana. He was arrested immediately, and the weapon was confiscated.

Before towing the truck, officers searched. They discovered a sleeping bag and a gym bag filled with duct tape. However, it was the unsettling cleanliness of Urdiales' vehicle that particularly caught Officer Fryer's attention.

Fryer observed, "The interior of the bed and cab was immaculate. The truck and cab appeared like they had just left the showroom... an uncommon sight against typical standards."

After Fryer's shift concluded, he examined Urdiales's records. Recognizing there was more context surrounding the arrest, he drafted a supplemental report and sent it to the detectives.

Alison Perona, Assistant State's Attorney in the Wolf Lake murder case, later stated, "Urdiales is a cunning, ruthless, and predatory killer who was apprehended due to a series of unfortunate incidents and dedicated police work."

Almost six months later, on April 1, 1997, Officer Fryer answered a call regarding a disagreement between a man and a woman at the American Inn, located at 4000 Calumet Avenue in Hammond. While Urdiales was preoccupied, expressing his grievances about a supposed theft to another officer, Patricia Kelly, a familiar prostitute from Hammond, made a startling remark to the police:

"This person has some unusual interests. He wants to take me to the back of his pickup truck, restrain me with handcuffs, and engage in anal sex."

Fryer, conscious of the recent killings of Lori Uylaki and Lynn Huber, quickly warned her, "Patricia, please don't do that. We're discovering dead girls up there."

Three weeks later, on April 22, 1997, Detectives Don McGrath and Raymond Krakausky set up surveillance in an alley just half a block from Urdiales's parents' home. At around 9:00 a.m., dressed in his security guard uniform and carrying a small brown lunch bag, Urdiales headed to work at an Eddie Bauer store in downtown Chicago. The detectives approached him to ask about a case from November 1996 regarding the seizure of his .38-caliber revolver.

Urdiales replied nonchalantly, saying, "The issue is settled, but I'm happy to discuss it regardless."

At the Area 2 police headquarters in Chicago, detectives escorted him into a small interrogation room to present photographs of Uylaki, Corum, and Huber.

Urdiales simply stated, "I don't know any of those three women."

Unaware of the detectives' intentions, they acted on a hunch. Earlier, he had been arrested in Indiana for illegal firearm possession, leading to the confiscation of his .38-caliber revolver. A week before its scheduled destruction, McGrath and Krakausky intervened, retrieving the weapon and promptly sending it to the Illinois crime lab.

McGrath later referred to it as "a shot in the dark," but it was successful.

Ballistics analysis confirmed that Urdiales's weapon had fired the bullets that killed the three women.

McGrath stepped closer. "Where did you get your revolver?"

Urdiales shrugged. "I purchased it for $300 in Calumet City around five years ago."

McGrath subtly smiled before landing the final blow: "The ammunition used in the murders of Tammie Erwin, Julie McGhee, and Mary Ann Wells was sourced from your firearm."

Urdiales's posture sagged. He removed his security badge, loosened his tie, and untied his shoelaces.

"It seems I won't be able to go to work today," he murmured.

After that, the floodgates swung wide open.

Without hesitation, Urdiales confessed. "I shot a White prostitute in her late 20s or early 30s in San Diego sometime between 1987 and 1989. I shot Julie McGhee, a 30-year-old local prostitute, in Cathedral City in 1988. I shot Tammie Erwin, a 19-year-old prostitute, in 1989. I stabbed Denise Maney, a 32-year-old prostitute, in 1995. I had no rational motive for any of it. I was just agitated when the women begged for their lives."

Curiously, he omitted the murder of 31-year-old Mary Ann Wells that took place in 1988.

Additional laboratory tests conclusively established his culpability by directly connecting him to the murders of Uylaki, Corum, and Huber.

Later, Lieutenant John Boot from Palm Springs noted, "Urdiales recalled every detail and dedicated the next several hours to providing a comprehensive confession regarding the murders of Jennifer Asbenson, Lori Uylaki, Cassandra 'Cassie' Corum, and Lynn Huber."

After Urdiales confessed, law enforcement in Illinois worked with officials from California to create an indictment.

An indictment against Urdiales was formally submitted on April 29, 1997. Nonetheless, legal and political discussions delayed the trial for five years.

In 2002, Andrew Urdiales was tried in Cook County, Illinois, for the murders of Laura Uylaki and Lynn Huber. He was convicted of first-degree murder in both cases and sentenced to death.

In 2004, Urdiales faced trial again, this time for murdering Cassandra Corum. He was found guilty of first-degree murder and received a death sentence once more. Following an appeal and the end of the evidentiary phase, he was extradited to California to be tried for the murders of Robbin Brandley, Julie McGhee, Mary Ann Wells, Tammie Erwin, and Denise Maney.

In July 2009, California passed legislation that allowed the merging of linked murder cases, leading prosecutors to combine five separate murder cases into one. Senior Deputy

District Attorney Howard Gundy of the Orange County District Attorney's Office supervised the case.

In the sentencing phase of the trial for Corum's murder, Detective Don McGrath disclosed that Urdiales stated, "I'm glad you caught me. I was beginning to feel the urge again." This prompted discussions about whether Urdiales should receive the death penalty, particularly as Illinois contemplated abolishing capital punishment.

His trial for the murders of Uylaki and Huber began on April 8, 2002. On April 30, 2001, the prosecutor formally announced the intent to seek the death penalty. Urdiales was found guilty on May 23, 2002, and sentenced to death seven days later, on May 30, 2002.

The Urdiales case highlighted issues identified by the Governor's Commission on Capital Punishment, which published a report outlining flaws in the criminal justice system and the capital sentencing method. This report pointed out that Urdiales faced severe mental health issues, which were overlooked as mitigating factors. Both the prosecution and defense acknowledged the difficulties in his upbringing, marked by experiences of physical abuse and neglect. When Urdiales was only three, his older brother's death in Vietnam plunged his mother into a profound depression. From 1991 to 1996, Urdiales participated in 90 hours of counseling with Veterans Administration therapists, seeking help for his anger and depression. His propensity for violence surfaced early, highlighted by the vicious killing of the family dog with a baseball bat before he reached the age of 13.

Defense attorneys argued that Urdiales had mild bipolar disorder, post-traumatic stress disorder, and brain abnormalities that affected his judgment. A doctor testified that Urdiales's brain cortex was smaller than average and showed tissue loss linked to his mother's alcohol consumption during pregnancy.

However, forensic psychiatrist Dr. Park Dietz dismissed these assertions, determining that Urdiales was merely a sexual sadist harboring profound resentment toward women.

Urdiales' situation shifted politically after a study by Northwestern University revealed wrongful convictions among death row inmates in Illinois. Alarmed by the state of the justice system, before leaving office, Governor George Ryan commuted all 167 death sentences on January 11, 2003. Consequently, his sentence was changed to life imprisonment.

Following that, the prosecution issued an indictment in the unresolved murder case of Cassandra Corum. The trial began on April 24, 2004. With Stephen Richards leading the defense, Urdiales altered his strategy by pleading guilty and blaming his actions on mental illness. Nevertheless, on May 10, 2004, Judge Harold Frobish sentenced him to death. In March 2011, Governor Pat Quinn abolished the death penalty in Illinois, causing Urdiales' second death sentence to be converted to life imprisonment.

Shortly after Governor Quinn arrived at his decision, Orange County prosecutors initiated extradition efforts to bring Urdiales to trial for five murders that occurred in California. On May 23, 2018, a jury found Urdiales guilty on all five counts of first-degree murder, supported by testimonies from several witnesses, including one of the victims who survived.

On June 13, 2018, the jury recommended the death penalty for every murder, resulting in his third death sentence on October 5, 2018.

Less than a month later, on November 2, 2018, at 11:15 p.m., officials found Urdiales unresponsive in his cell during a routine security check at San Quentin State Prison. He was by himself, and authorities concluded that he had committed suicide by hanging. At that time, Urdiales was 54 years old.

CHAPTER TWENTY-FOUR

Social Media Murderer
– Joshua Keadle

Tyler "Ty" Thomas, the daughter of LaTanya and Richard Thomas, was born on September 7, 1991. She was last seen at the intersection of 5th and Nebraska Streets in Peru, Nebraska, on December 3, 2010.

One evening, Tyler went to a party near the Southeast Nebraska Campus and drank heavily. Friends noted that she had several beers and many shots of tequila; it was time for her to leave. As she exited, she argued with her best friend, kicked a hole in the wall, and slurred, "I'm going to Omaha, even if I have to walk."

Unaware of the looming tragedy, Tyler departed the party and headed two blocks toward her dorm at Peru State College. The last known sighting of her took place near the town water tower, only a short distance from her dorm.

Campus security cameras captured Tyler outside at 1:06 a.m. and again at 1:08 a.m., notably without a coat and holding her phone. Shortly before 1:30 a.m., she messaged a friend to indicate she was lost. However, a witness spotted her near the dorm building around that time.

Tyler never returned indoors. Her friends quickly became worried, not only due to her intoxicated condition but also because the temperature had plummeted into the teens. At 3:00 a.m., only an hour and a half after she was last seen, Tyler was reported missing. Her friends scoured the area until 5:00 a.m., but their attempts were unsuccessful. Tyler Thomas disappeared without a trace.

Tyler's family and friends were heartbroken by her sudden disappearance, dismissing any idea she might have been left alone. She had abandoned her purse and coat, showing no signs of distress. In truth, she was flourishing in college. She was a member of the Peru State dance team and had already signed up for the upcoming semester. An Omaha Bryan High School graduate, she lived in Bellevue, Nebraska, when not in classes. She dreamed of becoming a teacher.

Just days following her disappearance, fellow Peru State student Joshua Keadle was identified as a person of interest. Keadle, who lived across the hall from Tyler in the dorm, had previously taken her on a date, yet she did not reciprocate his feelings and sought to avoid him.

Born on September 2, 1981, Joshua Keadle was a junior majoring in sports management and significantly older than Tyler. When the police questioned him, he first said, "I did see Tyler walking along the road the night she disappeared, but I never stopped to talk to her." However, his story soon took a different turn.

Just days later, Keadle was taken into custody on separate charges of felony rape and false imprisonment. Additionally, he faced allegations of indecent exposure stemming from an incident in which he reportedly exposed himself to a woman several months before Tyler's disappearance.

After additional questioning, Keadle changed his account, ultimately admitting, "Tyler entered my car, and we drove to the Peru Boat Dock on the Missouri River to smoke marijuana." Investigators found tire tracks matching Keadle's 1996 Ford Explorer close to the dock and noted drag marks leading from the pier to the riverbank.

Keadle's final statement was profoundly incriminating. He told police, "Tyler told me she would give me a blow job in exchange for a ride to Omaha. But after I finished all over her face, she accused me of raping her. She threw her cell phone at me, and we got into a verbal argument that turned physical. Around 2:00 a.m., I left her on the dock alone and returned to my dorm to shower."

Further investigation showed that Keadle had searched online to find out if fingerprints could be retrieved from a corpse discovered in a river.

On December 9, six days following Tyler's disappearance, Keadle was arrested for tampering with evidence and giving false information to the police. Shortly thereafter, he faced formal charges of felony rape and false imprisonment after another woman accused him of sexually assaulting her three times in the month prior to Tyler's disappearance.

Sadly, Tyler Thomas remains missing. Investigators, her family, and the community believe she fell victim to a serial predator whose actions ultimately led to his capture. For Tyler, that fateful December night initiated a nightmare from which she has yet to escape.

Another teenage girl came forward, alleging that in April 2008, when she was just 15 years old, Joshua Keadle raped her while she was staying overnight on the campus of Midland Lutheran College—now known as Midland University—in Fremont, Nebraska. At the time, Keadle was a student at the college. He was subsequently charged with first-degree sexual assault of a minor in connection with the case.

In another case, officials in Madison County, Nebraska, charged Keadle with indecent exposure for reportedly exposing himself to a woman in Norfolk, Nebraska, in April 2010.

In March 2012, Keadle was found guilty of the 2008 rape and received a prison sentence of 15 to 20 years, which is significantly less than the maximum penalty of 50 years. In the same year, Tyler Thomas's mother initiated a wrongful death lawsuit against Keadle and Peru State College.

In the week leading up to Tyler's disappearance, the director of campus security at Peru State College recommended Keadle's expulsion. He later informed the police, "Keadle was failing his classes. He had been charged criminally for breaking down the door of his dorm room. Two students had reported him for sexual harassment within the first two weeks of his stay in the residence halls, and I knew he had faced a previous rape accusation at another Nebraska college. Although the school did not expel him right away, we were determined not to let him return for the second semester."

Despite an ongoing investigation, Tyler remained missing, leading a judge to declare her dead in 2013 officially. Although her body was never recovered, the State awarded a death certificate for Tyler Marie Thomas.

After two years, a judge dismissed the lawsuit against Peru State College, stating that the institution could not have anticipated Keadle as a potential violent threat.

Many believe Tyler was thrown into the Missouri River, near her college campus.

In May 2016, the Thomas family won $2.64 billion in damages from Keadle in their lawsuit.

The decision included:

$80 million for wrongful death
$100 million for the pain and suffering endured by her family
$30 million for emotional distress
$2.4 billion in punitive damages

According to Nebraska law, punitive damages awarded in civil cases are directed to the local school district rather than the plaintiffs. Since Keadle was incarcerated and had no assets, Tyler's family realized they would not receive any form of compensation.

Unfulfilling satisfaction?

Certainly.

Keadle remained incarcerated for a separate conviction, but his parole opportunity in 2020 was nearing. Then, an unexpected disclosure changed everything.

After serving a 30-day sentence in the same jail as Keadle, Corey Pfeifer came forward with a stunning claim. Pfeifer alleged that Keadle had confessed to him, stating, "Keadle admitted to me that he had killed Tyler Thomas and disposed of her body. He told me he had taken Tyler down to the river, and they had sex, and they would never convict him because they would never find her body."

In October 2017, nearly seven years after Tyler's disappearance, Keadle was charged with first-degree murder. He was tried in early 2020, with prosecutors contending that he had killed Tyler at the Peru Boat Dock before disposing of her body in the river.

After nine hours of deliberation, a jury made up of eight women and four men found him guilty, not of first-degree murder, but of the lesser charge of second-degree murder.

After the verdict, Attorney General Doug Peterson expressed gratitude to the jury, the Peru State College community, and the volunteers who assisted in searching for Tyler. He acknowledged the tireless efforts of law enforcement and the commitment of the prosecution, stating, "Even though we have not been able to return Tyler's body, we hope this verdict will provide her family with some measure of closure after years filled with uncertainty and pain."

Kevin Semans, Tyler's father, shared his contentment with the verdict. "I'm relieved he won't be roaming the streets. Once the sentencing occurs, more details will emerge about how truly horrific he was. The past ten years have felt endless. Joshua Keadle deserves absolutely no mercy for his actions—none at all."

Latanya Thomas and her mother conveyed comparable emotions, stating, "This signifies the beginning of our healing journey. It has exceeded our expectations, especially since we have been holding our breath for so long... enduring nightmares."

Even with the verdict, one troubling question lingered: Where is Tyler's body?

DJ Thomas, her sibling, expressed his sorrow, saying, "We haven't had a chance to heal or grieve since there's no body to bury. We lack closure. It's just missing. She was my best friend and shaped my perspective on others."

During the sentencing, Tyler's family faced Keadle, expressing the deep effect his actions had on their lives. Tyler's grandmother, Violet Bennett, remarked, "We waited a long time for this."

Keadle claimed he thought of Tyler's mother every day while maintaining his innocence.

He later appealed his 2020 conviction to the Nebraska State Supreme Court. His attorney, Jeff Pickens, contended that the prosecution failed to establish "corpus delicti" beyond a reasonable doubt—a term that means "body of the crime." Pickens argued that no one should face conviction based solely on an unverified confession, noting that Keadle stated, "I didn't hurt her. I left her at the river; she was unharmed. I didn't do anything to her." He further pointed out the absence of blood or forensic evidence linking Keadle to Tyler's death, raising the possibility that her history of alcohol abuse and troubled relationships cast reasonable doubt on whether Keadle was responsible or if Tyler had even died at all.

Keadle's previous offenses overshadow his assertions of innocence. In March 2012, he was found guilty of raping a 15-year-old girl in 2009 at Midland Lutheran College.

In July 2020, Joshua Keadle was sentenced to 71 years in prison for murdering Tyler Thomas, who was only 19 when she was killed in 2010. Alarmingly, this serial rapist and murderer may be eligible for parole after serving just 35 years.

Judge Rick Schreiner of the First Judicial District Court delivered the sentence. The court upheld the conviction, declaring, "Tyler Thomas, a student at Peru State College (PSC) in Nebraska, has been missing since December 3, 2010, and her body has never been recovered. Joshua W. Keadle was the last person known to have seen her alive. In 2017, he was charged with first-degree murder related to Tyler's disappearance. A jury convicted Keadle of second-degree murder, resulting in a prison sentence. He is appealing, claiming the trial evidence was insufficient to prove the occurrence of homicide. We find no merit in this claim and affirm the judgment."

In January 2025, Keadle sought a retrial.

He is scheduled for parole in 2054 from the Nebraska Reception and Treatment Center in Lincoln. There, he will engage in clinical treatment, cognitive-behavioral programs, educational pursuits, vocational training, and life skills development.

Yet, suppose it weren't for Joshua Keadle's confession to a jailhouse informant regarding the murder of his final known victim, Tyler Thomas. In that case, justice might never have been served for the many innocent girls he had brutally raped and murdered before her.

CHAPTER TWENTY-FIVE

Hillside Stranglers – Kenneth Alessio Bianchi and Angelo Buono

Kenneth Alessio Bianchi, born on May 22, 1951, in Rochester, New York, is recognized as a serial killer. He gained notoriety alongside his cousin, Angelo Buono, Jr., as one of "The Hillside Stranglers." Currently, he is serving a life sentence in Washington. Furthermore, Bianchi is considered a suspect in the Alphabet murders, a series of three unresolved homicides in his hometown.

Bianchi stood almost six feet tall with a fit, muscular build. His dark hair was well-groomed and accompanied by a mustache. He lived with his long-time girlfriend, Kelli Boyd, and their infant son. Kelli struggled to accept that someone as lovely and gentle as Kenny could be connected to a murder case. His employer also viewed him as a dependable and respected team member.

Bianchi was given up for adoption by his mother, a prostitute, only two weeks after his birth. At three months, he was taken in by Frances Scioliono and her husband, Nicholas Bianchi, who also lived in Rochester.

From an early age, Bianchi experienced considerable turmoil, leading his adoptive mother to label him "a compulsive liar who was lying from the cradle." His habit of falling into trance-like daydreams often worried her. Though above average in intelligence, he struggled with his studies and frequently lost his temper. At the age of five, he was diagnosed with petit mal seizures. By age ten, he received a diagnosis of passive-aggressive disorder. After Nicholas died from pneumonia in 1964, Frances had to work while her son went to high school.

Soon after graduating from Gates-Chili High School in 1971, Bianchi wed his sweetheart. However, the marriage lasted only eight months, as she reportedly left without explanation. As an adult, he withdrew from college after just one semester. He moved between various low-paying jobs, becoming a security guard at a jewelry store. This position allowed him the opportunity to steal valuable items, which he often gave to girlfriends or prostitutes in return for their loyalty. Bianchi frequently found himself on the move due to his repeated petty thefts.

In 1977, he moved to Los Angeles and began to spend time with his older cousin, Angelo Buono. Buono was impressed by Bianchi's stylish clothing, jewelry, and tales of enticing any woman he desired while maintaining control over them.

Before long, they teamed up as pimps, and by late 1977, they had escalated to murder.

At the time of their arrest in early 1979, they had assaulted and murdered ten women.

Angelo Buono was not particularly attractive in terms of looks, personality, or intellect. His traits were marked by crudeness, vulgarity, egotism, ignorance, and a penchant for sadism. Nevertheless, he attracted numerous women and referred to himself as the "Italian Stallion."

He had multiple marriages and fathered several children, all of whom he physically abused and occasionally sexually abused.

Born in Rochester, New York, on October 5, 1934, he relocated to Southern California, specifically to Glendale, later that same year, following his parents' divorce. He resided with his mother, Jenny, and older sister, Cecilia. His mother earned a living through piecework at a shoe factory. Although he was raised in a Catholic environment, his interactions with religion and public education had little effect on him. Throughout his life, he remained unaware of spiritual, moral, and academic matters.

Although he acknowledged the importance of treating women with some kindness to fulfill his sexual desires, he concurrently held profound resentment toward them, coupled with an urge to demean and hurt them.

He called his mother a "cunt" and a "whore" to her face, but was emotionally tied to her until she died in 1978. Even as a 14-year-old, he boasted to his friends about raping and sodomizing girls.

Murders

A handful of murders hardly disturb a sprawling city like Los Angeles. Within this extensive metropolis, where violence often lurks in the shadows, homicides, especially those involving marginalized groups like sex workers, frequently remain unreported. Death simply blends into the backdrop of everyday life.

So, when three women were found strangled and dumped naked on remote hillsides northeast of the city between October and early November of 1977, the news barely caused a ripple.

The victims were seen by many as leading "high-risk lifestyles." Yet, amid the city's typical indifference, a few perceptive homicide detectives sensed that something more sinister was emerging—a pattern just starting to come to light.

Kenneth Bianchi and Angelo Buono cruised through the streets in Buono's vehicle, equipped with predator-like instincts and counterfeit police badges. They impersonated undercover officers, wielding their false authority to persuade unsuspecting young women that they were being detained for questioning.

Their targets ranged from 12 to 28 years old from all walks of life. Once inside the car, the girls were trapped. Bianchi and Buono would drive them to Buono's house, where the illusion of law enforcement dropped—and the nightmare began. There, behind closed doors, the women were tortured, brutalized, and murdered.

They routinely engaged in sexual assault before executing their victims by strangulation. In several instances, they deviated from this method, employing lethal injection, electric shock, or carbon monoxide poisoning to carry out the killings.

Amid a string of murders, Kenneth Bianchi boldly sought a job with the Los Angeles Police Department. In a chilling turn of events, he joined officers on a ride-along, participating in the investigation of the very crimes he had perpetrated as the Hillside Strangler.

Yolanda Washington, age 19 – October 17, 1977
She was a sex worker whose nude body was discovered on a secluded hillside near the Ventura Freeway at 6510 Forest Lawn Drive in Los Angeles. Her corpse had been carefully posed in a lewd position, suggesting a deliberate attempt to shock or degrade. Investigators noted that her body had

been washed before being dumped—an effort likely made to remove forensic evidence. Faint ligature marks were visible around her neck, wrists, and ankles, indicating that she had been restrained. The autopsy revealed she had been brutally beaten, raped, and ultimately strangled. She would become the first confirmed mutual victim of Kenneth Bianchi and Angelo Buono. The two men had lured her into their vehicle by posing as undercover police officers, a ruse they would use again to prey upon vulnerable women.

Judith Ann Miller, age 15 – October 31, 1977
On the morning of November 1, 1977, police responded to a disturbing scene on Alta Terrace Drive in La Crescenta, a quiet, middle-class neighborhood about 12 miles north of downtown Los Angeles. The body of a teenage girl had been discovered lying naked, face up, on a narrow strip of grass between the sidewalk and the street. In an act of compassion, the homeowner who found her had covered her with a tarp to shield the view from neighborhood children walking to school. Investigators noted ligature marks on her neck, wrists, and ankles—clear signs that she had been bound and strangled. The absence of blood or signs of struggle at the scene led detectives to conclude the body had been dumped there after she was killed elsewhere.

Miller was last seen alive on Halloween night, October 31, 1977, speaking with a man in a large, two-toned sedan parked along Sunset Boulevard near Carney's restaurant. The men—later identified as The Hillside Stranglers—posed as undercover police officers, convincing her she was under arrest. After handcuffing her, they drove her to Buono's Auto Upholstery Shop at 703 East Colorado Street in Glendale. It was there that Miller was brutally murdered.

Elissa Teresa Kastin, age 21 – November 6, 1977
Five days later, on November 6, 1977, the nude body of another young woman was discovered near the Chevy Chase

Country Club in Glendale. Like Judith Miller, this victim bore distinct five-point ligature marks—on her neck, wrists, and ankles—indicating she had been bound, strangled, and brutally raped. There was no evidence of sodomy, but the violence of the attack was unmistakable.

The victim was identified as 21-year-old Elissa Teresa "Lissa" Kastin, a full-time waitress and professional dancer with the all-female cabaret troupe, The L.A. Knockers. Unlike the previous two victims, Kastin had no known ties to prostitution, drugs, or the runaway scene. She was last seen the night before, leaving the restaurant where she worked.

According to investigators, Kastin was followed after her shift ended. As she neared her home, she was pulled over on her own street by men posing as law enforcement. Flashing a fake badge, they claimed to be detectives and told her she needed to come with them for questioning. She was handcuffed on the spot, never to be seen alive again.

Evelyn Jane King, age 28 – November 10, 1977

She was an aspiring actress and a devoted Scientologist, chasing dreams under the bright lights of Los Angeles. But beneath the surface of her hopeful journey, a silent horror loomed. On November 9, she vanished without a trace while waiting at a bus stop—no witnesses, no clues. Days later, her lifeless body was discovered in a tangle of overgrown brush near the Los Feliz exit off the Golden State Freeway. The extent of decomposition obscured key details, leaving investigators unable to confirm whether she had been raped or tortured. Yet the evidence pointed to a chilling end: she had likely been sodomized, then strangled—a savage death that extinguished a young life brimming with potential.

Delores Ann Cepeda, age 12 – November 13, 1977
She and Sonja Johnson were schoolgirls—close friends and the youngest victims of The Hillside Stranglers. Their

ordinary afternoon turned tragic shortly after they stepped off a bus at Eagle Rock Plaza. Kenneth Bianchi and Angelo Buono, posing as undercover officers and flashing counterfeit police badges, approached the girls with chilling authority. Deceived by the ruse, the two teenagers were coaxed into the strangers' car—unknowingly stepping into the hands of killers. The teenagers were taken to Angelo Buono's upholstery shop in Glendale, California, where they met a tragic end at the hands of their captors. On November 20, their lifeless bodies were discovered discarded in a heap of trash in Highland Park, a chilling testament to the brutality of their murders. Even as decomposition had already set in, the evidence left behind told a chilling story—both victims had been sexually assaulted and then strangled.

Sonja Johnson, age 14 – November 13, 1977
She and Dolly Cepeda were discovered in a trash-strewn heap, their bodies already in an advanced state of decomposition. Despite the decay, investigators determined that both girls had been raped and strangled to death.

Kristina Weckler, age 20 – November 20, 1977
Earlier that same day, hikers stumbled upon the naked body of 20-year-old Kristina Weckler, a quiet, soft-spoken honors student at the Art Center College of Design. She was described by Detective Bob Grogan of the Los Angeles Police Department as "a loving and serious young woman who should have had a bright future ahead of her."

Weckler had been left on a hillside between Glendale and Eagle Rock. When Detective Grogan arrived at the scene, he noted the now-familiar ligature marks around her wrists, ankles, and neck. Upon turning her over, he observed bruising on her breasts and blood seeping from her rectum—grim indicators of the brutality she had endured.

Unlike the previous victims, however, Weckler bore two puncture marks on her arm, though there were no signs of the track marks typically seen in intravenous drug users. Toxicology later confirmed that she had been injected with Windex, a household glass and surface cleaner containing ammonia.

Lauren Rae Wagner, age 18 – November 29, 1977
Wagner was a business school student found dead on the west side of Mount Washington at 1217 Cliff Drive in Glassell Park. She appeared to have been burned by an electrical cord while being tortured, based on the burn marks on the inside of her hands. Additionally, there was evidence that suggested Wagner was handcuffed before being strangled to death. At this time, investigators concluded that the perpetrator might have been a police officer or someone pretending to be one. They consequently cautioned female drivers whom policemen stopped to double-check that they were, in fact, law enforcement.

Kimberly Diane Martin, age 17 – December 9, 1977
She was a sex worker and model who was found naked on a deserted lot near Los Angeles City Hall. In the Silver Lake neighborhood, Kimberly's body had been dumped over the side of a hill, where it could be seen from police headquarters. She was working for an outcall escort service when she was called to 1950 Tamarind, Hollywood, on the night of her murder. She was slain in an empty apartment, and her body was thrown in Echo Park near 2006 North Alvarado. Before being cruelly strangled, Martin was raped and tortured.

Cindy Lee Hudspeth, age 20 – February 16, 1978
The last victim attributed to The Hillside Strangler case was discovered on February 17, 1978, in a remote section of Los Angeles. A helicopter pilot flying over the Angeles Crest Highway spotted an orange Datsun abandoned partway down

a steep cliff and alerted authorities. When police arrived at the scene, they located the nude body of 20-year-old Cindy Lee Hudspeth in the trunk of the vehicle. A student and part-time waitress, Hudspeth bore the now-familiar signs of the Stranglers' brutal methods—she had been raped, tortured, and strangled. Her body had been stuffed into the trunk before the car was deliberately pushed over the edge.

Unlike many of the previous murders, Hudspeth's killing had not been premeditated. On the evening of February 16, Kenneth Bianchi arrived at Angelo Buono's auto upholstery shop just as it was closing. Inside, Buono was speaking with Hudspeth about potential work on her car. Recognizing an opportunity, the two men stepped aside and quickly conspired to make her their next victim.

One evening, soon after their failed attempt to carry out an 11th murder, Bianchi disclosed to Buono that he had participated in an LAPD ride-along and was under investigation related to the strangler case. Upon hearing this, Buono exploded in anger.

A heated dispute broke out, with Buono threatening Bianchi's life if he did not relocate to Bellingham, Washington. In May 1978, Bianchi escaped to Bellingham, reuniting with his girlfriend and son, who were already residing there.

On January 11, 1979, Kenneth Bianchi lured two female students to a residence where he was employed as a security guard. The victims, 22-year-old Karen Mandic and 27-year-old Diane Wilder, were both attending Western Washington University.

Upon entering, Bianchi pushed Karen Mandic down a staircase in front of him and strangled her. He then also murdered Diane Wilder.

This time, Bianchi acted independently—unlike his earlier crimes, where he included his cousin and accomplice, Angelo Buono. Consequently, he committed significant errors, leaving behind numerous clues that quickly led investigators to him. Crucial evidence comprised a California driver's license and other documents that, via a standard background check, linked him to the residences of two confirmed Hillside Strangler victims.

The next day, he was captured.

After his arrest, Bianchi confessed that he and Buono had impersonated police officers in 1977 to apprehend a young woman named Catharine Lorre, planning to abduct and murder her.

They released her when it was revealed that she was actor Peter Lorre's daughter. It was only after his arrest that Catharine realized the true identities of the men she had encountered.

Trial

During his trial, Bianchi asserted he was not guilty due to insanity, alleging that an alternate personality named "Steve Walker" was responsible for the crimes. He managed to persuade several expert psychiatrists about his assertions related to multiple personality disorder. Nevertheless, investigators sought input from their own team of psychiatrists, led by Dr. Martin Orne, a professor of psychology and psychiatry at the University of Pennsylvania.

When Orne informed Bianchi that disorder cases often involve three or more personalities, Bianchi quickly adopted another alias: "Billy."

Eventually, investigators uncovered that the name "Steven Walker" originated from a student whose identity Bianchi had previously tried to usurp to practice psychology illegally.

Authorities discovered a small collection of books in Bianchi's residence covering modern psychology topics, which further suggests his capability to feign the disorder.

After intense scrutiny of his claims, Bianchi confessed to creating a false disorder. In hopes of leniency, he agreed to testify against Buono. However, Bianchi was uncooperative during his testimony and frequently contradicted himself, seemingly trying to obstruct Buono's conviction. In the end, his efforts were in vain, leading to Buono's conviction and life sentence.

In 1980, Bianchi started dating Veronica Compton, whom he met while in prison.

During his trial, she took the stand for the defense, offering the jury a vague and fabricated account of the crimes in a brazen attempt to exonerate Bianchi—while also revealing her disturbing plan to purchase a mortuary with another convicted killer to engage in necrophilia.

She was later convicted and imprisoned for attempting to strangle a woman she had lured to a motel—an elaborate ruse intended to convince authorities that The Hillside Strangler was still active and that the wrong man had been imprisoned. In a disturbing twist, Bianchi had smuggled her a sample of his semen, which she planned to plant on the victim to stage the scene as a sexual assault and murder in the Strangler's signature style.

The Los Angeles County District Attorney's Office offered Bianchi a deal. If he pled guilty, he would get life with the possibility of parole and be able to serve his time in

California, where the prisons were supposedly more humane than in Washington.

In return, Bianchi was to agree to testify truthfully and fully against Angelo Buono. For Bianchi, the choice was between death in Washington or life in California. However, he remained in Washington to serve his life sentence at the Washington State Penitentiary in Walla Walla.

Angelo Buono was sent to Folsom Prison in California, where he remained in his cell, fearing injury from other inmates. He died of a heart attack on September 21, 2002.

CHAPTER TWENTY-SIX

Damsel of Death – Aileen Wuornos

Aileen Wuornos, known as "The Damsel of Death," was born Aileen Carol Pittman on February 29, 1956, in Rochester, Michigan. Her mother, Diane Wuornos, was just 14 when she married 18-year-old Leo Dale Pittman on June 3, 1954. They welcomed their first son, Keith, on March 14, 1955, but their marriage soon began to unravel. Less than two years after their wedding—and merely two months before Aileen was born—Diane sought a divorce. At only 16 years old, she gave birth to Aileen, initiating a childhood filled with instability and feelings of neglect.

Aileen was unaware of her father, who had been imprisoned for the rape and attempted murder of a 7-year-old girl when she was born.

Leo Pittman, reportedly struggling with schizophrenia, had a concerning criminal record featuring convictions for sexual offenses against minors. His existence was characterized by a relentless cycle of imprisonment followed by short periods of freedom, which ultimately resulted in his repeated return to jail. In 1969, while serving yet another sentence, Pittman took his own life by hanging in his cell.

Wuornos began engaging in sexual activities in school and with her brother in exchange for cigarettes, drugs, and food at the age of 11. She claimed that her alcoholic grandfather had sexually assaulted and beaten her when she was a child.

On May 27, 1974, 18-year-old Aileen Wuornos was arrested in Jefferson County, Colorado. She faced charges of driving under the influence, disorderly conduct, and shooting a .22-caliber pistol from a moving vehicle. Additionally, she was charged with failing to appear in court.

From ages 14 to 22, she made six suicide attempts. In 1978, at 22, she survived a notably severe attempt after shooting herself in the abdomen.

Over a year, Wuornos killed seven men, all of whom were aged 40 to 65 and traveling by car.

Murders

On November 30, 1989, 51-year-old electronics store owner Richard Charles Mallory encountered Aileen Wuornos while driving along a state highway in Clearwater, Florida.

According to Wuornos, what began as a transactional encounter quickly turned violent. She later claimed that Mallory had driven her to a remote, wooded area under the pretense of seeking sexual services. Still, once there, he allegedly beat, raped, and sodomized her.

Wuornos asserted that she fired in self-defense.

Mallory was the first victim officially recognized in the case of Aileen Wuornos. Her testimony was initially met with skepticism, but later revelations shifted public perception. During the trial, it was revealed that Mallory had a prior conviction for attempted rape in Maryland, a crucial detail that Wuornos withheld until the court proceedings commenced. Additionally, Wuornos's longtime partner, Tyria Moore, pointed out that she had never heard Wuornos mention anything regarding Mallory's past.

Two days after the murder, a deputy sheriff from Volusia County located Mallory's abandoned car. Nearly two weeks later, on December 13, authorities found Mallory's body in a wooded area several miles away.

He had suffered several gunshot wounds, with two rounds entering his left lung, which resulted in his death.

Victims

David Andrew Spears, 47, was a construction worker in Winter Garden, Florida. He was last seen on May 19, 1990.

Almost two weeks later, on June 1, 1990, authorities found his body exposed along U.S. Highway 19 in Citrus County. Spears had suffered six gunshot wounds from a .22 caliber pistol, pointing to a vicious and intentional act of violence.

Charles Edmund Carskadon, age 40, was involved in rodeo part-time and met a tragic end on May 31, 1990. His lifeless, unclothed body was discovered a week later, on June 6, in rural Pasco County, Florida.

It had been wrapped in an electric blanket and left to decompose in the sweltering heat, making identification and investigation more difficult. An autopsy revealed that Carskadon had been shot nine times with a .22 caliber weapon.

The numerous gunshot wounds indicated a chaotic and violent assault.

Peter Abraham Siems, 65, was a retired merchant seaman living in Jupiter, Florida. In June 1990, he began a road trip to visit family in Arkansas, but never arrived. His abandoned car was found in Orange Springs, Florida, on July 4, 1990. Witnesses later reported seeing Tyria Moore and Aileen Wuornos leaving the area. Forensic analysis uncovered Wuornos's palm print inside the car's door handle. Despite extensive searches, Peter Siems's remains were never found.

On July 31, 1990, Troy Eugene Burress, a 50-year-old sausage salesman based in Ocala, Florida, embarked on his usual delivery route but did not return. Since he didn't check in and was unreachable, his family and employer reported him missing, raising significant alarm.

Four days later, on August 4, 1990, a grim discovery was made. Burress's body was found in a wooded area off State Road 19 in Marion County, not far from Ocala. He had been shot twice, and investigators quickly determined foul play. The remote location and manner of death suggested a targeted, execution-style killing—one that would later be linked to a broader pattern of homicides.

Charles Richard "Dick" Humphreys, a retired major from the United States Air Force at 56, previously worked as a child abuse investigator for the state and served as Chief of Police. A devoted public servant and justice advocate, Humphreys dedicated much of his life to protecting others—first in uniform, then law enforcement, and ultimately by probing crimes against society's most vulnerable individuals.

On the morning of September 12, 1990, Humphreys' body was found in Marion County, Florida. He was fully clothed, a somber indication of the brutality he endured—shot seven times in the head and torso.

The murder was both brutal and deliberate, executed with evident intent.

His vehicle was found far away in Suwannee County, which complicated the investigation and heightened worries about the killer's movements and motives. The brutal murder of a man committed to enforcing the law appalled and angered many, contributing another name to the growing list of victims in what would soon be recognized as a concerning series of murders.

Walter Gino Antonio, 61, devoted his life to service and hard work. Professionally, he was a truck driver, a security guard, and a reserve police officer. On November 19, 1990, his nearly naked body was discovered along a secluded logging road in rural Dixie County, Florida.

He suffered four gunshot wounds, and his remains were abandoned in the woods. Five days afterward, authorities discovered his vehicle more than 150 miles away in Brevard County, deepening the mystery surrounding his brutal murder.

On January 9, 1991, Aileen Wuornos was apprehended at The Last Resort biker bar in Volusia County, Florida, due to an outstanding warrant issued under the name of Lori Grody.

On January 16, 1991, Aileen Wuornos confessed to multiple murders, asserting that each was committed in self-defense against men she claimed had attempted to rape her.

In November 1991, an unexpected event occurred when 44-year-old Arlene Pralle, a born-again Christian who had never met Wuornos, opted to adopt her legally. Pralle came across Wuornos's photograph in a newspaper and felt a compelling desire to reach out, which led to a close and widely publicized relationship with the accused serial killer.

On January 14, 1992, Aileen Wuornos stood trial for the murder of Richard Charles Mallory. While previous crimes typically cannot be introduced in court, the prosecution leveraged Florida's Williams Rule for a significant advantage.

This statute allows the introduction of evidence from other crimes to demonstrate a pattern of behavior. This enabled the jury to hear about Wuornos's involvement in several additional killings, providing a broader and more damaging perspective on her actions.

On January 27, 1992, the jury reached a guilty verdict in Mallory's case, in part due to the harmful testimony provided by Wuornos's former lover, Tyria Moore, who collaborated with law enforcement.

In the sentencing phase, defense attorneys brought in mental health specialists who described Wuornos as deeply troubled. She had received diagnoses of borderline personality disorder and antisocial personality disorder—conditions that the defense argued contributed to her violent acts.

Despite these arguments, the court showed little compassion. Just four days later, Aileen Wuornos was sentenced to death.

On March 31, 1992, Aileen Wuornos pleaded no contest to the murders of Charles Richard Humphreys, Troy Eugene Burress, and David Andrew Spears, expressing in court her desire to "get right with God."

In her statement, Wuornos reiterated her long-standing claim that her first victim, Richard Mallory, had violently attacked her, saying, "But these others did not; they were just beginning to." Although she sought spiritual redemption, the court remained largely inflexible.

On May 15, 1992, she was sentenced to death for three murders.

In June of that year, Wuornos admitted to murdering Charles Edmund Carskadon, leading to her fifth death sentence in

November 1992. In February 1993, she received her final conviction after confessing to the murder of Walter Jeno Antonio, resulting in another death sentence. Authorities decided against pursuing charges for the murder of Peter Abraham Siems because his body had never been recovered.

At the end of the legal proceedings, Aileen Wuornos was sentenced to death six times—an unmatched count for any female serial killer in American history.

Wuornos provided several conflicting accounts regarding the circumstances of the killings. Initially, she maintained that all seven victims had either raped or attempted to rape her. At the same time, she was engaged in prostitution, framing each killing as an act of self-defense.

In the end, she altered her story, withdrawing her self-defense argument and confessing that her actions were motivated by robbery and a desire to hush witnesses. During a candid interview with a documentary filmmaker, she reverted to her initial self-defense claim, mistakenly thinking the cameras were turned off.

She conveyed that her earlier withdrawal had stemmed from her struggle to cope with life on death row, where she had spent ten years, and her wish to hasten her execution.

Wuornos initially resided on death row at the Broward Correctional Institution (BCI) for women before her transfer to Florida State Prison for execution.

Her appeal to the U.S. Supreme Court was denied in 1996. In 2001, Wuornos petitioned the Florida Supreme Court to dismiss her legal counsel and terminate all pending appeals. In her petition, she candidly wrote, "I killed those men, robbed them as cold as ice. And I'd do it again, too. There's no chance of keeping me alive or anything because I'd kill again. I have hate crawling through my system... I am so sick of hearing this 'she's crazy' stuff. I've been evaluated so many times. I'm competent and sane and trying to tell the truth. I'm one who seriously hates human life and would kill again."

Despite her lawyers' claims of mental incompetence, Wuornos maintained her stance, supported by a court-appointed panel of psychiatrists who determined she was mentally competent.

Florida Governor Jeb Bush directed three psychiatrists to conduct a 15-minute interview with Wuornos. The competency test requires the psychiatrists to determine whether the condemned individual comprehends the reasons for her execution and understands that she will die. All three assessed her as mentally fit for execution.

In 2002, Aileen Wuornos began voicing allegations of mistreatment at the hands of prison personnel. She accused prison matrons of deliberately contaminating her meals with dirt, saliva, and urine. Wuornos claimed she had overheard conversations among prison staff aimed at pushing her "over the brink" to the point of suicide before her scheduled execution. She further alleged that she heard personnel expressing intentions of sexually assaulting her before the execution.

Wuornos expressed multiple grievances, including repeated strip searches, overly tight handcuffs, door slamming, constant surveillance through her cell window, low water pressure, and mold on her mattress. She reported ongoing verbal abuse, citing episodes of "cat-calling" characterized by "disdain and blatant hatred."

In response to this treatment, Wuornos threatened to skip showers and refuse food trays when hen certain officers were on duty in her cell block. "Meanwhile," she remarked, "my stomach is growling, and I'm showering in my cell's sink."

Her attorney addressed these concerns publicly, emphasizing that "Ms. Wuornos genuinely seeks humane and proper treatment until the day of her execution." He also affirmed her sincerity, stating clearly, "She believes what she's written."

Aileen Wuornos was executed via lethal injection on October 9, 2002, at 9:47 a.m. EDT. Instead of choosing a final meal worth up to $20, she opted for just a cup of coffee. Her last words were puzzling: "Yes, I'd just like to say I'm sailing with the rock, and I'll return, like Independence Day, with Jesus. June 6, like the movie. Big mother ship and all, I'll be back, I'll be back."

Following her execution, Wuornos was cremated, and her ashes were scattered beneath a tree in Michigan by her childhood friend, Dawn Botkins. Per Wuornos' wishes, her funeral featured the song "Carnival" by Natalie Merchant from the 1995 album *Tigerlily*, a track she frequently listened to during her time on death row.

Wuornos became the second woman executed in Florida and the tenth across the U.S. following the Supreme Court's reinstatement of the death penalty in 1976.

THE KILLERS

Chapter 1 - Rodney James Alcala

Chapter 2 - Ángel Maturino Reséndiz

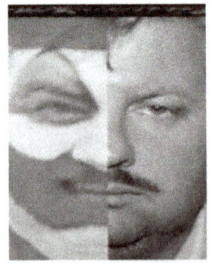

Chapter 3 - John Wayne Gacy

Chapter 4 - John Albert Gardner III

Chapter 5 - Cameron Hooker

Chapter 6 - Adam Leroy Lane

Chapter 7 - Richard Ramirez

Chapter 8 - Israel Keyes

Chapter 9 - James Michael Biela

Chapter 10 - Lonnie David Franklin Jr.

Chapter 11 - Ted Bundy

Chapter 12 - Tommy Lynn Sells

Chapter 13 - David Parker Ray

Chapter 14 - Bobby Joe Long

Chapter 15 - Todd Kohlhepp

Chapter 16 - Harold David Haulman III

Chapter 17 - Jesse L. Matthew Jr.

Chapter 18 - Brian Lee Golsby

Chapter 19 - Brandon Scott Lavergne

Chapter 20 - Khalil Wheeler-Weaver

Chapter 21 - Kylr Yust

Chapter 22 - Robert Christian Hansen

Chapter 23 - Andrew Urdiales

Chapter 24 - Joshua Keadle

Chapter 25 - Kenneth Alessio Bianchi

Chapter 25 - Angelo Buono

Chapter 26 - Aileen Wuornos

www.ingramcontent.com/pod-product-compliance
Lightning Source LLC
Chambersburg PA
CBHW061552120626
46550CB00004B/1459